THE PRONUNCIATION OF
AMERICAN ENGLISH

The Pronunciation of

AMERICAN ENGLISH

An Introduction to Phonetics

ARTHUR J. BRONSTEIN

Lehman College

of The City University of New York

Prentice-Hall, Inc., Englewood Cliffs, New Jersey

Printed in the United States of America

ISBN: 0-13-730887-6

Library of Congress Catalog Card Number: 60-6750

10 9 8 7 6 5 4 3 2

PRENTICE-HALL INTERNATIONAL, INC., *London*
PRENTICE-HALL OF AUSTRALIA, PTY. LTD., *Sydney*
PRENTICE-HALL OF CANADA, LTD., *Toronto*
PRENTICE-HALL OF INDIA PRIVATE LIMITED, *New Delhi*
PRENTICE-HALL OF JAPAN, INC., *Tokyo*

To

Elsa, Nancy, and Nabby

Preface

THIS BOOK details a most important section of the study of our language. It deals with the sounds of American English, the base upon which such other areas of study as grammar, syntax, and the rhetoric of spoken and written discourse are built. In these and other branches of the study of our language, words are used to express thoughts, and the words of any language are the results of the sounds and silences we make when we speak.

The student is surely aware of the fact that each language has a special sound system. From that system the speakers of that language select certain combinations to construct the many varieties of words used by them. The student is equally aware that different speakers may be saying these same words somewhat differently. We have come to call one such sound system "American English." It is the subject of this book.

The study of the sound system of our language encompasses much that we know and much we still must seek. Within the past few decades especially, investigations in the special areas of phonetics, phonemics, dialect study, acoustics, and general linguistics have brought to light much additional information about the major sound segments of our language—the consonants, vowels, consonant clusters, complex vowel nuclei, and their modifications in American English. The stresses, pitches, pauses, and melodies we use when we speak, and their effects on these sound-segments, have been the object of much study too. These areas of study comprise the subject matter of this text. There are other parts of the sound system of American English, to be sure. These would include tense and lax qualities, loud and soft levels, rapid and slow rates, prolonged and abruptly produced sounds, uninflected and highly inflected melodic patterns, and the pertinent or distinctive "shades" between such noted extremes. Speech and language scientists know much about these aspects of our language, although much more study and research are needed before we shall be able to identify their special places in our language system. Such investigations are now under way. As the knowledge resulting from these researches becomes available, it will need to be added to the other phonological features about which our evidence is more complete.

This text is written for use in classes in the phonetics and pronunciation of American English, as its title indicates. Such study is recognized as a necessary part of the background of all students of our language. It is applied in many specialized fields of study: public speaking, oral interpretation of literature, dramatics, speech correction and audiology, voice and diction or articulation, grammar, linguistics, radio and television performance, and any other area of study where the knowledge and understanding of the English language is essential.

Perhaps the last part of this book should be the part the student might want to look at first. Appendix A surveys the language we have come to call "English," from the time of the invasions of the British Isles by the Anglo-Saxons. Most schools present such a study as a separate course, and if programs and time permit, such a study of the history of our language will prove rewarding as well as provide a sound basis for understanding the streams of our language as they have developed. Such a study, most valuable as it is, is not *necessary*, however, for an analysis of the language we speak today, which can proceed from the evidence at hand. The chapter surveying the history of our language is, therefore, placed in the Appendix section, but it is hoped that the student will not overlook it. Once the student has a chance to learn the phonetic alphabet, he will be especially interested to "see and hear" how contemporaries of Alfred the Great, Chaucer, Shakespeare, and Samuel Johnson might have sounded during their days.

The analysis of current American English is presented in three major divisions. The first, "Our Language Today," provides the student with certain basic concepts, definitions, and attitudes. Here the student is introduced to the International Phonetic Alphabet, the sound system of American English, a careful analysis of the concept of the phoneme, and an opportunity to practice and develop his skill in simple transcription exercises. This part of the text presents the student with the realization that there are many dialects of American Speech, some regional, some social, some cultivated, some less-cultivated or substandard. The subjects of standard usage, disputed usages, the influences that cause and resist change in the language, and a discussion of the regional divisions of American speech are included in this section.

Part Two details the consonants, vowels, and complex consonant and vowel clusters of American English. The formation and acoustic values of these sounds, their modifications and variations in the stream of speech, in the different regional areas, and in cultivated and less-cultivated varieties, are presented. Part Three discusses certain special aspects of our sound system: the nature and types of sound change; the pronunciation of words and the influences affecting such pronunciations; spelling pronunciations, alternative pronunciations, and the pronunciation of foreign words in American English; pitch levels, stress, and pause—their forms and effects on the other sounds we use; the melodies of American English. Innumerable examples appear throughout the text, as do maps, charts, and drawings. Bibliography, question-review, and exercise sections appear after each subject and a special group of maps, charts, and selections for phonetic practice appear in Appendix B.

The problem of symbolization has been a particularly knotty one. The many publications in phonetics, phonemics, and linguistics with slight symbol variations in so much of the writing has resulted in unfortunate confusion. I consulted a number of respected teachers and scholars in different sections of the country for advice. The resolution of the problem, as it appears in this text, is based on their answers. One of the respondent's comments is especially worth noting: "Transcription is merely the means of identification; hardly the end. One transcription decision can be as useful as the next." I hope that the transcription system used in this text will satisfy most, if not all, of its users. With very few modifications, it is probably the one most widely used by teachers of phonetics in this country.

Where the evidence is incomplete and where respected scholars differ in their conclusions, the student will find appropriate mention of such facts. The student will soon learn that this is not a field where the evidence is all there and where opinions are set and static. Like any other area of study about man and his functioning in this world, such evidence is never complete. The language we use is constantly changing as it adapts itself to the many influences upon it. As new evidence becomes available, it must be introduced into the already established system of knowledge.

ACKNOWLEDGEMENTS

No text is written by one author. The teachers, scholars, and writers whose lectures, articles, and books are listened to and studied are, of course, responsible for the ideas and knowledge which, thereafter, each recipient begins to call his own. The works of Leonard Bloomfield, W. Cabell Greet, Daniel Jones, John S. Kenyon, and Hans Kurath stand apart, for hardly any text in the phonetic study of current English can overlook the contributions and influence of these men on our thinking today. The works of their colleagues and students have been studied, and for much of this text, I am indebted to them in turn. Special mention must be made of the published writings of B. Bloch, A. F. Hubbell, L. S. Hultzén, R. I. McDavid, Jr., K. L. Pike, H. L. Smith, Jr., C. K. Thomas, G. L. Trager, and C. M. Wise. Without the contribution of these phoneticians and linguists, this text would not have been possible.

Two friends, Wilbur E. Gilman, Chairman of the Department of Speech at Queens College, and Allan F. Hubbell of the Department of English at New York University and Managing Editor of *American*

Speech, read almost the entire manuscript. I am deeply indebted to them both for their suggestions and corrections. My colleagues in the Department of Speech at Queens College, Jon Eisenson, Beatrice Jacoby, John Newman, Mardel Ogilvie, Dorothy Rambo, Elizabeth Goepp Scanlan, and Norma S. Rees, graciously consented to read selected sections and to give me their reactions and suggestions. Samuel Lieberman of the Classics Department at Queens College and Stanley Greenfield of the English Department at the University of Washington were good enough to check special notes dealing with certain references to Chinese and Old English, respectively. Esther K. Sheldon of the English Department at Queens College read the entire section on the history of the English language and gave me the benefit of her expert knowledge in that field. Ruth P. Jackson of the Education Department at Queens College read the first few chapters of an earlier version for style and readability. Clarence Barnhart, Editor-in-Chief of the *American College Dictionary*, and Robert Sonkin of the Department of Public Speaking at The City College of New York were the stimulants to the discussion on standards as it appears in the beginning of this text, begun when we were preparing a session on that subject for one of the regional conventions of a few years back. Pierre Delattre of the University of Colorado was good enough to read critically and verify my impressions of the acoustic value of certain consonants. Jess Stein, Managing Editor of the *American College Dictionary*, and Laurence Urdang of the editorial staff of the *American College Dictionary* read Chapters 12 and 13, suggesting appropriate improvements and additions to the presentation. Kenneth Freyer of the Queens College Library helped secure certain hard-to-get bibliographical items. I owe a special thanks to A. C. Gimson of the Department of Phonetics at the University College of London. He not only granted permission for the reproduction of the IPA chart in his capacity as Secretary-Treasurer of the International Phonetic Association, but so kindly offered to supply a phonetic transcription of his own speech as a sample of current Southern British. I am grateful too to those publishers and authors who permitted me to quote from their works. Appropriate acknowledgements for these quotations and for the reproduction of certain maps and charts appear in the text.

It is a pleasure to make special acknowledgement to each of the following for their technical and pedagogical advice, with special reference to certain problems of phonemic and phonetic symbolization: James Abel of Brooklyn College, Harold B. Allen of the University of Minnesota, William K. Archer of Fairleigh Dickenson University, Marshall Berger of The City College of New York, Bert Emsley of Ohio State University, George W. Hibbitt of Columbia University, Sumner Ives of Tulane University, John P. Moncur of the San Francisco Hearing and Speech Clinic, John Newman and Mardel Ogilvie of Queens College, Raven I. McDavid Jr. of the University of Chicago, and Milton Valentine of the University of Colorado.

There are many unacknowledged sources from whom I've borrowed—from colleagues at conventions and association meetings over many years, and from my most important teachers, my students. For all the assistance from all sources, I am deeply appreciative. For the mistakes, I alone am to blame.

No family should enjoy the situation that results when one member thereof is writing a book, for too much time must be spent away from the normal pleasures of family life. My wife, Elsa, and our two children, Nancy and Nabby, have been most patient and understanding, in addition to helping with the typing, proofreading, indices, and the planning and executing of the first drafts of the illustrative material. For their assistance and encouragement over these many, many months, and for the joys which they manage to provide at almost all times, I am most grateful. Therefore, my dedication page to them.

A. J. B.

Contents

Figures

PART ONE

Our Language

Today

CHAPTER 1

Viewing Our Language

Today

INTRODUCTION

OUR STUDY of the pronunciation of American English is divided
into three major parts. The first provides an explanation of those
concepts and terms necessary for an introduction to this study.
This background deals with the attitudes toward language usage, the
levels and varieties of usage, phonetics and phonemics, dialect and
regional speech. Part II, the detailed analysis of the sounds of
American English, is the core of our study. Part III will apply the
previous data to four major areas: sound change, its nature and
forms; the pronunciation of words; the nature of stress or accent;
the pitch and melody patterns we use. All of the above comprise the
study of American-English phonology, the study of the sounds we
use and the forms they take as we speak to each other.

Our concern throughout this text is the study of the nature and
structure of the sounds of the language around us. It is our intent
to analyze the available evidence pertaining to current American
pronunciation. It should be obvious that, since *all* the facts about

3

current pronunciation are not known, additions to our body of knowledge must be made as new studies appear and as further evidence is submitted. Our study is a *synchronic* one, for it deals with those facts of our language of a given place and time. The place leads to the label "American-English"; the time is today.

Although some illustrations of the speech of earlier times will appear throughout this text, the major task will be the consideration of the language of the present day. Historical data and evidence are surveyed separately, in the Appendix, where you will find a review of the language from Old English times to the present. No complete study of American English can overlook the language of yesterday, as it was spoken by the Americans of the Reconstruction period, the time of the War Between the States, the Revolution, and the Colonial period, as well as by our English-speaking forbears across the ocean. Such a study is a course unto itself, and except for the survey chapter already mentioned, it is not included as part of this text. A complete understanding of the phonology includes, therefore, two closely related, yet clearly separable, bodies of linguistic information—the one we have labeled *synchronic*, the other we call *historical* or *diachronic*.

Such questions as "What is correct?," "What is standard?," or "Is it wrong to say—?" are the basis for the first concept that we shall consider. You will soon see that the answers to these questions are not fashioned easily and that quick pronouncements are avoided. As is stated elsewhere in this text, if pronouncements must be made, let them come when, after the study of our linguistic behavior, we are more capable of not only having an opinion, but of defending it.

"STANDARD SPEECH"

The term *standard speech* describes the socially acceptable patterns of speech as used by the educated persons of any community. The very breadth of the term, as defined, raises a number of questions.

1. If usage differs from community to community, is there one preferred standard of American English?

2. How does one actually know what the preferred standard in a given community is?
3. Does the standard remain the same for any definite period of time?
4. What are the influences, if any, that help to establish and maintain standard usage?
5. Are there any influences that force changes in the standard speech?
6. When should we accept new forms and discard old ones?
7. What do people speak when they use a dialect other than that known as "standard speech"?

This chapter discusses the concept of standard speech today, the different levels of speech, how we arrive at them, and the major influences that cause and retard changes in the spoken language.

THE CONCEPT OF STANDARD USAGE: IS THERE A "RIGHT" AND "WRONG"?

British and American Standard

The speech patterns of the educated persons in England vary from region to region, as they do in this country. One such dialect however, spoken and maintained by the graduates of the great English Public Schools (actually expensive, private ones) and their families, has come to represent the socially preferred standard of British English. This dialect, once spoken only by the upper classes of the southeast midlands (London and its environs), has come to be known as "Southern British" or "Southern English" speech. Actually, this preferred pattern or dialect is found in use today all over England, possessing no real distinctive or local flavor. It is not, as commonly thought, the geographical dialect of educated London English. It is rather the dialect spoken by the educated leaders of England, a dialect not of region but of the highest social status. This particular dialect of standard British English is also the dialect you would learn if you were a student in a European University, studying English as a foreign language.

This standard of British English, the "accent of social standing," is the speech commonly used by parliamentary leaders, bankers, industrialists, and professionals. It is the "accent" you hear spoken by visiting British dignitaries. You have probably heard it in the newsreels as spoken by the members of the royal family. You have heard it spoken by British actors on the stage, in the movies, and on your radio and television sets. This standard has many characteristics that distinguish it from our own patterns of speech. The most noticeable are: a melody pattern which possesses greater extremes in inflection when compared to our own; the words *dog*, *cross*, *log*, *hot*, and *odd* all contain the same vowel; the *r* sound is not pronounced except before a vowel (*park* as "pahk" and *far* as "fah"); the *r* between two vowels is a single flapped sound, sometimes respelled in our newspaper comic strips as "veddy" for *very*. The pattern closest to it in America is heard on the stage, and is known as "stage speech." It is known in England as "Received Pronunciation," meaning heard or "received" in the "best" circles.

It has been carefully described by the leading British phonetician Daniel Jones, former professor of phonetics at the University of London.[1]

The United States does not possess a socially preferred standard of speech, as is found in England; nor is there one geographical standard that is considered more acceptable than another. To some persons, a standard of speech used by educated Bostonians or Chicagoans might be considered preferable. Speaking with persons from all over the country, however, will soon convince you that no such general preference exists. The speech of educated Bostonians is no more "standard" than the educated speech of Tulsa, except in Boston. And the educated patterns of speech of Chicago or Charleston are not more acceptable than are those of New York. The speech you use in this country, then, is considered standard *if it reflects the speech patterns of the educated persons in your community*.

[1] See his *An Outline of English Phonetics*, 8th ed. (Cambridge, Eng., W. Heffer and Sons, 1956); *The Pronunciation of English*, 3rd ed., rev. (Cambridge, Eng., Cambridge University Press, 1950); and *Everyman's English Pronouncing Dictionary*, 11th ed. (New York, Dutton, 1956).

Your best reference is the actual speech of the educated members of the community. How do you get to know it? Listen! Your ear is your best guide. On questions of disputed pronunciation usage, where your sources seem to differ, you must refer to current, reputable dictionaries, your teachers, the manuals on pronunciation, and texts such as this.

Standard and Disputed Usages

Standard speech is characterized by patterns of speech that call least attention to themselves. Inasmuch as the purpose of language is the communication of ideas, we normally avoid usages that detract from that purpose. Widespread educated usage, therefore, is an important factor to consider, especially when judging the acceptability of disputed forms. This concept may be demonstrated best by referring to certain commonly disputed grammatical usages of today.

You have certainly heard such constructions as "different than" for "different from," "it is me" for "it is I," and the use of "none are" for "none is." For a long while, most teachers and writers considered these usages "incorrect." Widespread use by many educated writers and speakers necessitated some consideration as to the acceptability of any or all of these forms. Many grammarians and teachers objected strongly, claiming that "traditional" usages are not only more "correct," but they are more easily understood. Many teachers today no longer frown upon some or all of the above mentioned forms. Their acceptance is based on the assumption that although such usages may well be questioned from a structural view by some, their widespread usage by so many educated persons in informal speaking situations necessitates their acceptance into the standard pattern.

The speaker of any language soon finds that the primary need is to be understood. He comes to realize that his language must do the job in as efficient a manner as possible. His language must meet the test of both "acceptability" and "competence." It is on this basis that grammarians struggle to analyze the "right" and "wrong" of language usage. To some, "right" means merely "widely used"; to others, it is defined as "grammatically acceptable." Their decisions regarding "right" and "wrong" are, therefore, colored by their approach.

Standard Speech at the Educated Level

The student of our language must be careful to distinguish between that pattern which is *commonly used* and that which is considered *standard*. The commonly used forms in a given community *may* be part of the standard pattern. But "standard speech" is actually not the "average speech" of all members of the community. It is not the common denominator between the speech used by the most highly educated members of the community and that used by the least educated members of the society. It is rather the habitual, or normal, speech used by the cultivated members of our society in both formal and informal situations. Its grammatical constructions are those of the well-considered books, newspapers, and periodicals you read. Its pronunciation, melodic, articulatory, and vocal patterns are those used by the persons who read such materials and who talk about them. The standard spoken language is, therefore, neither "affected," "uneducated," nor "illiterate."

VARIETIES OR LEVELS OF SPEECH

You will gain a clearer understanding of our language as you begin to recognize the existence of the different varieties or levels of usage found in any community. These levels reflect the societal structure of the community. Like the levels of that society, they overlap, showing no clear-cut lines of demarcation. Usages of one level may be found in a neighboring level. Charles C. Fries describes these levels in his article "Usage Levels and Dialect Distribution," in the *American College Dictionary.* He pictures them as a series of interlocking circles. Keep in mind that these levels are peculiar to all regional areas of the country.

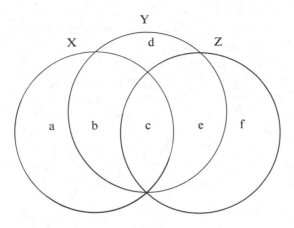

FIG. 1. The interlocking circles of formal, colloquial, and illiterate English. (After Charles C. Fries in *The American College Dictionary* (New York, Random House, 1953), p. xxviii, with permission from Random House, Inc.)

X—formal, literary English
Y—colloquial, informal English of cultivated people
Z—illiterate, uneducated English

b, c, e, represent the overlappings of the three types
c—that which is common to all three
b—that which is common to formal and colloquial
e—that which is common to colloquial and illiterate
a, d, f represent the portions peculiar to that set of language habits

Educated Formal Speech

The three interlocking circles represent *formal literary* English (the expressions used in serious books), *colloquial* English (the usages of informal, educated conversation), and *illiterate* English (usages of the uneducated). The first two circles represent different degrees of formality of standard usage. Both belong to a social status different from the third. These same levels exist for both written and spoken English. Formal speech may be heard from the pulpit, in a public address by a government official, in the speech of the. well-educated person in a formal situation. Colloquial expressions are held to a minimum. The precision of this style of speech necessitates restrictions on the use of many unstressed forms, and the speaker assumes a careful and deliberate manner. *Record, actor,* and other such disyllables may possess some degree of stress on both syllables. The auxiliary forms *was, have,* and *had* may not be fully unstressed, the vowels of each tending to retain their full value. Contractions such as *haven't, weren't,* and *hadn't* are avoided in favor of the full forms *have not, were not,* and *had not.* This style of speech is used by the platform speaker and reader in a formal situation. It is formal, deliberate, and educated.

Educated Colloquial Speech

Colloquial or informal speech possesses characteristics of speech common to the classroom, the business conference, the dinner table, and the everyday situations in which we conduct our affairs. This style differs from the more formal and deliberative style in the greater use of unstressed syllables and the normal use of contractions common to the spoken language. It is the style of speech most commonly used by all but the uneducated levels of society. It is grammatically "correct" and acceptable. Its pronunciations and enunciations are those commonly found in our dictionaries. New pronunciations find their way into this style more easily than they do into the more formal type of speech. *Both formal and colloquial English comprise the standard of the language. Both are functional varieties of the standard form.*

Substandard Speech

Substandard speech contains the expressions and pronunciations commonly found in the language of the uneducated members of the community. Grammatical regulation is at a minimum and excessive assimilations and deletions of sounds take place. "D'jeat" may be heard for "did you eat?," "fir" for "first," and "wanna" for "want to." The speech of this level sounds careless, slovenly, and unacceptable to habitual speakers of Standard English.

Not only are certain usages found in more than one level, but the pronunciation patterns we use in any one level are often the results of shifts from another level. The pronunciations of *nature* and *picture* as "natshure" and "piktshure" were previously common only in substandard speech. Today, such pronunciations are part of standard speech. The stressed vowel sound in *father* was considered substandard and "rural" little more than 150 years ago, when *father* (with the vowel of *cat*) was the commonly-used standard form. The pronunciation "close" for the noun *clothes* (the verb still retains the original form, as spelled), a formerly uneducated form, was already common in informal educated speech by the beginning of the eighteenth century. All our dictionaries today show this pronunciation (klōz) as well as the older pronunciation (klōthz).[2] "Idear" for *idea*, although used by many educated speakers, has not been able, as yet, to bridge the gap into the standard pattern.

There is a strong and valid objection to depicting these forms of speech as "levels," especially if the reader will then assume that "very good" speech is at one end of the diagram, "very bad" speech at the other, and the colloquial pattern somewhere in between. Formal and informal speech are both used by the same people and either is as "good" as the other. Colloquial speech is neither "worse" than formal speech, nor lacking in any aspect of social acceptability. Each is merely used in different situations. Furthermore, it is important to note that the informal and formal varieties do not differ greatly from each other. In most instances, they make use of the identical forms. It might be useful, therefore, to think of these differently described speech patterns as "forms" or "varieties," rather than as "levels" of speech.

As a student of the English language, you are faced with the need for recognizing the existence of varieties of speech and of conforming to those common to your social and intellectual community. You

---

[2] Robert Herrick's *Upon Julia's Clothes*, written in 1684, contains the following lines:

> Whenas in silks my Julia goes,
> Then, then, methinks, how sweetly flows
> That liquefaction of her clothes.

will find that the habitual speech of your community is that which we label "informal-colloquial." In actuality, this style varies little from community to community and even from region to region. Although fairly definite regional variations exist (see Chapter 3), the language from region to region is much more alike than it is different. Many influences account for this remarkable uniformity of educated speech found in America. This uniformity may be traced to the fact that all of us go through a school system for a number of years, to the mass media (newspapers, radio and television shows, and movies we see and hear), to the ease of travel from area to area, the similar books we read and study, and most importantly, to the language used by the earlier settlers who took with them, in their moves westward from the eastern seaboard areas, the similar patterns of those areas.

Although our speech in different regions is more alike than it is different, we are still able to recognize regional speech sources. Our language is certainly not entirely uniform, as you will see in Chapter 3. Educated speech is certainly more varied in the United States than in England, where speakers of Received Pronunciation do not give a clear indication of their geographic origins. If you have four professors—from Montgomery, Alabama; Springfield, Massachusetts; Dallas, Texas; and Lincoln, Nebraska—you are surely aware that each comes from a different section of the country. This might not be so if they came from four sections of England, for their regional differences would probably be concealed by the Received Pronunciation patterns they all would use.

This educated informal-colloquial style is the speech you accept and expect of those speaking to you. It is the style of speech that will persist about you after your schooling ends. Your recognition of these patterns has already taken place. Your acceptance of them is unavoidable.

CHANGE AND STANDARD USAGE

Our discussion of standard speech, so far, might lead you to the conclusion that we have been talking about a "static," "fixed," or "set" language. Nothing could be farther from the truth. Our language is constantly changing. New words, meanings, and pronunciations are added to the standard levels, while others become obsolete through disuse. Some of these factors that cause change are subtle, hardly detectable at first. Others are the result of more obvious influences.

You know that the speech of all persons will show some differences in the same sounds, even when the sounds appear in the same context. Part of the reason for this may be attributed to the different speeds with which a word or phrase is spoken, or the slight shifts in stress on a given word in different phrases. Thus, the vowel sound in the word *good* in the following phrases may show some differences when it is read at different speeds, or because the word possesses different degrees of stress in different phrases.

> Take good care to make a good showing.
> For goodness sake!
> "Good!" said the teacher.
> "Am I good or bad?" was the child's persistent question.

You have also heard two persons with the same linguistic background pronounce the same words slightly differently. When the regional background differs, the differences are even more obvious. Thus, the vowels in the words *forest, candy, fine,* and *town* might be pronounced differently by members of your class who come from the same regional area. *Half* and *third* are heard with clearer differences when spoken by Southern, New York, and Middle-Western people.

Finally, sounds show some differences when they appear near different sounds (*k*eep—*c*ool), or before differently stressed vowels (*p*en—u*pp*er), in different positions of a word (*t*ea—bu*t*ter), or in differently stressed syllables (I *was*—I was *here*).

All of these factors influence or cause change in the language we speak. If unchecked, these changes become more obvious and the language assumes different forms in time. This is what happened to words like *mission, nature,* and *father,* formerly pronounced "mis-i-un," "natyur," and "fǎther." Such changes account, in part, for our developing language and for our present modern English sounds from earlier forms.[3]

THE INFLUENCES THAT RESIST CHANGE

The influences that cause change in our standard are somewhat counterbalanced, not only by our general resistance to rapid change (the almost instinctive desire to conserve), but by other factors. These are the schools, the dictionaries, and the written word.

The Schools and the Dictionaries

Schools and dictionaries play a most important part in interpreting and prescribing acceptability of language usage. As keepers of fashion, they tend to act as greater or lesser conservative agents. Their purpose is to teach and list the language in its recognizably acceptable form. Schools draw the line of acceptability, indicating what is permissible, questionable, or unacceptable. As the pressures of changes exert their influence, schools wait for widespread acceptance and then offer their sanction. They move slowly before sanction is granted. Widespread usage by educated speakers prepares the way for such acceptance by the schools.

The dictionary is actually a generalized reference record of current, cultivated usage (sometimes formal, sometimes colloquial, sometimes both). For many of its readers, it tends to act as a permanent, ultimate authority. As such, unless a current edition is available, the reader finds his authority representing a static, unchanging language.

It is perhaps not unnecessary to state that many of us are rather naïve in our attitudes toward dictionaries. Firstly, we assume that only one "verdict" is found in all dictionaries for any given entry. A rapid check of the pronunciation entries for such words as *adult*, *abdomen*, *aerial*, *clangor*, *ask*, and *advertisement* will show quite a divergence of opinion. The unabridged editions of Webster's *New International* and Funk and Wagnall's *Standard* include long lists of

---

[3] A detailed analysis of sound change is found in Chapter 11.

words for which different dictionaries present different "authorita-tive" pronunciations, demonstrating noticeable disagreement among reputable dictionaries. There is no real consensus as to the "educated" pronunciations of all the words we commonly use.

Secondly, we should be aware that dictionaries exclude many variant pronunciations of words that are actually in common use in different sections or regions of the country. Editors do so because inclusion of all such known variations would be financially pro-hibitive. They select those forms which represent the most widely used forms.[4]

Of greater importance is the recognition that dictionary entries are "word entries" and not always the entries of words as spoken in the context of speech. We speak in groups of words, in phrases, and sentences, not in single words, one at a time. The same words in different contexts may sound different because of the immediate phonetic environment or the degree of stress the word receives. Although some dictionaries attempt to insert such variants as may appear in our speech, they do not, and probably cannot, include all such forms of the words we use. Thus, the word *the* is hardly ever pronounced (thē), with a fully stressed vowel, nor are the words *was*, *have*, and *and*. The variant pronunciations of these words are dis-cussed later in this text. Suffice it to say here, that if we followed the pronunciation listed in some dictionaries for such words, our speech would sound stilted and unnatural, a sort of "word-by-word" speaking.

The schools and dictionaries are not the first to accept changes in the language. Nor should they be. When enough substantiating evidence is available, the teacher and the lexicographer must be willing to subscribe thereto. If they (or you) are too hesitant to

---

[4] Sometimes the bias of the editor may show. Southern pronunciations appear with a reasonable degree of consistency in Kenyon and Knott's *Pronouncing Dictionary of American English*, not in any of the others. And one well-known dictionary still lists the broader "a" [a], in such words as *ask* and *dance* despite the fact that the great majority of Americans normally pronounce these words with the "short ǎ" of *cat*, while the broader sound is found only sporadically in the eastern part of the United States.

sanction usages clearly current in standard circles, they (and you) soon find themselves behind the times.

The Written Word

One of the strongest deterrents to pronunciation change is the spelled form of the written language. How many times have you decided on a disputed or unknown pronunciation by merely checking the spelling of the word? Actually, most of us tend to pronounce words new to us in a manner consistent with their spelling, at least until we get a chance to check. The tendency to retain these pronunciations, once spoken and heard, is a strong one. Over the years, there have been many movements to change the spelling of our language to reflect current pronunciations. The nineteenth century saw a strong spelling-reform movement spearheaded by Isaac Pitman, the creator of the well-known method of shorthand. At George Bernard Shaw's death, his will created a special fund to be used for the purpose of spelling reform. But none of these attempts has been successful as yet. The spelled form has remained a strong influence on our habits of pronunciation and will continue to do so as long as we are a literate people. Spelling changes occur very slowly, if at all. Pronunciation changes, though more rapid, are checked by the very presence of the spelled forms. As a single example, note how American speakers retain the many syllables and the secondary stress in such words as *secretary*, *dictionary*, *tertiary*, and *primarily*. And if you didn't use the word *every* so frequently, might not the spelled form kindle a desire to say this as a three syllable word, instead of as a two syllable word, as you normally do? We must recognize the written word, along with the schools and dictionaries, as a force that prevents variation in the language.

SUMMARY

The view of our language has now expanded to include a number of new horizons for you. You now realize that answering the question "What is right?" may not be simple. You are aware that our language differs from British English, in more ways than one; that we have no socially-preferred regional pattern of speech; that one geographical standard is really no "better" than another.

Since the purpose of language is simply to be understood by those to whom we speak, you now realize the need for language efficiency, and that such efficiency is closely related to the concepts of standard speech and to the varieties of usage. The language we use is both changing and being restrained from too rapid change. We are aware of forces that change or prevent change, how they work, or how they affect the language we speak.

One segment of our subject still needs to be discussed in this connection. What are these geographical or regional standards, where are they spoken, and how did they come about? This subject must wait until we can understand an important tool with which we can analyze the spoken language. This tool, the phonetic alphabet, is the subject of the next chapter.

QUESTIONS FOR FURTHER STUDY

1. Add the following terms to your vocabulary, being sure you understand them: *colloquial-cultivated English; spelling pronunciation; standard American English; usage levels* or *varieties of speech.*
2. Why is the term *correct speech* actually a misnomer? What would you substitute?
3. Should your cousin from Des Moines change his speech when he visits you in Savannah? Why?
4. Is a spelling book published at the turn of the century out-of-date, as far as "correct spelling" is concerned? Why?
5. Are the pronunciation entries in a dictionary, published about the same time, suitable for checking your own pronunciation questions? Why?
6. What levels or varieties of speech would you use when speaking to a classmate; the president of your university; a well-known friend, not seen since elementary school days?
7. Would you expect your younger brother to be corrected if he should say the following to his second-grade teacher? Why?

   "madder" for *matter*   "yeah" for *yes*
   "boid" for *bird*   "close" for *clothes*

"ev'ry" for *every*   "at's right" for *that's right*
"goverment" for *government*   "mebbe" for *maybe*

SOURCES FOR FURTHER STUDY

FRIES, Charles C., "Acceptable Pronunciation," *The Teaching of English* (Ann Arbor, Mich., George Wahr Publishing Co., 1949), pp. 46–73.

———, "Usage Levels and Dialect Distribution," in *The American College Dictionary* (New York, Random House, 1953), pp. xxvii–xxxviii.

GREET, W. Cabell, "Pronunciation," in *The American College Dictionary* (New York, Random House, 1953), p. xxii.

JONES, Daniel, "Types of Pronunciation," *The Pronunciation of English*, 3rd ed., rev. (Cambridge, Eng., Cambridge University Press, 1950), Ch. 1, pp. 3–5.

KANTNER, Claude E., and WEST, Robert, "American Speech Style," *Phonetics* (New York, Harper, 1946), Ch. 16, pp. 261–283.

KENYON, John S., *American Pronunciation*, 10th ed. (Ann Arbor, Mich., George Wahr Publishing Co., 1951), pp. 12–16.

———, "Cultural Levels and Functional Varieties of English," *College English*, Vol. 10 (October, 1948), pp. 31–36.

———, and KNOTT, Thomas A., *A Pronouncing Dictionary of American English* (Springfield, Mass., Merriam, 1944), pp. xv–xvi.

KRAPP, George P., "English Dialects," and "The Levels of English Speech," *The Knowledge of English* (New York, Holt, 1927), Ch. 3, pp. 22–28 and Ch. 6, pp. 55–76.

LLOYD, Donald J., and WARFEL, Harry R., "The Speech Community," *American English in its Cultural Setting* (New York, Knopf, 1956), Ch. 3, pp. 42–56.

PYLES, Thomas, "Linguistic Nationalism and the Schoolmaster," and "Purity by Prescription," *Words and Ways in American English* (New York, Random House, 1952), Ch. 4, pp. 74–92 and Ch. 11, pp. 271–292.

THOMAS, Charles K., "Standards of Pronunciation," *An Introduction to the Phonetics of American English*, 2nd ed. (New York, Ronald, 1958), Ch. 24, pp. 253–260.

"Urbanization and Standard Language." (Six papers by W. F. Twadell, Einar Haugen, Robert A. Hall, Jr., Paul L. Garvin, Margaret Mead, Hans Wolff.) *Anthropological Linguistics*, Vol. 1, No. 3 (March, 1959), 41 pp.

Webster's New International Dictionary 2nd ed. (Springfield, Mass., Merriam, 1934), pp. xxiii–xxvi.

WILSON, George L., "Standards of Correct Pronunciation," *The Quarterly Journal of Speech*, Vol. XXIII (December, 1937), pp. 568–576.

CHAPTER 2

Analyzing the Spoken Language

THE PHONETIC CONCEPT

Introduction

PHONETICS IS CONCERNED with the study of the sounds of speech as they are made by a speaker and heard by a listener. With a knowledge of phonetics we can recognize and analyze the sounds of our language, and classify, describe, and study each sound in relation to other sounds of the language. It is a most important branch of the study of any language. It uses the pertinent research of acoustics, the physiology and anatomy of the speech and hearing mechanisms, and the principles of the science of linguistics. With a knowledge of phonetics, you are capable of understanding the actual sound structure of the language you speak and hear. With an understanding of phonetics, the variations within a language can be made clear, and the reasons for sound change can be explained more easily.

An understanding of the phonetic approach, then, is basic to any language study. Language, as we know and use it, is the spoken tongue, the normal means of face-to-face communication.

The written form records the spoken language. A written form uses a system of letters or other written shapes to represent the sounds of speech which the writer would use if he were with the receiver of his message. The notes written on your paper by your professor are the substitute for the words he would use in conference. The combinations we make with the letters of our alphabet arbitrarily refer to a system of sounds which, when spoken, is the language we use. This relation of the spoken to the written form has been succinctly stated:

> Writing is not language, though it usually represents language. Letters are not sounds, though they may represent sounds. Combinations of letters are not words, though they may represent words.[1]

The study of a language begins, then, with a study of its spoken form, its sounds and sound system. And the alphabet of concern is phonetic rather than the one containing the conventional spelling such as is used to represent the words you have just read on this page.

Why a Phonetic Alphabet?

It is common to think of a language as represented by the letters of an alphabet and the combinations thereof. Actually, these symbols represent the *sounds* used by the speakers of that language. The written form of the language we use today continues to show little change from one generation to another. The alphabetical way of representing our speech has successfully resisted pressures for change, even when it no longer reflects many current pronunciations. Since the sixteenth century, spelling changes have been few indeed, but our pronunciations have changed in many ways. Although the spelling of many words still conforms to the pronunciations we use for them *(stir, carve, hit, get, ship, art)*, there are many others for which the spelling hardly reflects modern pronunciation usage. Your pronunciation of *night, through, isle, calm, nature, looked, Worcester,*

---

[1] W. Nelson Francis, *The Structure of American English* (New York, Ronald, 1958), p. 38.

cupboard, one, soldier, and *slough,* exactly as spelled, would raise quite a few eyebrows among your associates.

A need for an alphabet that can and does recognize these spoken changes when made, and that can represent them accurately, has been obvious for a long time. By the end of the nineteenth century the realization of this need was strong enough to motivate a convention of an international group of language teachers who concerned themselves with the establishment of principles and symbols for such an alphabet. The basis for the IPA (International Phonetic Alphabet) was established in 1886 and the first alphabet was designed in 1888. Although concerned at first with phonetics as applied to the teaching of English, the international membership of the association led to a demand for phonetic texts in languages other than English. As a result, the association has developed, over the years, a system containing different characters for the phonetic representation of the principal languages of the world.

Since first established, these characters have undergone some modification, but the principles that established them have remained relatively unchanged.[2] The basic principle of any phonetic alphabet is that one symbol shall represent one distinctive sound, regardless of how many different ways it may be spelled.

In each of the following pairs of words there is an identically spelled form: *this* and *thin; cite* and *city; gem* and *gate.* Yet we pronounce the *th* in the first pair, the *i* in the second pair, and the *g* in the third pair differently. We all pronounce the *ough* spellings in *through, though, cough,* and *rough* differently. The *s* in *his* is not an "s" sound and the *b* in *dumb* as well as the *t* in *often* are normally silent or unpronounced, while the *tion* and *sion* of *nation* and *mission* are pronounced identically.

Unlike our Latin alphabet, a phonetic alphabet represents the same sounds by the same symbols, regardless of the spelled form.

---

[2] A copy of the current IPA chart appears in the Appendix. It is published by the International Phonetic Association. The chart and *The Principles of the International Phonetic Association,* 1949, are obtainable from the Secretary of the IPA, Department of Phonetics, University College, London.

Where different speakers pronounce a given word or phrase differently, the use of the phonetic alphabet allows for the representing of such differences. Phonetic study can proceed best, then, if the language is represented by a *sound* rather than by a *written* or *spelled* alphabet.

THE PHONEMIC CONCEPT

Before we attempt to learn this new "sound alphabet," we will need to recognize and understand the process or method by which we can isolate the different sounds of our language. This method is based on a recognition of the *phonemes* of a language. For our purposes at the moment, a phoneme may be defined as a sound that is significantly different from the other sounds of the language. Once we can recognize and identify these significantly-different sounds, our task of analyzing our speech is made easier. Firstly, we must recognize that there may be certain other sound-features we shall hear whenever a person talks. The problem before us is to separate those sound-features essential to the speaker's message from those which may be disregarded without hindering our understanding of what he is saying.

One person speaks "through his nose," another in a high tenor voice, another with exceptional rapidity, and still another with great volume. Each says the same sentence: "Please pass the butter." What shall we indicate as the significant sounds of this sentence in this language? Certainly none of the factors of rate, pitch, volume, or quality of speech and voice is as important for our understanding the message as the words being spoken. Those words are made up of certain very specific sounds, which, when put together, convey the intended request. *What* is said, rather than *how* it is said, is of first and immediate concern. We receive the message when we hear and recognize the combinations of those significant sounds which ultimately have a certain effect on our behavior. Had we heard the similar-sounding, but quite different, "Please gas the brother," our resultant behavior would have been changed considerably.

Phonemics is that area of linguistic study concerned with the identification of the significant sounds of a given language. This then must be our first concern. We must identify those sounds of our language, which, when combined with other sounds, represent meaningful concepts to the users of that language. In order to accomplish this task, it will be useful to look at our language from a new vantage point.

Let us assume you come across English as a new language, completely unknown and strange to you. As you listen to the speakers of this strange language and attempt to understand it, one of your first problems is to break the language down into its meaningfully-different, or significantly-different, sounds. You are not concerned with slight differences, or with variations that different speakers make of the same sound. Such detailing of insignificant variations at this stage would merely confuse you. You may hear what seem like two different initial sounds in *key* and *cool*, and two different initial sounds in *sue* and *sure*. In time, as you continue to listen to the speakers of this language, you will be able to conclude that the initial sounds of *cool* and *key*, although somewhat different from each other, are really only different "k" sounds, analogous to the two "shades" of the same color. The initial sounds of *sue*, and *sure*, although acoustically similar, turn out to be different sounds in this language—they are not shades of the same color, they are different colors. The sounds you hear in *cool* and *key* can be heard in *kite*, *cough*, and *hike*. The sound you hear in *sue* can be heard in *see*, *sore*, and *lass;* that of *sure* in *she*, *shore*, and *lash*. You can readily note that the similar sounds of *cool* and *key* may be replaced by those in *kite*, *cough*, and *hike*, yet the words when pronounced will still have the same meanings for us. But the similar sounds in the pairs *see* and *she*, *sore* and *shore*, *lass* and *lash* cannot be substituted for each other, unless the speaker desires to change the meaning of the word. "I love the lass" may sound like "I love the lash," but it cannot be used in place of it. Replacing the initial sound of *see* with the initial sound of *sure* in *see*, *sore*, *lease*, and *crass* creates four new words in English. The similar initial sounds in *see* and *she* are significantly different. You cannot replace one with the other without changing the meaning intended for the listener.

Continuing analysis of this language will lead you to recognize other differences, some significant, some not. *Fend* and *bend* begin with different phonemes in English. They make for significantly-different words. *Life* and *rough*, however, end with the same phonemes in our language. If interchanged, their pronunciation will still signify the same meanings. The vowels in *heat* and *beat* will be recognized as significantly different in English from those in *hit* and *bit*. Although acoustically similar, when one is substituted for the other, the result is a different word in the language.

If your native tongue were French, the vowels in the two words *heat* and *hit* would not be recognized by you as two essentially different sounds at first, for in French these two vowel sounds are not significantly different from each other. They would sound like variations of the same phoneme, as spoken by two speakers, or by the same speaker in different phonetic contexts. As a student of French, you might say the word *ici* (meaning "here" and normally pronounced as though spelled "ēēsēē") or the word *qui* (meaning "who" and normally pronounced as though spelled "key") with a sound closer to the vowel of *it* than to the more commonly used vowel of *eat*. Your French friend might wince, but he would know the words you were saying. The vowels of *it* and *eat* do not appear as significantly-different sounds in French. They do not create, when substituted for each other, semantic or meaningful differences in words, as they do in English. Therefore, a speaker of English, listening to his French friend trying to speak English, would notice that his friend says the same sounds for both *sit* and *seat*. When the Frenchman first tries to speak English he might say the sentence "Heat the ball," when he means "Hit the ball," or "It does not feet," when he means "It does not fit." To the Frenchman, then, the vowels of *it* and *eat* are different varieties of one sound, or of one phoneme, in his language, like the different varieties of the initial phoneme we use in the two words *key* and *cool.* These different varieties, which do not contrast significantly from each other, are known as *allophones* of the same phoneme; they are merely different members of the same phoneme.

Let us continue the illustration a bit further. The speaker of English may note that his pronunciation of the *t* sound in *team* and *steam* varies. To him, however, the two *t* sounds do not vary so much that they are actually different phonemes in English. He knows them, if he recognizes the differences at all, as minor variations of the same sound in his language. They are allophones of the phoneme known to him as /t/. When he analyzes the two *t* sounds of *team* and *steam* he may note that the *t* of *team* is followed by an explosive puff of air, while the *t* of *steam* is not followed by this same aspiration. As we can readily see, the presence or absence of this aspiration after the *t* does not make for a phonemic difference in our language. The sound with the following aspiration or without it is still a *t* sound. If, however, he should study Chinese, he would soon note that the presence or absence of this same aspiration (or explosive puff of air) after a consonant does create a significant change in a word. In Pekinese, *tao*, with no aspiration after the *t*, means "to pray," while *tʰao*, with aspiration after the *t*, means "to demand"; *kung*, without aspiration, means "respectful," *kʰung*, with aspiration after the *k*, means "to fear." Hence, in Chinese the presence of aspiration after a sound changes it significantly from the sound with no following aspiration, thus indicating two different phonemes. In English the same variations would merely indicate two allophones of the same phoneme.

Similarly, the words *see, yes, bits,* and *lace* all possess a common phoneme: /s/. The words *zebra* and *has* are pronounced with the phoneme /z/. The words *cat* and *cash* possess the same initial conso- nant and, for most of us, the same vowel phonemes. We may conclude then, that although different speakers of the English language might say each of these phonemes slightly differently in each of these words, they are merely using variations of the same phonemes. We recognize phonemically-different pronunciations as different sounds: *(ten* and *den)*. We recognize allophonic differences, when they occur, as aspects or insignificant variations of the same sound: *(pen* and *happy)*. *Allophonic variants, when substituted for each other, do not make for meaningful differences in a word. Phonemically-different sounds, when substituted for each other, do make for meaningful differences.*

    We are now ready to take the next step in phonemic recognition, namely, that the sounds of a language are found in certain characteristic patterns. This means that any one allophone of a phoneme may occur in a special context in which none of the others occurs, and secondly, that different phonemes can and do occur in the same contexts. Let us return to the small "puff of air" mentioned earlier as noticed in the word *team.* Our normal pronunciation of this word could be demonstrated by writing a small *h* after the *t* sound to distinguish *t^heam* from *steam.* The same "puff of air" is sounded after other sounds too, when in identical environments: *peak* vs. *speak; care* vs. *scare.* In the first word of each pair, the same puff of air is heard, while in the second word it is not present. You will notice that in each pair, the *p, t, k* sounds are followed by the same stressed vowels, but that the aspirated sounds are initial, while the unaspirated ones are preceded by *s* sounds. A test with other words will show that same presence or absence of this puff in the same environments: *pace* and *space; pie* and *spy; pore* and *spore; pin* and *spin; tie* and *sty; toe* and *stow; kin* and *skin; kill* and *skill.* It is now possible to make a generalization about an aspect of each of the three phonemes /p, t, k/, namely, that two different varieties of each sound exist in certain contexts, and that these two variations do not result in significantly-different sounds but in different allophones of the same sound. Further, you can also observe from the above samples that the one variety of /p, t, k/ is never found in the phonetic environment of the other. The *p* sound with the explosive puff is not heard when it follows an *s* sound, and the *p* sound with the following puff of air is always heard when it begins a stressed syllable. Since these two varieties, or allophones, of /p/ (or /t/ or /k/)

do not appear in the same contexts, they are said to be in *complementary distribution*, and, as such, qualify as members of the same phoneme.

The second part of the generalization, that different phonemes can and do occur in the same contexts, is easier to recognize. Phonetically-similar sounds, like *p* and *b*, or *s* and *z*, may appear in identical contexts, as in *pin* and *bin*, *park* and *bark*, *rip* and *rib*, *sue* and *zoo*, *racer* and *razor*. These are significantly-different sounds that result in different words, and they cannot be substituted for each other without confusing the listener. These sounds are not like the phonetically similar *t* sounds in *team* and *steam*, for the substitution of one of these *t* sounds for the other is quite possible in our language, even if such would sound strange to our ears. "St^heam" for "steam" sounds like a mispronunciation of *steam;* "pin" for "bin" isn't a mispronunciation; it is a different word because of a significantly-different initial sound. We conclude again, then, that /p/ and /b/ are different phonemes, while the *t* sounds of *team* and *steam* are different allophones of the same phoneme.

Some Different Phonemes in English		*Some Different Allophones of the Same Sound in English*	
*t*en	*d*en	*t*an	*st*and
*s*ue	*z*oo	*k*eep	*c*ool
la*c*y	la*z*y	*p*en	*Sp*ain
*s*eat	*s*it	*l*ive	fu*ll*
*g*et	*g*ate	*c*ar	*sc*ar
*g*et	*y*et	*s*it	*w*in
men*d*	mean*t*	*s*ue	*c*ool

Each language has its own set of phonemes. It is necessary for you, as a student of phonetics, to isolate these phonemes and to recognize them no matter in what context they appear. As a student of phonetics, you will note that different adjacent sounds influence a particular sound under consideration so that it varies slightly from the way it is heard in other contexts. It remains the same phoneme as long as no significant difference results. Since *t* and *d* in *ten* and *den* are different phonemes in our language, they are represented by different symbols: /t/, /d/. The initial sounds in *geese* and *goose* are variants or members of the same phoneme in our language. As such they are represented by the same symbol: /g/.

THE PHONETIC ALPHABET

The following table lists the sounds we use for the English language in America. It is based on the alphabet of the International Phonetic Association. It includes only those symbols needed for transcribing American English, with some slight modifications commonly used in American phonetic study. You do not use all of these sounds in the particular dialect you speak. It will be useful, however, to be able to recognize each of them when you hear it. Pronounce each symbol with the sound you normally use in the key word. Where the sound does not appear as a special sound of your dialect, a footnote may explain the reason. Check with others and with your teacher to be sure that the symbol and sound go together. Variations will be discussed in detail later in the text.

Learn to identify each sound with the symbol, each symbol with the sound, remembering there is one, and only one, symbol for each sound. This is a new alphabetical system for you. You will find it necessary to practice with it before you can apply it. If you will give it a few minutes each day, you will master it in a short while.

THE SOUNDS OF AMERICAN ENGLISH

Vowel Sounds	Key Words	In Phonetic Transcription	Respelled in the Diacritic Systems of	
			American College Dict.	*Webster's New Collegiate Dict.*
i	*each, free, keep*	[itʃ, fri, kip]	ēch, frē, kēp	ēch, frē, kēp
ɪ	*it, bin*	[ɪt, bɪn]	ĭt, bĭn	ĭt, bĭn
e[1]	*ate, made, they*	[et, med, ðe]	āt, mād, t̶h̶ā	āt, mād, t̶h̶ā
ɛ	*end, then, there*	[ɛnd, ðɛn, ðɛə-ðɛɚ]	ĕnd, t̶h̶ĕn, t̶h̶âr	ĕnd, t̶h̶ĕn, t̶h̶âr
æ	*act, man*	[ækt, mæn]	ăkt, măn	ăkt, măn

[1] Pronounced either as a single vowel or as the diphthong [eɪ].

Vowel Sounds	Key Words	In Phonetic Transcription	American College Dict.	Webster's New Collegiate Dict.
a²	ask, half, past	[ask, haf, past]	ăsk, hăf, păst; äsk, häf, päst	åsk, håf, påst
ɑ	alms, father	[ɑmz, fɑðə-ə˞]	ämz, fäthər	ämz, fäthĕr
ɒ³	hot, odd, dog, cross	[hɒt, ɒd, dɒg, krɒs]	hŏt, ŏd, dôg or dôg, krôs or krŏs	hŏt, ŏd, dô̆g, krô̆s
ɔ	awl, torn	[ɔl, tɔ(r)n]	ôl, tôrn	ôl, tôrn
o⁴	obey, note, go	[obe, not, go]	ōbā, nōt, gō	ȯbā, nōt, gō
ʊ	good, foot	[gʊd, fʊt]	go͝od, fo͝ot	go͝od, fo͝ot
u	ooze, too	[uz, tu]	ōoz, tōo	ōoz, tōo
ə⁵	alone, among circus, system	[əlon, əmʌŋ] [sɜ˞kəs, sɪstəm]	əlōn, əmŭng sûrkəs, sĭstəm	ălōn, ămŭng sûrkŭs, sĭstĕm
ə, ə˞	father, singer	[fɑðə-ə˞, sɪŋə-ə˞]	fäthər, singər	fäthĕr, sĭngĕr
ʌ	up, come	[ʌp, kʌm]	ŭp, kŭm	ŭp, kŭm
ɜ, ɝ	urn, third	[ɜn, ɝn, θɜd, θɝd]	ûrn, thûrd	ûrn, thûrd
ɨ⁶	children, swim	[tʃɨldrən, swɨm]	———	———

Consonant Sounds	Key Words	In Phonetic Transcription	American College Dict.	Webster's New Collegiate Dict.
p	pie, ape	[paɪ, ep]	pī, āp	pī, āp
b	be, web	[bi, wɛb]	bē, wĕb	bē, wĕb
m	me, am	[mi, æm]	mē, ăm	mē, ăm

² A sound intermediate between [æ] and [ɑ]. Not a common American English vowel. Found in such words as those listed in Eastern New England and sporadically in the New York City area. Speakers in other parts of the country use [æ] in these words. Southerners commonly use this sound in such words as *blind*, *mine*, and *five*.

³ A sound intermediate between [ɑ] and [ɔ]. Not a common American English vowel. Found in such words as those listed in Eastern New England and in the western part of Pennsylvania, as well as in the Received Pronunciation of England. Speakers in other parts of America would normally use [ɑ] in *hot* and *odd*, and [ɔ] in *dog* and *cross*.

⁴ Pronounced either as a single vowel or as the diphthong [oʊ].

⁵ [ə] and [ʌ] may be considered as unstressed and stressed forms of the same sound, as are [ə˞] and [ɝ], [ə] and [ɜ]. The symbolization used in this text, however, follows that commonly used in American speech texts as illustrated in the Kenyon and Knott *Dictionary*, rather than that school of American linguists who use [ə] and [ʌ] as stressed or unstressed varieties of the same phoneme, both represented by [ə].

⁶ This controversial "barred i" sound is commonly overlooked as a vowel sound separate from [ɪ] or [ə]. It does not seem to appear in all persons' speech, and there are many who use it in certain words at certain times, but not at all times. It is discussed in detail in Chapters 7 and 9.

Consonant Sounds	Key Words	In Phonetic Transcription	American College Dict.	Webster's New Collegiate Dict.
w	we, woe	[wi, wo]	wē, wō	wē, wō
ʌ[7]	why, when	[ʍaɪ, ʍɛn]	hwī, hwĕn	hwī, hwĕn
f	free, if	[fri, ɪf]	frē, ĭf	frē, ĭf
v	vine, have	[vaɪn, hæv]	vīn, hăv	vīn, hăv
θ	thin, faith	[θɪn, feθ]	thĭn, fāth	thĭn, fāth
ð	then, clothe	[ðɛn, kloð]	then, klōth	then, klōth
t	ten, it	[tɛn, ɪt]	tĕn, ĭt	tĕn, ĭt
d	den, had	[dɛn, hæd]	dĕn, hăd	dĕn, hăd
n	no, one	[no, wʌn]	nō, wŭn	nō, wŭn
l	live, frill	[lɪv, frɪl]	lĭv, frĭl	lĭv, frĭl
r	red, arrow	[rɛd, æro]	rĕd, ărō	rĕd, ărō
s	see, yes	[si, jɛs]	sē, yĕs	sē, yĕs
z	zoo, as	[zu, æz]	zoo, ăz	zoo, ăz
ʃ	show, ash	[ʃo, æʃ]	shō, ăsh	shō, ăsh
ʒ	measure, azure	[mɛʒɚ, æʒɚ]	mĕzhər, ăzhər	mĕzhĕr, ăzhĕr
j	you, yes	[ju, jɛs]	ū, yĕs	ū, yĕs
ç[8]	huge, human	[çudʒ, çumən]	hūj, hūmən	hūj, hūmăn
k	key, ache	[ki, ek]	kē, āk	kē, āk
g	go, big	[go, bɪg]	gō, bĭg	gō, bĭg
ŋ	sing, long	[sɪŋ, lɔŋ]	sĭng, lông	sĭng, lŏng
h	he, how	[hi, haʊ]	hē, hou	hē, hou

Consonant Combinations (Affricates)	Key Words	In Phonetic Transcription	American College Dict.	Webster's New Collegiate Dict.
tʃ	chew, each	[tʃu, itʃ]	choo, ēch	choo, ēch
dʒ	gem, hedge	[dʒɛm, hɛdʒ]	jĕm, hĕj	jĕm, hĕj

Vowel Combinations (Diphthongs)[9]	Key Words	In Phonetic Transcription	American College Dict.	Webster's New Collegiate Dict.
eɪ[12]	aid, may	[eɪd, meɪ]	ād, mā	ād, mā
aɪ[10]	aisle, sigh	[aɪl, saɪ]	īl, sī	īl, sī
ɔɪ	oil, joy	[ɔɪl, dʒɔɪ]	oil, joi	oil, joi
aʊ[11]	owl, cow	[aʊl, kaʊ]	oul, kou	oul, kou
oʊ[12]	own, go	[oʊn, goʊ]	ōn, gō	ōn, gō

[7] A voiceless [w] sound; also written as [hw].
[8] [ç] is a voiceless [j] sound; also written as ʾ[hj].
[9] For other diphthongs, see Chapter 10, pages 191–193.
[10] Or [ɑɪ]. See Chapter 10, page 195.
[11] Or [ɑʊ]. See Chapter 10, page 198.
[12] See [e] and [o].

Some Special Symbols Used in Phonetic Transcription

In order to permit more distinctive markings, certain "narrow" symbols are used to represent variant forms of sounds as we hear them. These symbols are not normally used for general or broad transcription purposes. Since these symbols are used to explain certain variations covered in Part II, you will be wise to learn them prior to studying Chapters 4, 5, 6, 7, 8, 9, and 10.

Symbol	Description	Key Word	Transcription
ˀ	the glottal stop; often heard initially before a stressed vowel	*ever*	[ˀɛvɚ]
~	nasalization of a sound	*can*	[kæ̃n]
̥	unvoicing a sound that is normally voiced	*his*	[hɪz̥]
̌	voicing a sound that is normally voiceless	*notice*	[not̬ɪs]
˗	fronting; making a sound towards the front of the mouth	*cat*	[kæ˗t]
˗	retracting; making a sound farther back in the mouth	*fall*	[fɔ˗l]
⊥	tongue raised	*many*	[mɛni⊥]
⊤	tongue lowered	*many*	[mɛnɪ⊤]
¨ or -	centralized vowel	*ship*	[ʃïp, ʃɪp]
		too	[tü, tʉ]
˒	lip over-rounding of a sound	*hall*	[hɔˀl]
ω	labializing a consonant sound	*live*	[lʷɪv]
:	lengthening mark	*rode*	[roːd]
·	half-lengthened sound	*wrote*	[ro·t]
ˌ	dentalizing a sound	*fill the cup*	[fɪˌ ðə kʌp]
̩	syllabifying a consonant	*beetle*	[bitl̩]

As you may have noticed, both slant lines, / /, and brackets, [ ], may be used to enclose sounds. When discussing a phoneme, the sound class that includes all the spoken modifications, the sound will be italicized or enclosed in slant lines: *p* or /p/. In discussions of the actual pronunciations of sounds, the sound will be enclosed in brackets: [p]. (In the word *pen*, the normal allophone of /p/ is the aspirated [pʰ], so that the English pronunciation of this word is heard as [pʰɛn].) Brackets will be used to enclose the phonetic transcription of all words, phrases, and sentences. In many instances either / / or [ ] can be used with equal justification. You will not find it confusing if you keep in mind that the slant lines enclose the theoretical sound (the sound concept or the sound class). Brackets enclose the actual pronunciations we use, be they sounds, words, phrases, or sentences.

Practice in Transcription and in the Application of Phonetic Symbols

You will find it advantageous to spend a few moments during the next few days transcribing your pronunciation of simple objects around you. Like any habit, the habit of transcribing the sounds of our language in phonetic script is strengthened with practice. Be sure that you transcribe what you hear, writing the words as you say them aloud. An easy way to accomplish this is to transcribe as someone dictates to you. When you have gained some assurance, try transcribing some phrases and sentences such as those listed below.

no one	When did you see him?
once more	if I can
The book is on the table.	Paint the wall and the ceiling.
The boy came to my house.	When will he arrive?
They were seen at church.	He cut his finger on the glass.
Her sister studies the flute.	Both football and lacrosse can be dangerous sports.

GAINING SKILL IN READING PHONETIC SCRIPT*

I was born in the year 1632, [ɪn ðə] city of York, of a [gʊd] family though not [əv ðæt kʌntri], my father being a foreigner of Bremen, [hu sɛtld] first at Hull; [hi gɑt ə gʊd əsteɪt] by merchandise, and leaving [ɔf] his trade, lived [æftəwɚdz] at York, from whence he married [maɪ mʌðɚ, huz] relations were [neɪmd rɑbɪnsən], a very [gʊd fæməli ɪn ðæt kʌntri],

---

*Since no one transcription can indicate the different regional variations of American English, some of the following pronunciations may not be typical of your own speech pattern. Regional variations are noted later in the text. The pronunciation noted in the following samples is fairly typical of the northern section of the coastalmidland area of the country.

and from whom [aɪ wəz kɔld] Robinson Kreutznaer; but [baɪ ðə juʒuəl kərʌpʃən əv wɜdz ɪn ɪ̃ŋglənd, wi] are now called, nay, we call ourselves and write our name [rɑbɪnsən krusoʊ, ænd so maɪ kəmpænjənz ɔlwəz kɔld mi].

Daniel Defoe, The Life and Adventures of Robinson Crusoe

At exactly fifteen minutes past eight in the morning, on [ɔgəst sɪksθ naɪntin fɔᵊti faɪv] Japanese time, at the [moʊmənt hwɛn ði ətɑmɪk bɑm flæʃt əbʌv] Hiroshima, Miss Toshiko Sasaki, [ə klɝk ɪn ðə pɝsənəl dɪpɑᵊtmənt əv ðə ist eɪʒə tɪn wɝks], had just sat down at her place in the plant office and [wəz tɝnɪŋ hɝ hɛd tə spik tə ðə gɝl æt ðə nɛkst dɛsk].

John Hersey, Hiroshima (New York, Alfred A. Knopf, Inc., 1946)

[naʊ wi] are about to begin, [ænd ju mʌst ətɛnd ænd hwɛn wi gɛt tə ði ɛnd] of the story, you will know more [ðən ju du naʊ əbaʊt ə vɛri] wicked hobgoblin. [hi wəz wʌn əv ðə wɝst kaɪnd, ɪn fækt hi wəz ə] real demon. [wʌn deɪ, ðɪs dimən wəz ɪn ə haɪ steɪt əv dɪlaɪt] because he had invented a mirror with this peculiarity: [ðæt ɛvri gʊd ænd prɪti θɪŋ] reflected in it [ʃræŋk əweɪ] to almost [nʌθɪŋ]. On the [ʌðɝ hænd] every bad [ənd gʊd fɝ nʌθɪŋ θɪŋ] stood out and looked its worst.

Hans Christian Andersen, The Snow Queen

There was commotion in Roaring Camp. [ɪt kəd nɑt əv bɪn ə faɪt] for in 1850, that was not novel [ɪnʌf tu həv kɔld təgɛðɝ ði əntaɪɝ sɛtl̩mənt]. The ditches and claims were [nɑt oʊnli dəzɝtɪd], but "Tuttle's grocery" had [kəntrɪbjutɪd ɪts gæmblɝz hu, ɪt wɪl bi rɪmɛmbɝd, kɑmli kəntɪnjud ðɛɝ geɪm ðə] day that French Pete and Kanaka Joe shot each [ʌðɝ tə dɛθ oʊvɝ ðə bɑɝ ɪn ðə frʌnt rum].

Bret Harte, Tales of the Gold Rush (Boston, Houghton Mifflin Co.)

PHONETIC TRANSCRIPTION SAMPLES FOR READING AND LISTENING PRACTICE

wɛn ɪn ðə koɝs əv hjumɪn ɪvɛnts ɪt bɪkʌmz nɛsəseri fɝ wʌn pip!tu dɪzɑlv ðə pəlɪtəkəl bændz wɪtʃ əv kənɛktɪd ðəm wɪð ənʌðɝ ənd tu əsjum əmʌŋ ðə paʊəz əv ði ɝθ ðə sɛprɪt ənd ikwəl steɪʃn tu wɪtʃ ðə lɔz əv neɪtʃɝ ənd əv neɪtʃɝz gɑd ɪntaɪtl ðəm ə disənt rɪspɛkt tə ði opɪnjənz əv mænkaɪnd rɪkwaɪɝz ðət ðeɪ ʃud dɪkleɝ ðə koziz wɪtʃ ɪmpɛl ðəm tə ðə sɛpəreɪʃn̩ ‖

Declaration of Independence

ɔl naɪt ðə tʃifs bɪfɔɚ ðɛɚ vɛslz leɪ |
ænd lɔst ɪn slip ðə leɪbɚz əv ðə deɪ |
ɔl bʌt ðə kɪŋ | wɪð vɛriəs θɔts əprɛst |
hɪz kʌntriz kɛɚz leɪ roʊlɪŋ ɪn hɪz brɛst ||

Homer, *Iliad*, English verse translation by Alexander Pope

ðə kɑk kroʊd	aɪ geɪv hɪm maɪ bʊk	oʊvɚ ðə fɛns
ʌndɚ ðə haʊs	dɪd maɪ mʌðɚ kɔl	əraʊnd ðə blɑk
wi kænt oʊpən ɪt	ə pɪloʊ faɪt	ðɪs sʌmɚ wɪl bi hɑt
bi ʃʊɚ tə sɪŋ laʊd	ʃiz ðə hɑki goʊli	traɪ ridɪŋ ə gʊd bʊk
stʌdi ət hoʊm	spik ðə spɪtʃ aɪ preɪ ju	kæri ɑn
fənɛtɪks ɪz izi	təmɑroʊ krips ɪn ðɪs peti peɪs	wɛst pɔɪnt
kip jɚsɛlf hɛlθi wɛlθi ənd waɪz	doʊnt kəmpleɪn	aɪ wʌndɚ ʍɑt ʃil du nɛkst
fʊtbɔlz ə rʌf spɔɚt	ðə ruf keɪvd ɪn	ðə sɛvən geɪbəld haʊs

səpoʊz | aɪ ansɚd | ðət ə dʒʌst ənd gʊd mæn ɪn ðə kɔɚs əv ə næreɪʃən |
kʌmz ɑn səm seɪɪŋ ɚ ækʃn̩ əv ənʌðɚ gʊd mæn | aɪ ʃʊd ɪmædʒɪn ðæt hi
wɪl laɪk tə pɚsəneɪt hɪm | ænd wɪl nɑt bi əʃeɪmd əv ðɪs sɔɚt əv ɪmɪteɪʃən ||

Plato, *Republic*, Jowett translation

ɪn ðə bɪgɪnɪŋ gɑd krieɪtɪd ðə hɛvən ənd ði ɚθ || ænd ði ɚθ wəz wɪðaʊt
fɔɚm | ənd vɔɪd ənd dɑɚknɪs wəz əpɑn ðə feɪs əv ði ɚθ | ənd ðə spɪrɪt
əv gɑd mʊvd əpɑn ðə feɪs əv ðə wɔtɚz ||

Genesis

roʊmənz | kʌntrimɪn | ənd lʌvɚz || hɪɚ mi fɔɚ maɪ kɔz | ænd bi saɪlənt |
ðət ju meɪ hɪɚ | bəliv mi fɚ maɪn ɑnɚ | ənd hæv rɪspɛkt tu maɪn ɑnɚ | ðæt
ju meɪ bəliv || sɛnʃɚ mi ɪn jʊɚ wɪzdəm | ænd əweɪk jʊɚ sɛnsɪz | ðæt ju
meɪ ðə bɛtɚ dʒʌdʒ ||

Shakespeare, *Julius Caesar*

QUESTIONS AND PROBLEMS FOR REVIEW

1. Why is an understanding of the phonemic concept necessary in studying a language?
2. Indicate the number of sounds in the following words:

see	scream	make	cigar	knock
tree	trigger	making	accuse	debt
live	penny	phlegm	jump	thumb
hand	pencil	lucky	knee	jerked
city	any	feet	wrong	accent

3. Define the following terms:
   a. phonetics
   b. phoneme
   c. allophone
   d. spelling form
   e. respelling
   f. transcription
4. Can you identify any sounds in a foreign language you have studied which do not appear in English?
5. How many consonants are there in American English? How many vowels appear in your dialect of American English? Which are they?

SOURCES FOR FURTHER STUDY

Phonetic Texts for Ear-Training Practice

BENDER, James F., and FIELDS, Victor A., *Phonetic Readings in American Speech* (New York, Pitman, 1939); fables and other simple selections in phonetic transcription by persons from all over the United States.

FIELDS, Victor A., and BENDER, James F., *Voice and Diction* (New York, Macmillan, 1949); transcriptions of simple to difficult selections.

KANTNER, Claude E., and WEST, Robert, *Phonetics* (New York, Harper, 1941), pp. 357–363; drills in reading phonetic script, nonsense verse, and sentences.

JONES, Daniel, *The Pronunciation of English* (Cambridge, Eng., Cambridge University Press, 1950), pp. 181–185; phonetic transcriptions of short literary selections in the Received Pronunciation standard of British English.

MANSER, Ruth, and MULGRAVE, Dorothy, *Conversations in Phonetic Transcription* (New York, Dutton, 1941); transcriptions of simple conversations.

Le Maitre Phonétique. Any issue of this bulletin of the International Phonetic Association contains samples of phonetic transcription sent in by phoneticians from various parts of the world, demonstrating Russian, French, English, Italian, or any other language, depending on the author's native tongue; also short articles and reviews, all in phonetic transcription.

Background Readings

BLOCH, Bernard, and TRAGER, George L., "Phonetics," pp. 10–37 and "Phonemics," pp. 38–52, in *Outline of Linguistic Analysis* (Baltimore, Linguistic Society of America, 1942), Chs. 2 and 3.

EMSLEY, Bert, THOMAS, Charles K., and SIFRITT, Claude, "Phonetics and Pronunciation," in Karl Wallace and others, eds., *A History of Speech Education in America* (New York, Appleton-Century-Crofts, Inc., 1954), Ch. 15.

GLEASON, Harry A., "The Phoneme," *An Introduction to Descriptive Linguistics* (New York, Holt, 1955), Ch. 12, pp. 158–171.

HEFFNER, R-M S., *General Phonetics* (Madison, University of Wisconsin Press, 1949), pp. 1–6.

HULTZÉN, Lee S., "Phonetic Transcription as Communication," *The Quarterly Journal of Speech*, Vol. 34 (April, 1948), pp. 194–201.

——, "Phonetics, Phonemics, and Teachers of Speech," *The Quarterly Journal of Speech*, Vol. 33 (April, 1947), pp. 202–206.

JONES, Daniel, "The History and Meaning of the Term 'Phoneme,'" *Supplement to Le Maitre Phonétique*, (July-December, 1957).

KENYON, John S., *American Pronunciation*, 10th ed. (Ann Arbor, George Wahr Publishing Co., 1951), pp. 65–73.

MARCKWARDT, Albert H., "Phonemic Structure and Aural Perception," *American Speech*, Vol. 21 (April, 1946), pp. 106–111.

POTTER, Simeon, "Sound and Symbol," *Modern Linguistics* (Fairlawn, N. J., Essential Books, Inc., 1957), Ch. 2, pp. 36–58.

STURTEVANT, Edgar H., *An Introduction to Linguistic Science* (New Haven, Yale University Press, 1947), pp. 9–18.

SWADESH, Morris, "The Phonemic Principle," *Language*, Vol. 10 (1934), pp. 117–129. Reprinted in *Readings in Linguistics*, Martin Joos, ed. (Washington, D. C., American Council of Learned Societies, 1957), pp. 32–37.

TRAGER, George L., *Phonetics: Glossary and Tables. Studies in Linguistics, Occasional Papers*, No. 6 (1958), 27 pp.

VOEGELIN, C. F., and VOEGELIN, M. F., "Guide for Transcribing Unwritten Languages in Field Work," *Anthropological Linguistics*, Vol. 1, No. 6 (June, 1959), pp. 1–28.

CHAPTER 3

Our Language Here
and There

ENGLISH AS A NATIVE language is spoken in many places throughout the world. It is the first language you hear as a child in Great Britain, the United States, most of Canada, Australia, and the Union of South Africa. It is native to British Guiana and Jamaica, and to many who live in India, Israel, Malta, and Ceylon. If you add the many persons who use English as a foreign language, it is the most widely used language in the world.

As you travel to each of these places where English is spoken, you will hear English with a slightly different "flavor": certain sounds are made differently; the speech rhythm may be slower or more rapid; the melody of the speech becomes noticeable, and even the vocal quality may sound strange. Although all English-speaking people use the same language, they do so somewhat differently.

These noticed differences result in new "languages" within the English language, which we have come to label as British English, American English, Canadian English, or Australian English. Within each of these branches, you will find certain differences. These

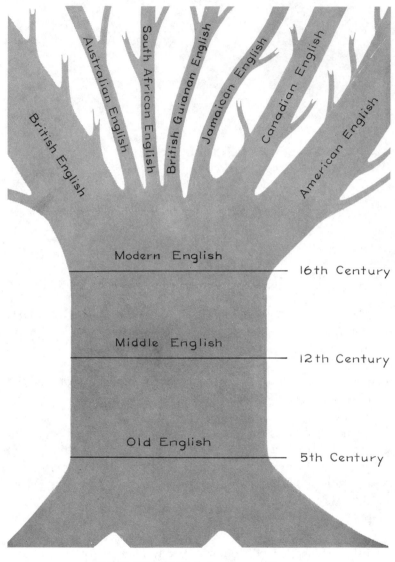

FIG. 2. The English Language Tree.

differences may be noticed as you move from one region to another. The smaller branches represent the different regional dialects of the language. Although we label the language of all such speakers as "English," we are actually talking about many dialects of the same language.

Despite these differences, we know that these regional patterns are more similar to each other than they are different. And although each of our American friends from Providence, New York, Jacksonville, Madison, and Seattle speaks a little differently, his speech sounds enough like that of the others so that we say that we all speak the same language—the language we call *American English*.

THE DIALECTS OF AMERICAN ENGLISH

The Term *Dialect* Defined

We can best understand the speech of the United States as we understand the dialect patterns spoken throughout the country. Many define the term *dialect* as that language peculiar to a district or a social class. As such, it is distinguished from the standard pattern of the region or that used in the country as a whole. Often the connotation when used in this sense is derogatory. "His speech is dialectal," or "He speaks a strange dialect," may well mean "His speech is uneducated, substandard, or not used in the best circles." The term has also been used to signify a "literary language," like that used in certain countries by scholars and authors when it differs from the language used by the large mass of society, usually uneducated and illiterate. Or the "literary dialect" may be the same as the standard-educated form where education is widespread and where many have access to the literary form as listeners, readers, and playgoers. And *dialect* has been known to possess the connotation implied in the phrase "dialect of social prestige," when it is supposed to represent that speech presumed to be the "best," and therefore to be imitated by other speakers, regardless of regional origin.

We think of the term *dialect* today as merely a variety of language, more or less different from other varieties of the same language. As such, there are no actual or implied judgments involved, of either "good" or "bad" or any of the shades in between, or on either side. The term includes the language habits peculiar to an area or a section of a country, including the standard usage found therein. A study of American dialects comprises a study of the speech patterns found in many sections of the country, including the study of the levels or the functional varieties of speech in each area. The *Publications of the American Dialect Society*, the materials collected by the *Linguistic Atlas* since 1931, the articles printed in *American Speech*, the *Quarterly Journal of Speech*, and similar journals, have given us a fuller understanding of the dialects and speech habits of the people in this country.

The term *dialect* as used in this text, then, refers to local or regional usages, rather than to levels or varieties of speech discussed in a previous chapter. No one dialect of American speech is considered preferable to any other. It is merely different, and is as acceptable in the regional area(s) described as is any other dialect found in its particular area. For example, the chart on pages 48–50 represents some typical pronunciations found in five regional areas.

The Study of Dialect and Regional Speech

A systematic and detailed study of the speech of the United States and Canada was begun in 1931 under the sponsorship of the American Council of Learned Societies. At that time, Professor Hans Kurath, in charge of the project, and his staff began a systematic recording of the speech habits found in the Atlantic coastal states. The field work for the New England states was completed in 1933 and in 1939 Kurath edited the *Handbook of the Linguistic Geography of New England*, detailing the background of the area studied and the methodology used, to provide the apparatus for interpreting the *Atlas* findings. By 1943, the three volumes of *The Linguistic Atlas of New England* were published, presenting pronunciation, vocabulary, and grammatical data about the speech of New England. In 1949, Kurath published his *Word Geography of the Eastern States* and in 1953, E. Bagby Atwood published *A Survey of Verbal Forms in the Eastern United States,* both based on the collected materials of the *Atlas.*[1] These special volumes, various articles by some of Kurath's associates, and a few Ph. D. dissertations based on the field records have presented us with considerable information about the speech of the northeastern seaboard. Studies for the *Atlas* made in other sections of the country are now going on. The field work for the Middle and South Atlantic areas was completed in 1949, that for the North Central states in 1956, and the Upper Midwest in 1957. Field work in other parts of the country is, as yet, incomplete. Some studies interpreting the data already collected have been published. In addition to the *Atlas* project, special studies and investigations by individual scholars have detailed aspects of the speech of given localities and areas throughout the country. Some of these are listed in the bibliography at the end of this chapter. They are all worthy of your study.

The Causes of Regional Differences

The causes of the differences of the spoken dialects of any language are many and varied. To the question "Why do Bostonians pronounce certain words (such as *cot* and *park*) differently from the way we hear them pronounced in certain other parts of the country?" the answer is dependent on many factors. Chief among these is the historical precedent—the language used by previous generations, the source of that particular language or dialect, and the changes that have taken place since. Neighboring languages or dialects also exert an influence. Infiltration by users of different dialects, radio and television speakers, the movies, and the stage all exert an influence on the speech we use, and cause the dialect we speak to differ from, or be similar to, others.

Modern American English had its start in the dialects of the language first spoken in the colonies of the Atlantic coastal regions during the seventeenth century. We sometimes forget that the language spoken by the earliest English colonists who came to

[1] The *Word Geography* and the *Survey of Verbal Forms* were both published at the University of Michigan, the present headquarters of the *Atlas.*

Jamestown in 1607 and to Plymouth in 1620 (and by those who came here very soon thereafter) was the Elizabethan English of the time of William Shakespeare, Francis Bacon, and Ben Jonson. Our earliest speech forms stemmed, then, from the variable forms of London English and the other regional dialects of Elizabethan English spoken in the British Isles. Each of the American colonies during the early seventeenth century existed as a comparatively separate geographic and social entity. Each developed a somewhat distinctive dialect of its own, the result of the particular character of British speech arriving with the settlers and the influences upon it as the years progressed.

The diversity of the speech of the coastal regions stems from the diversity of the speech of the colonial settlers and the early isolation of the colonies from each other. There was comparatively little intercommunication for almost a century after settlement. The inconvenience of travel, the difficult terrain, and the unfriendly, if not hostile, Indians kept the colonial settlements apart. Culture patterns and speech habits had some chance to settle and develop their own peculiarities and distinctive colorations before inland expansion burst through the mountains to the west, during the eighteenth century. In time, closer relationships between adjacent colonial areas were established, and settlements increased and expanded inland away from the seaboard areas. But the coastal patterns had already been established, and the major regional dialects of the eastern coast reflect the history of the settlement areas.

As we move away from the eastern coastal regions, it is the history of the large settlement waves therefrom that again provide the clues to the beginnings of the regional patterns of speech to be found. Three such large waves took place during the eighteenth century. One, beginning in the western section of New England, west of the Connecticut River line, traveled westward across New York and northern Pennsylvania to the basins of the Great Lakes. In another, Pennsylvanians moved south through western Maryland to the Carolinas and Georgia. After the Revolution, their descendents crossed the mountains, settling in Kentucky, Tennessee, southern

Ohio, Indiana, and Illinois. Still others, mostly from Pennsylvania and western New Jersey, moved into the Ohio Valley and what is now West Virginia. In the third large migration, Southern settlers moved south along the coast, inland around the Appalachians and across the Gulf states into eastern Texas.

As we can see, the settlement westward into the interior country was predominantly from western New England, upper New York State, the inland and southern Midland areas, with eastern New England, the coastal midland, and the South contributing comparatively little. The inhabitants of the South found it to their advantage to retain their plantation agriculture, remaining where they were or moving further south along the coast, or into the Gulf states, the lower Mississippi valley, and east Texas. Nor did the inhabitants of Eastern New England, New York City and its environs, nor of the coastal Middle Atlantic regions join the eighteenth century migrations. They were part of the large urbanizing process already under way as a result of the growing industries of the region and the growing trade with the European mother countries.

By the nineteenth century, travelers from abroad, as well as native persons traveling to different sections of the country, began to note distinctive speech patterns. Roles in certain plays were written with special respellings to indicate geographic dialects. Spelling books, although clearly imitative of the widely-used Webster's *Blue-Backed Speller*, footnoted certain pronunciations as peculiar to a geographic region. By the end of the first third of the twentieth century, writers of texts and articles on the pronunciation of American speakers had categorized the United States into three major regional areas: *Eastern* or *New England* (the New England states from Maine through Connecticut and New York City and its environs), *Southern* (all the former states of the Confederacy and parts of Maryland, West Virginia, Kentucky, and Oklahoma), and *General American* or *Northern* (the speech of the remainder of the country). A dialect map of the United States prior to the 1940's was commonly thought of as pictured in Figure 3.

In 1947, C. K. Thomas published the first edition of his *Phone-*

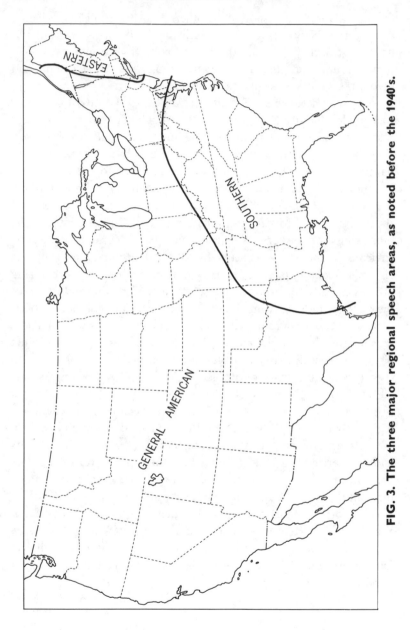

FIG. 3. The three major regional speech areas, as noted before the 1940's.

tics of American English and designated seven major regional areas of the country, based on an analysis of thousands of recordings of native Americans. He separated western New England and New York City and its environs from the *Eastern* area, the middle Atlantic region and the western part of Pennsylvania from the *General American* area, and parts of Tennessee, Kentucky, West Virginia, and sections of the bordering states as distinctive enough from the remainder of the South to be labeled separately. In the 1958 edition of the same book, he increased the regional areas to ten, breaking up the General American area into *Central Midland*, *North Central*, *Northwest*, and *Southwest*, as in Figure 4.

The evidence of the studies based on the data of the *Linguistic Atlas* is not too different from some of the conclusions reached by Thomas, at least as concerns the eastern coastal region. Kurath's plotting of the major dialect areas of the eastern states is based upon vocabulary evidence rather than upon pronunciation data, and is reported in his *Word Geography of the Eastern United States*, 1949. His conclusions indicate the need to change our older designations of *Eastern*, *Southern*, and *General American* to *Northern*, *Midland*, and *Southern* for the eastern area of the United States, as noted in Figure 5, with the westward extensions of the lines to be completed at a later date.

Our conclusions about regional pronunciations throughout the country are still tentative. They must wait upon the interpretations and analyses of the field data already collected and those still to be collected, both in the United States and Canada. Conclusions, other than tentative ones, about the directions of the boundary lines separating major speech areas in the Middle West and beyond cannot be drawn without this information. With it, it will be possible to designate not only such major regional areas of speech but also any noticeable subareas, as has been done for the Atlantic coastal regions. As the information and analyses thereof become available, it will be possible to confirm or change the tentative conclusions about our regional speech already noted. We can, however, draw some conclusions from the evidence already in: (1) A clearly defined

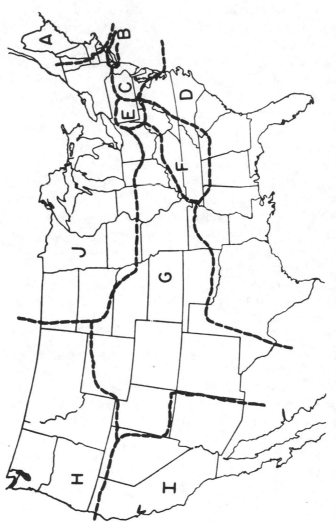

FIG. 4. The ten major regional speech areas: A: Eastern New England; B: New York City; C: Middle Atlantic; D: Southern; E: Western Pennsylvania; F: Southern Mountain; G: Central Midland; H: Northwest; I: Southwest; J: North Central. (From Charles K. Thomas, *An Introduction to the Phonetics of American English*, 2nd ed., p. 232. Copyright, 1958, The Ronald Press Company.)

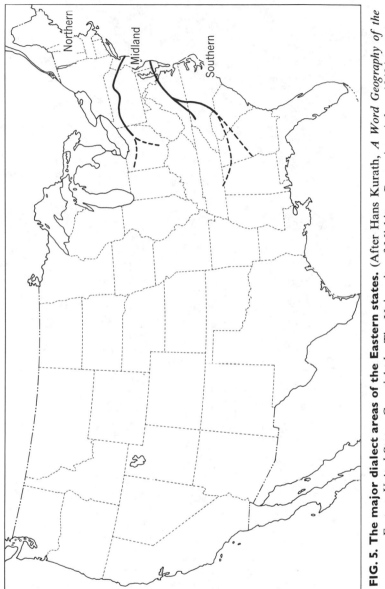

FIG. 5. The major dialect areas of the Eastern states. (After Hans Kurath, *A Word Geography of the Eastern United States.* Copyright by The University of Michigan Press, Ann Arbor, 1949.)

Word	Eastern New England	New York City	Coastal Midland	South	Northern Middle West
far, barn, poor, third	[fɑː, baːn, pʊə, θɜːd]	[fɑɜ, baːn, pʊə, θɜːd] frequently, though not universally; others say [fɑɜ, baɜn, pʊə, θɜːd]	[fɑɜ, baɜn, pʊə, θɜːd]	[fɑː, fɑɜ, baːn, baɜn, pʊə, θɜːd]. [ɜ] is occasionally diphthongized to [ɜɪ] before consonants: [θɜɪd, bɜɪd]	[fɑɜ, baɜn, pʊə, θɜːd]
park, farm	[pɑːk, paɜk, faːm, faɜm]	[pɑːk, paɜk; paɜk; faːm, faɜm], loss of postvowel [r] frequent although not universal	[pɑɜk, faɜm]	[pɑːk, paɜk, faːm, faɜm]	[pɑɜk, faɜm]
orange, foreign	[ɑrɪndʒ, fɑrɪn] predominantly; also [ɒrɪndʒ, ɔrɪndʒ, fɒ-, fɔrɪn] esp. in more western sections	[ɑrɪndʒ, fɑrɪn]	[ɑrɪndʒ, fɑrɪn]	[ɑrɪndʒ, fɑrɪn] predominantly; also [ɒrɪndʒ] and [ɔrɪndʒ]	[ɒrɪndʒ, fɔrɪn] and occasionally [ɑrɪndʒ, fɑrɪn]
greasy	[grisi]	[grisi]	[grisi] in northern section, [grizi] in southern section	[grizi]	[grisi]

tune, duty	[tun, dutɪ], sometimes [tɪun, tɪun] and [drutɪ, djutɪ]	[tɪun], often [tun], occasionally [tjun]	[trun]; sometimes [tjun, tun]	[tjun, trun]; occasionally [tun]	[tun, trun; dutɪ, drutɪ]
hog, frog, dog	[hɑg, frɑg]; also [hɒg] and [frɒg]; [dɔg]	[hɑg, frɑg]; occasionally [hɒg, frɒg]; [dɔg]	[hɑg, frɑg] in the northern midland sections, with common use of [hɒg, frɒg] in more southern sections, as in Delaware, Maryland; [dɔg]	[hɒg, frɒg]; [dɔg]	[hɒg, frɒg]; also [hɑg, frɑg]; [dɔg]
four, hoarse	[foɚ, hoɚs]; and [fɔɚ, hɔɚs] especially in southern sections	[fɔ, fɔɚ, foɚ; hɔːs, hoɚs, hoɚs]	[fɔɚ, hɔɚs] in northern sections; use of [o] as in [foɚ], etc. in southern midland and in western Pennsylvania sections	[foɚ, hoɚs]	[foɚ, hoɚs]
ask, dance	[ask, dans]; use of [æsk, dæns] growing especially in urban areas	[æsk, dæns]	[æsk, dæns]	[æsk, dæns]; and [a-ɑsk, da-dɑns] by some in tidewater Virginia	[æsk, dæns]

Word	Eastern New England	New York City	Central Midland	South	Northern Middle West
worry, courage	[wʌri, kʌrɪdʒ]	[wʌri, kʌrɪdʒ]	[wari, kʌrɪdʒ]	[wʌri, kʌrɪdʒ]	[wɜri, wɝi, kɜrɪdʒ, kɝɪdʒ]
when, where	[ʍɛn, ʍɛə]; [wɛn, wɛə] in larger urban areas	[wɛn, wɛə-ə]	frequently [wɛn, wɛə]; also [ʍɛn, ʍɛə]	[ʍɛn, ʍɛə] with growing use of [wɛn, wɛə] in larger urban areas	same as South
nice, blind	[naɪs-nɑɪs, blaɪnd-blɑɪnd]	[naɪs-nɑɪs, blaɪnd-blɑɪnd]	[nɑɪs-nɑɪs, blɑɪnd-blɑɪnd]	[na·s, na·ᵊs, naɪs; blaɪnd, bla·ᵊnd, blaɪnd]; [aɪ] before voiceless consonants, as in *nice*, and [ɑ·ᵊ, a·ɪ] before voiced consonants as in *nine* in eastern Va. (and Ontario, Canada)	[nɑɪs-nɑɪs, blɑɪnd, blɑɪnd]

Midland speech separates the regional dialects of the North and South in the eastern part of the United States. (2) The political boundaries of the North and the South have proved inaccurate for designating regional speech areas. (3) The older designations, "New England Speech," or "Eastern Speech," are misleading. Coastal New England, western New England, New York City, and the Hudson Valley are fairly distinct speech areas and are better thought of separately or grouped as subareas of the northeastern part of the United States.

Some Regional Differences Charted

The chart (pp. 48–50) highlights a few typical pronunciations found in different regional areas of the country. Do not interpret the listing as meaning that all speakers, in the areas noted, consistently use the listed pronunciation. Rather interpret it to mean that *most* educated speakers in these areas use such pronunciations in words of the type noted. Five dialect or regional areas are represented.

This chart does not attempt to isolate the phonemic aspects of the indicated dialects, although we all recognize that every regional dialect (if not each person's dialect) has its own phonemic structure. Nor should we assume that these variations, as shown, represent departures from one over-all pattern of American English. Since there are so many differently-structured major dialect types of American English, linguistic geographers of our language are understandably hesitant to present one such over-all pattern. The features presented are based on some of the reported phonetic impressions of collectors of data about American-English dialect geography. No phonemic conclusions are drawn here.

A NOTE ON THE SPEECH OF THE STAGE, SCREEN, RADIO, AND TELEVISION

The speech of the actor in the American theater reflects the history of the American theater itself. During colonial times, the American stage played host to actors from England who presented to the American public its only acquaintance with dramatic fare. Ofttimes,

"American" speech was actually written into the plays, to be spoken by characters considered uneducated, "rustic," or "common." The predominant dialect of the stage was clearly British. This influence is present today, not only because of the influence of the vast amount of literature written by English playwrights, but also because of the continuing influence of the British stage itself. Most American actors today adhere to British patterns of speech in all plays by British or continental authors, while many will use "stage speech" (based on British "Received Pronunciation") even in plays about the American scene. Indigenous regional accents are, however, clearly indicated for those roles portraying characters from particular regions of the country and today the American theater-goer expects such speech in these roles.

Screen, radio, and television actors must all meet the basic requirement of possessing not only clearly audible voices, but patterns of speech that could be classified as "educated-standard." The nature of these media requires speech of somewhat greater informality than that of the stage. British patterns of speech are found in use only by British-born and British-bred actors. American actors retain the normal patterns of educated American speech, unless the roles call for special dialects or varieties of speech. Commentators, newscasters, announcers, and speakers are expected to use these educated patterns of speech. Preferably, their speech should not be associated with the dialect patterns of any particular or local region. Elongated vowels associated with Southern speech, or the excessive tongue inversions found in certain sections of the West are avoided.[2]

QUESTIONS FOR FURTHER STUDY

1. Review the causes of regional differences of a language. Check with your foreign-language instructors about the reasons for the differences

[2] H. L. Mencken in *The American Language, Supplement II*, presents a most readable account of the problems besetting the radio industry in tackling the problem of pronunciation, on pages 33–38. You will find his account both enlightening and entertaining. J. F. Bender's *NBC Handbook* and W. C. Greet's *World Words*, present appropriate advice on pronunciation to the announcing staffs of the National and Columbia Broadcasting Systems.

between Castillian and Mexican Spanish; Marseilles, Lyons, and Parisian French; Berlin and Hamburg German.

2. Which regional area is represented by each of the following? Why?

   a. I saw him first: [aɪ sɔ ɪm fɝst].

   b. The log in the park lay in the furrow: [ðə lɔg ɪn ðə pɑˑk leɪ ɪn ðə fɝˑo].

   c. He parked his car: [hi pɑːkt hɪz kɑə]; or [hi paːkt hɪz kaː].

   d. He bought four kinds of oranges: [hi bɔt foɝ kaɪndz əv ɔrəndʒəz]; or [hi bɔt foə kaɪndz əv ɑrəndʒəz]; or [hi bɔt foə kaˑəndz əv ɑrəndʒəz].

3. Which speech pattern would be expected of you as: *(a)* an actor in a Shakespearian play? *(b)* a radio announcer on a national network? *(c)* a local announcer? *(d)* a television actor? *(e)* the lead in each of the following plays: *A Doll's House, The Importance of Being Earnest, Abe Lincoln in Illinois, Hamlet?*

4. Check each of the following words in Kenyon and Knott, *Pronouncing Dictionary of American English*. Note the variant pronunciations given for different regional areas.

fear	*water*	*poor*	*courage*	*wash*
hurry	*hat*	*thirty*	*hoarse*	*mock*

5. Read some of the selections in the Appendix. Note those forms that indicate dialect markers.

SOURCES FOR FURTHER STUDY

ANDREWS, Charles M., *Our Earliest Colonial Settlements: Their Diversities of Origin and Later Characteristics* (New York, New York University Press, 1933).

BENDER, James F., *NBC Handbook of Pronunciation*, 2nd ed. (New York, Crowell, 1951).

BLOOMFIELD, Leonard, "Dialect Geography," *Language* (New York, Holt, 1933), Ch. 19, pp. 321–345.

GLEASON, H. A., Jr., "Variation in Speech," *An Introduction to Descriptive Linguistics* (New York, Holt, 1955), Ch. 20, pp. 284–300.

GREET, W. Cabell, "A Standard American Language?" *New Republic*, Vol. 95 (1938), pp. 68–70.

———, *World Words*, 2nd ed., rev. (New York, Columbia University Press, 1948).

IVES, Sumner, "Use of Field Materials in the Determining of Dialect Groupings," *Quarterly Journal of Speech*, Vol. 41 (December, 1955), pp. 359–364.

————, "American Pronunciation in the Linguistic Atlas," *Tulane Studies in English*, Vol. 3 (1952), pp. 179–193.

KANTNER, Claude E., and WEST, Robert, *Phonetics* (New York, Harper, 1941), pp. 267–270.

KENYON, John S., and KNOTT, Thomas A., *A Pronouncing Dictionary of American English* (Springfield, Mass., Merriam, 1944), esp. "The Main Regional Divisions," pp. xxxii–xxxiii.

KURATH, Hans, *Handbook of the Linguistic Geography of New England* (Washington, D. C., American Council of Learned Societies, 1939).

LLOYD, Donald J., and WARFEL, Harry R., "Our Land and Our People," *American English in its Cultural Setting* (New York, Knopf, 1956), Ch. 1, pp. 9–26.

MARCKWARDT, Albert H., "Regional and Social Variations," *American English* (New York, Oxford University Press, 1958), Ch. 7, pp. 131–150.

McDAVID, Raven I., Jr., "American English Dialects," in W. Nelson Francis, *The Structure of American English* (New York, Ronald, 1958), Ch. 9, pp. 480–543.

MENCKEN, H. L., *The American Language*, 4th ed. (New York, Knopf, 1946), esp. "The Materials of Inquiry: The Hallmarks of American," pp. 90–97, "What is an Americanism?" pp. 97–103, and "The Pronunciation of American: Dialects," pp. 354–378.

————, *The American Language, Supplement II* (New York, Knopf, 1948), esp. "The Pronunciation of American: Dialects," pp. 101–270.

POTTER, Simeon, "Linguistic Geography," *Modern Linguistics* (Fair Lawn, N. J., Essential Books, Inc., 1957), Ch. 6, pp. 123–140.

ROBERTSON, Stuart, "Pronunciations, Variations, Standards," *The Development of Modern English*, 2nd ed., rev. by Frederic G. Cassidy (Englewood Cliffs, N. J., Prentice-Hall, Inc., 1954), Ch. 12, pp. 386–400.

THOMAS, Charles K., "Regional Variation in American Pronunciation," *An Introduction to the Phonetics of American English*, 2nd ed. (New York, Ronald, 1958), Ch. 21, pp. 191–215.

WILSON, George P., "Instructions to Collectors of Dialect," *Publications of the American Dialect Society, No. 1* (April, 1944), 14 pp.

WISE, Claude M., "Speech Regions of America," and "Stage Speech," *Applied Phonetics* (Englewood Cliffs, N. J., Prentice-Hall, Inc., 1957), Ch. 6, pp. 171–181, and Ch. 10, pp. 239–244.

Special Regional Studies

DECAMP, David, "The Pronunciation of English in San Francisco" Part, 1, *Orbis*, Vol. 7 (1958), pp. 372–391, and Part 2, *Orbis*, Vol. 8 (1959), pp. 54–77.

GREET, W. Cabell, "Delmarva Speech," *American Speech*, Vol. 8 (1933), pp. 57–63.

HANLEY, Miles L., "Observations on the Broad *A*," *Dialect Notes*, Vol. 5 (1925), pp. 347–350.

HUBBELL, Allan F., "Curl and Coil in New York City," *American Speech*, Vol. 15 (1940), pp. 372–376.

———, *The Pronunciation of English in New York City* (New York, Kings Crown Press, 1950).

KENYON, John S., "Flat *A* and Broad *A*," *American Speech*, Vol. 5 (1930), pp. 323–326.

KIMMERLE, Marjorie M., McDavid, Raven I. Jr., and McDavid, Virginia Glenn, "Problems of Linguistic Geography in the Rocky Mountain Area," *Western Humanities Review*, Vol. 5 (1951), pp. 249–264.

KURATH, Hans, *A Word Geography of the Eastern United States* (Ann Arbor, University of Michigan Press, 1949), esp. Ch. 1, "The English of the Eastern States: A Perspective," pp. 1–10, and Ch. 2, "The Speech Areas of the Eastern States," pp. 11–49.

——— and McDAVID, Raven I., *The Pronunciation of English in the Atlantic States* (Ann Arbor, University of Michigan Press, 1961).

STANLEY, Oma T., "The Speech of East Texas," *American Speech*, Vol. 11 (1936), pp. 3–36.

THOMAS, Charles K., "The Place of New York City in American Linguistic Geography," *Quarterly Journal of Speech*, Vol. 32 (1947), pp. 314–320.

———, "Pronunciation in Downstate New York," *American Speech*, Vol. 17 (1942), pp. 30–41, 149–157.

———, "Pronunciation in Upstate New York," *American Speech*, Vol. 10 (1935), pp. 107–112, 208–212, 292–297; Vol. 11 (1936), pp. 68–77, 142–144, 307–313; Vol. 12 (1937), pp. 122–127.

TRESSIDER, Argus, "The Sounds of Virginia Speech," *American Speech*, Vol. 18 (1943), pp. 268–269.

TURNER, Lorenzo D., *Africanisms in the Gullah Dialect* (Chicago, The University of Chicago Press, 1949).

WHEATLEY, Katherine E., "Southern Standards," *American Speech*, Vol. 9 (1934), pp. 36–45.

WISE, Claude M., "Southern American Dialect," *American Speech*, Vol. 8 (1933), pp. 37–43.

PART TWO

The Sounds
of American
English

CHAPTER 4

The Consonants

of American English

THE CLASSIFICATION OF AMERICAN ENGLISH CONSONANTS

EACH CONSONANT of American English is commonly classified as to its place and manner of articulation, and the presence or absence of voice. The terms used to analyze any particular sound will be descriptive of the position of the articulators, of the presence of voice, and of acoustic value. For example, the consonant in the word *me* is classified as a sound made with both lips, voiced, and nasally emitted. The consonant in the word *fee* is a voiceless, lip-teeth sound, emitted orally as a fricative.

Voiced and Voiceless Consonants

There are fourteen voiced consonants in the English language, or consonants made while the vocal folds are vibrating. These consonants are found in the following words:

/b/	*big*	/m/	*me*	/ð/	*they*	/z/	*zoo*
/d/	*dig*	/n/	*no*	/v/	*view*	/ʒ/	*measure*
/g/	*go*	/ŋ/	*sing*	/w/	*we*		
/l/	*live*	/r/	*red*	/j/	*you*		

59

There are nine voiceless consonants in the English language, or consonants made while the vocal folds are at rest. These consonants are found in the following words:

/f/ fee	/k/ key	/t/ tea	/ʃ/ she
/h/ he	/p/ pea	/s/ sea	/θ/ thin
/ʍ/ when			

There are two consonant-blends, or affricates, in English. The voiced and voiceless affricates /tʃ/ and /dʒ/ appear as the initial sounds in *chew* and *gem*.

Voiceless consonants are normally more strongly articulated, held, and/or released with greater energy and pressure than are their voiced counterparts. The energy used in making the voiced sound is in part dissipated by the amount used to activate the vocal cords into vibration. Voiceless consonants tend to be *fortis*, or strong, sounds. Voiced consonants tend to be *lenis*, or weak, sounds.

Stops and Continuants

All consonants are characterized by a complete or partial closure of the channel through which the breath stream flows, from the larynx, or voice box, through the mouth or nose. The articulators (tongue, teeth, lips, palate) act either to form a complete stoppage of the breath stream in order to produce sounds known as stops or plosives, or to form a partial closure of the breath stream to produce sounds known as continuant sounds.

Stops. There are six stops in the English language, represented by the symbols /p, b, t, d, k, g/. They are heard as the initial sounds in the words *pen, be, ten, den, key, go*. One other stop is heard as an unintentional sound in our language. It is known as the glottal sound and is represented phonetically by the symbol [ʔ]. We do not hear it, normally, as a separate sound in our language. The glottal stop is not, of course, one of the consonantal phonemes in American English. It may appear as the initial sound in the word *ice* [ʔaɪs].

Continuants. All open or continuant sounds are either fricative or frictionless consonant sounds. For fricative sounds, also known as spirants, the breath stream is hindered by the articulators to the extent that a noticeable frictionlike quality is present. There are ten fricative sounds in English: /θ/, /ð/, /f/, /v/, /s/, /z/, /ʃ/, /ʒ/, /h/, and /ʍ/. The frictionless consonants are either glide, nasal, or lateral sounds. They are also known as semivowels because of their vowel-like quality. For glides, the breath stream is altered during the formation of the sounds by the motion of the articulators from one position to another. The second position of the glide is the position of the following sound. There are three such sounds in English: /w/, /r/, and /j/. For nasal sounds, the breath stream is forced through the passageway behind the mouth cavity and out through the nose. The soft palate, acting as a valve, is forward and lowered (see Figure 16), so that the sound may be nasally emitted. The /l/ is the only sound in English made with the breath stream forced over the sides of the tongue. It is classified separately as a lateral sound.

The Speech Producing Mechanism

Some simple diagrams of our sound-producing mechanism appear below. Since we label sounds according to the articulators that make them or by their areas of phonation or resonance, it will be useful to "see" these areas in relation to each other. The same mechanism produces the consonants and the vowels and all their variants. The consonants are charted in this section, the vowels in Chapter 7.

We know, of course, that the lungs provide the source of energy for speech—the outgoing breath. Driving bursts of air are emitted periodically through the space (or *glottis*) between the vocal cords, which are housed in the larynx. The rate of these escaping bursts of air determines the pitch or frequency of the emitted sound. The sound, now a laryngeal tone, is shaped, hindered, obstructed, and reinforced by the articulators and resonators of speech.

The articulators which we must know to identify the sounds of the language are the lips, teeth, tongue, hard palate, soft palate, uvula, and the parts thereof. The resonators, or areas of reinforce-

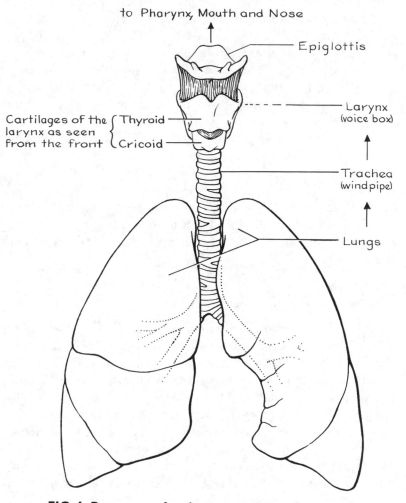

to Pharynx, Mouth and Nose

Epiglottis

Larynx
(voice box)

Cartilages of the { Thyroid
larynx as seen
from the front { Cricoid

Trachea
(windpipe)

Lungs

FIG. 6. Passageway for the energy source for speech.

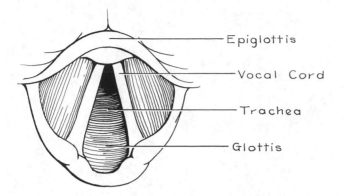

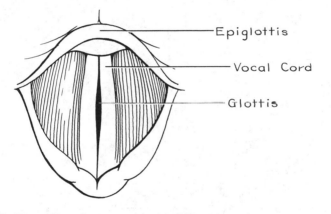

FIG. 7. The vibrating source: (Top) Vocal cords at rest. (Bottom) Vocal cords vibrating producing voice.

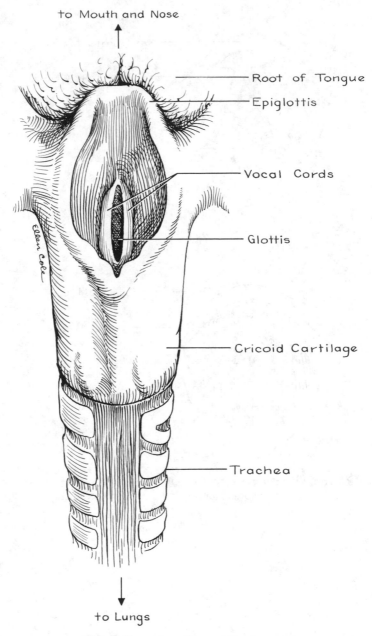

to Mouth and Nose

Root of Tongue

Epiglottis

Vocal Cords

Glottis

Cricoid Cartilage

Trachea

to Lungs

FIG. 8. Superior view of the larynx.

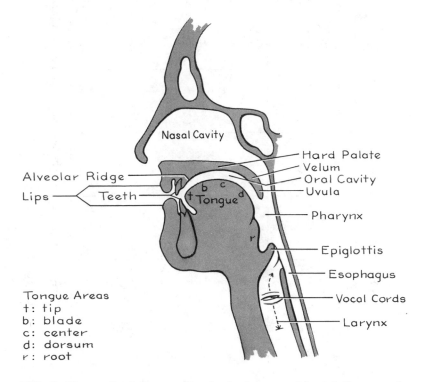

Nasal Cavity

Hard Palate
Velum
Alveolar Ridge
Oral Cavity
Lips
Teeth
Uvula
Tongue

Pharynx

Epiglottis

Esophagus

Vocal Cords

Larynx

Tongue Areas
t: tip
b: blade
c: center
d: dorsum
r: root

FIG. 9. The articulators and principal resonators of the speech mechanism.

ment, through which the sound travels, is altered, and emitted, are the pharynx, the mouth or oral cavity, and the nasal cavity, and parts thereof. In addition, we shall find that the vocal bands act as articulators, and as already noted, the larynx is the first place in which the sound is reinforced.

A detailed study of the anatomy, physiology, and acoustics of speech and hearing is out of place in this text. Its usefulness to any serious student of the science of speech is obvious, and you will find it worth your while to pursue such study in such sources as indicated below.[1]

[1] Charles Van Riper and John Irwin, *Voice and Articulation* (Englewood Cliffs, N. J., Prentice-Hall, Inc., 1958): Ch. 11, "The Anatomy of Articulation,"

CLASSIFICATION OF THE AMERICAN ENGLISH CONSONANTS*

	Both Lips (bilabial)	Lip—Teeth (labio-dental)	Tongue—Teeth (lingua-dental)	Tongue—Ridge (alveolar)	Tongue—Hard Palate (post-alveolar)	Tongue Blade—Palate (palatal)	Tongue—Velum (velar)	Glottis (glottal)
Stops	p b			t d			k g	ʔ†
Continuants								
Fricatives	ʍ	f v	θ ð	s z	ʃ ʒ	ç†	(ʍ)	h
Frictionless Sounds								
Nasals	m			n			ŋ	
Laterals				l				
Glide-semivowels	w				r	j	(w, r)	
Affricates					tʃ dʒ			

* Voiceless consonants appear to the left of each column, voiced consonants to the right. Secondary forms of the same sounds are shown in parentheses.

† [ʔ] and [ç] are not phonemes in English. See pp. 79 and 124.

The remainder of this chapter analyzes the stop consonants in detail. The fricatives and frictionless consonants are discussed in the following chapters. Each sound is discussed as it is heard in various positions of a syllable or phrase, as well as in cluster combinations with other sounds. Following each set of consonants, you will find pertinent review material.

THE STOP-PLOSIVE SOUNDS

Introduction

All stop sounds possess the same characteristic stages of formation and release. A set of articulators, or two different articulators, are in contact. Slight pressure of the breath stream builds up behind the closure. Upon relaxation of the closure, or occlusion, the sound is exploded. The three stages can be simply diagrammed as follows:

1. *articulators closed*   2. *building up of*
                                                pressure

3. *release of articulatory closure*
with resultant explosion of sound

---

pp. 354–385; Ch. 12, "Positions and Muscles Used in Articulation," pp. 386–417; Ch. 13, "Phonation," pp. 418–456.

Giles W. Gray and Claude M. Wise, *The Bases of Speech*, 3rd ed. (New York, Harper, 1959): Ch. 3, "The Physiological Basis of Speech," pp. 135–199; Ch. 2, "The Physical Basis of Speech," pp. 66–134.

Claude W. Wise, *Applied Phonetics* (Englewood Cliffs, N. J., Prentice-Hall, Inc., 1957): Ch. 3, "Production and Classification of Speech Sounds," pp. 33–79.

Bruce P. Bogert and Gordon E. Peterson, "The Acoustics of Speech," in Lee Edward Travis and others, *Handbook of Speech Pathology* (New York, Appleton-Century-Crofts, Inc., 1957), Ch. 5, pp. 109–174.

Any two articulators may act as the agents of occlusion. The two lips are used in forming the /p/ and /b/ sounds. The tongue tip and gum ridge are in contact when the /t/ and /d/ sounds are made. The back of the tongue and the velum are closed for the /k/ and /g/ sounds. In each instance the breath stream is interrupted and held back by the occlusion of the articulators. (See Figure 10.)

Upon release, the stop may take one of two forms. It is *aspirated* when the release is accompanied by a vigorous puff of air. When no such vigorous puff of air accompanies the release, the sound is *unaspirated*. Similarly, when the held energy of the breath stream is great, the resultant stop is emitted as a strong, or *fortis*, sound; when not, the sound is emitted as a weak, or *lenis*, sound.

When the stop is adjacent to other consonants, the acoustic value

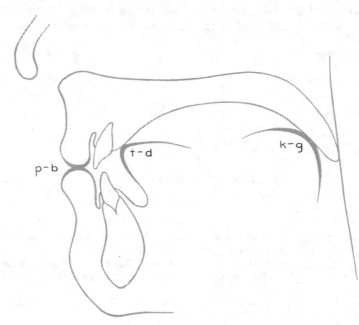

FIG. 10. The articulators that act as obstructors to the breath stream to form the stops. /p—b/: both lips; /t—d/: tongue tip and alveolar ridge; /k—g/: back of tongue and velum.

of the release may change. This change is especially likely if the stop in question precedes another sound made in the identical area of the mouth. In such instances, the plosive quality of the sound is completely absorbed by the following *homorganic* sound. (Sounds are homorganic when they are articulated in the same part of the speech mechanism, but differ in one or more features. Alveolar /t, d, n/ are homorganic, as are the bilabials /p, b, m/ or the fricatives /θ, ð/.) When saying the phrases *hot dog, hip boot,* and *take good aim,* you will note that the plosive at the end of the first word of each phrase is not released with an aspirate quality. When the following sound is not a homorganic consonant, a lesser degree of absorption of the plosive release takes place. Check your pronunciation of *take five, send Gary,* and *hogpen.*

Stops immediately preceding one of the nasal sounds or the /l/ sound are exploded through the nose or over the sides of the tongue. In the words *hidden, topmost, button, Cragmore* the sounds /d, p, t, g/ are released through the nasal passage. This resultant explosion is known as *nasal plosion. Laterally ploded* sounds are heard in the clusters *beetle* and *made less.* Nasal and lateral plosion occur easily when the sound following the stop is homorganic, and no pause intervenes between the two sounds.

Voiced plosives are normally devoiced when they appear initially or finally in a phrase, or when they precede voiceless consonants in the same phrase. This devoicing may be heard in such phrases as:

Buy a nice rug.
Go on that ride. } At beginning or end of a phrase

Rub some oil.
He paid for it. } When immediately before voiceless consonants

Partial, rather than complete, devoicing is heard, when the speaker begins the first sentence with [b̥] the second with [g̊], which quickly turn into the normal voiced [b] and [g]. Similarly, the /d/ of *ride* and the /g/ of *rug* trail off into the following silence by partially devoicing the last part of the voiced plosive: [rʌg̊g], [raɪd̥d]. If we did not partially devoice such voiced plosives, the result would probably sound like [rʌgᵊ], [raɪdᵊ]. Complete devoicing of these plosives when in final position is considered a fault of careless usage.

The Stop-Plosives /p/ and /b/

The /p/ and /b/ sounds are bilabial sounds, orally emitted. /p/ is the voiceless *cognate* of /b/. The /p/ sounds in *pen*, *happy*, and *stop* differ in their release and thus possess slightly different acoustic values. These allophonic differences (see page 25) are accounted for by the degree of aspiration, and the degree of pressure and release. The /p/ in *pen* is a strongly aspirated sound, while the /p/ in the other words tends to be weakly aspirated or unaspirated. The *fortis*, or strongly aspirated, /p/ is used before stressed vowels, the *lenis*, or weakly aspirated, /p/ before consonants, at the beginning of an unstressed syllable, or at the close of a syllable. The stronger aspiration may be noted in phonetic transcription as a small puff mark, [ʰ], following the sound:

> The ˈpen was given to ˈPaul. (strongly aspirated *p*'s)
> The top of the slipper was bent. (weakly aspirated *p*'s)

/p/ when preceded by /s/ in the same syllable, as an initial cluster, is an unaspirated sound, even when followed by a stressed vowel. Note the lack of strong aspiration in your pronunciation of the words *spine*, *spot*, *whisper*, and *respite*. /p/ in final positions is often an unaspirated or weakly aspirated sound. In some instances, /p/ in this position is unreleased, although many persons give the sound full aspiration when in the final position of the word. Compare your own pronunciation of *pen*, *happy*, *Spain*, and *tap*, checking whether the degree of aspiration changes. You will normally hear no aspiration of /p/ when the plosive immediately precedes another consonant: *topmost*, *ripped*, *clasps*. /b/ is always unaspirated.

Excrescence of /p/ and /b/

An unconsciously-made intrusion, or excrescence, of a /p/ or /b/ may be found in the speech of many persons in such words as *something* and *dreamed*. Such excrescence is formed as the articulators move from the position of one sound to that of another. Earlier spelling of *glimpse* for earlier *glimse*, and *empty*, formerly *emty*. Historically excrescent *b* is noted in such words as *slumber, humble, thimble*, formerly spelled without the *b*.[2]

The /b/ Sound

Like other voiced plosives, the /b/ in English has both a strong and a weak form, as well as a voiceless form. Initially, before a stressed vowel, the /b/ sounds, in such words as *big, burn*, and *beg*, are voiced, unaspirated sounds, relatively strongly exploded. In medial and final positions, as in *cabby* and *tub*, the sounds are made with weaker explosions. A devoiced *b*, [b̥], occurs in the words *lobster, grubstake*, and *tubful*, where the following voiceless sounds are anticipated by devoicing the /b/. When final in a phrase, both released and unreleased forms of /b/ exist, and when released in this position, as in "He turned the knob," or "The baby was in the crib," the final plosive sound is weak and partially devoiced.

Consonant Clusters with /p/ and /b/

When followed by one of the glide or semivowel sounds /l/, /r/, /w/, or /j/, the /p/ sound normally shows the influence of the following phoneme, and exerts some influence of voicelessness on them. In *play, pray, pure*, and *tap with*, the lips assume a closed position, but are slightly protruded in anticipating the following sounds. In turn, these glides or semivowel sounds are either devoiced, or at least partially so, in such consonant clusters. Before the other stops /t/, /d/, /k/, /g/ in the same word or phrase, there is normally no exploded release of the /p/ and /b/ sounds, while before the fricative sounds, the ploded quality is absorbed by the fricative sounds. *Apt, rubbed, depth, taps*, and *rubs* do not show the aspirated or strongly exploded characteristic of the initial /p/ and /b/ in *pen* and *big*.

[2] See John S. Kenyon, *American Pronunciation*, 10th ed. (Ann Arbor, George Wahr Publishing Co., 1951), pp. 122–123.

Other Varieties of /p/ and /b/

In less cultivated speech, these sounds are made with excessive aspiration or as fricative sounds. The latter variety is noticed in the "careless" pronunciation of *obvious* and *cupful*, when the /p/ and /b/ sounds are not made with both lips as stopped sounds, but approximate the /f/ and /v/ fricative openings: [ɑβvɪəs], [kʌɸfʊl]. The strange phonetic symbols [β] and [ɸ] indicate sounds normally found in the Spanish pronunciation of *Havana* and the German word *Pferd*, that is, as bilabial fricative continuant sounds.

Complete devoicing of the /b/ when in the final position of a phrase, as in "... tribe," [... traɪb̥], is a foreignism (as is the use of an unaspirated /p/ when normal usage dictates otherwise). This should not be confused with *partial* devoicing of /b/ before a pause, as discussed earlier.

THE STOP-PLOSIVES /t/ AND /d/

The voiceless /t/ and the voiced /d/ are tongue tip to gum ridge, or alveolar, sounds orally emitted. The voiceless sounds in *tea*, *stay*, *bitter*, and *hit* differ in their release, possessing different acoustic values. These are noted by the presence or absence of aspiration, following the release of the sound. Similarly, the /d/ sounds released in *den*, *larder*, and *bud* possess slightly different acoustic values, a stronger release being used for the first /d/ and a weaker one for the second and third sounds. The /t/ sound may be either fully aspirated or lesser aspirated, and the /d/ sound may be strongly or weakly ploded. Like the voiceless /p/ sound, the alveolar /t/ exists as a strongly aspirated sound when it initiates a stressed syllable, and as a lesser aspirated sound when it begins an unstressed syllable or ends a syllable.

Like the /p/ and /b/, the /t/ and /d/ may be unreleased sounds when final in a phrase, although many speakers do complete the plosion in this position, some with distinct aspiration for /t/, others with a lightly aspirated /t/ or weakly ploded /d/. A check of these sounds in the following phrases will probably reveal all three varieties of the final plosive sounds:

Give it to Ne*d*.   He's going to the cour*t*.
I won'*t*.   Have you read the tex*t*?
Did you see i*t*?   It's not too ba*d*.

/t/ preceded by /s/ is an unaspirated sound even when the two sounds precede a stressed vowel. Compare your pronunciation of *steam, stop,* and *stone* with *team, top,* and *tone.* You will note that the /t/ sounds differ in the acoustic value of the released sound,

Medial /t/ and /d/

The medial /t/ assumes either a fully aspirated or weakly aspirated quality depending on whether it initiates a stressed syllable. When we compare our pronunciations of *attempt* and *better, a tame bird* and *atom, he's a tall man* and *she doesn't like him at all times, why tell* and *white elephant,* we notice that the first of each of the words or phrases contains a *fortis,* aspirated /t/, while the second of each pair contains a weakly aspirated, *lenis* /t/. Those medial /t/ sounds that initiate the stressed syllables have the same aspirated quality as the /t/ of *ten* and time. Weakly aspirated medial /t/ may be heard:

1. when /t/ precedes an unstressed vowel, like in *city, yesterday, fitting,* and *liberty;*
2. when /t/ precedes a stressed vowel of a following word, but does not initiate the word, like in "Set only four places," "Right over here," and "white elephant";
3. when /t/ precedes a syllabic [l] like in *beetle* and *bottle.*

Medial /t/ and /d/ between two vowels (in intervocalic position) possess a slightly different incisiveness of formation and release when they precede unstressed vowels. Being sure you listen to the /t/ each time, compare the pronunciations of the /t/'s in *together,* *ten,* and *bitter, tomorrow* and *fitting, top* and *mutter, tore* and *bottom.* Similarly when the intervocalic /d/ precedes an unstressed vowel, as *divide, divorce,* it does not possess the incisive plosive quality in *den* and *do.* Compare these with *fodder, ladder,* and *rider.* Note that when the /t/ or /d/ sounds appear initially or before a stressed vowel, the plosive quality is precisely and sharply released, while the inter-vocalic sounds before unstressed vowels are released with less in-cisiveness, less sharpness. The acoustic value of this sound is almost identical with the intervocalic flapped sound of British English in such words as *worry* and *faraway* (IPA symbol [ɾ]). The intervocalic /t/ is of the same quality, with the voice quality removed.

Voiced /t/

A voiced variety of /t/ is commonly heard in all regional areas of the country when: *(a)* in intervocalic position before an unstressed vowel, as in *butter, let him in,* and *get another; (b)* preceding a syllabic /l/ as in *beetle* and *subtle; (c)* between a nonsyllabic /l/ and an unstressed vowel as in *malted, altogether, consulted,* and *salted; (d)* between /n/ and an unstressed vowel as in *twenty, wanted, seventy, want to see,* and *He went in to Allen's store; (e)* between unaccented vowels as in *at another place* and *if it is convenient.* The voiced variety does not occur when the sound is in initial or final position of a phrase, when it begins an accented syllable, nor when it precedes syllabic /n/ as in *Today is Monday, Where is it?, atone,* and *button.* Some phoneticians have labeled this an allophone of /t/ and call it a "voiced t," [t̪], the subscript [.] depicting the voicing. Others consider it an allophone of /d/.[3] Regardless of where it "belongs" there is little doubt as to its consistent existence in less cultivated American speech and its fairly widespread use in informal, educated speech. It varies freely with the voiceless variety in educated speech, but in more formal situations and when the speaker desires

[3] For excellent discussions of this phenomenon in American English, see the previously cited John S. Kenyon, *American Pronunciation,* 10th ed., 1951, pp. 126–127; Allan F. Hubbell, *The Pronunciation of English in New York City* (New York, Kings Crown Press, 1950), pp. 23–24; Victor A. Oswald, "Voiced T—A Misnomer," *American Speech,* Vol. 18 (1943), pp. 18–25; Donald J. Sharf, "Distinctiveness of 'Voiced T' Sounds, *American Speech,* Vol. 35 (1960), pp. 105–109.

greater precision of speech, the use of the voiceless variety is common, and a clear distinction is made between *bitter* and *bidder*, *atom* and *Adam*, *latter* and *ladder*.

The /t/ and /d/ in Dental Position

When immediately preceding the *th* sounds /θ/ and /ð/, the /t/ and /d/ are dentally made, the tongue tip being in contact with the upper incisor teeth. In the words *breadth* and *width*, and in the phrases *hit the ball* and *put the book*, it is normal for these sounds to be made in either the interdental position (tongue tip between upper and lower teeth) or in dental position (tongue tip in contact with the upper teeth).

Excrescent /t/ and /d/

An unconsciously inserted /t/ and /d/ sound is made by many speakers in such words as *once*, *fence*, *sense* and *fans*, *bans*, *sins*. The tongue, as it moves from the alveolar position of /n/ to the open position of the tongue for /s/ and /z/, moves through the released plosive position for /t/ and /d/. Compare your pronunciation of *prince* and *prints*, *sense* and *cents*, *bans* and *bands*, *fins* and *finds*, *gains* and *hands*. In each of the first words of these pairs, the tongue motion, from the /n/ to the /s/ or /z/ sound, allows the speaker to insert a /t/ before the /s/, and a /d/ before the /z/. Unless the speaker is most careful, and practically interrupts the word before either of the sibilant sounds, he will tend to insert the excrescent sound in such combinations as those listed above. Authorities are beginning to recognize this excrescence as standard, acceptable pronunciation. A typical comment on this point states "... indeed these words *(dense, mince, prince)* ... are pronounced more often than not as homonyms of *dents, mints, prints*."[4]

[4] R-M. S. Heffner, *General Phonetics* (Madison, University of Wisconsin Press, 1949), p. 186.

Consonant Clusters with /t/ and /d/

Like /p/ and /b/, the /t/ and /d/ show the influence of the semi-vowels /l/, /r/, /w/, and /j/ when these sounds follow the plosives. In turn, they are influenced by a preceding alveolar stop in cluster position. In comparing the formation of *time* with *twice, too* with *true, hit* with *hit Lucy*, and *to* with *tune* (when pronounced as [tjun]), the following can be noticed:

twice: the lips begin the formation of /w/ while the /t/ is being formed; the /w/ is either fully or partially devoiced.

true: the lips assume the position of the /r/ and the tongue has greater blade contact while making the /t/, anticipating the formation of the /r/; the /r/ sound is emitted with greater fricative quality than is normal; the /r/ is either fully or partially devoiced.

Can you note similar influences in the other two examples listed above?

Before other stops in the same words or phrases, there is no exploded release of the /t/ and /d/ except in careful, deliberate speech. Before fricative sounds, the quality of the exploded /t/ is absorbed by the fricative sound. Thus, *at camp, light bomb, could go, hits, bids,* and *catch* do not normally show the aspirated or strongly ploded characteristic possessed by the initial /t/ and /d/ of *ten* and *dig*.

Other Varieties of /t/ and /d/

A form of /t/ and /d/ commonly found in substandard speech results from the placement of the tongue tip on the inner surfaces of the upper or lower teeth. The plosive nature of the sound results from release of contact between the blade of the tongue and the gum ridge. This changes the plosive quality of the sound from an incisively ploded form of the alveolar sound to an affricative one (a plosive followed by a fricative sound similar to a /ts/ or /dz/ cluster).

In careless or indistinct speech, the /t/ and /d/ may be lost, especially when final or in certain clusters, as in *he had it̬, it's in the sand̬, eighth̬, width̬, breadth̬, lists̬,* and *posts̬*.

After /n/ and before an unstressed vowel, /t/ and /d/ may be dropped in careless speech as in *wanť to, twenty, finď another, center, wonderful, blinding storm,* and *lanď of plenty.*

When immediately preceding a syllabic /n/ or /l/, the /t/ is often dropped and a glottal plosive inserted (see page 79). A transcription of such pronunciations may be seen in the words *kitten, mitten, bottle,* and *settle:* [kɪ²n̩], [mɪ²n̩], [bɑ²l̩], and [sɛ²l̩].

Full devoicing of /d/ when in the final position of a phrase is considered a foreignism, as in "... on a steep grade." [... greɪd̥].

THE STOP-PLOSIVES /k/ AND /g/

The voiceless /k/ and voiced /g/ sounds are back of tongue-velum stops, orally emitted. They are known as velar stops. Like the other stops already discussed, they differ in the quality of their release, possessing different acoustic values. These differences result from the presence or absence of aspiration. Compare *king, liking,* and *make* with *go, bigger,* and *hog.* You will note again that a fully aspirated sound is made when the voiceless plosive precedes a stressed vowel, and that the voiceless stop is less aspirated when it precedes a lesser stressed vowel, or when final. (/k/ and /g/ are heard as released or unreleased plosives when final in a phrase. They behave like /p-b/ and /t-d/ in this regard.) The voiced /g/ is normally made with a stronger release when it precedes a stressed vowel, with a weaker release when it precedes a lesser stressed vowel and when final. When preceded by /s/, as in *sky* and *skate,* the /k/ is weakly aspirated or unaspirated. No aspiration is heard when the voiceless plosive precedes another consonant, as in *taǩe more* and *picǩ two.*

Excrescence of /k/ and /g/

There are few instances of an excrescent velar plosive in our language. The added /k/ or /g/ is not heard after the velar nasal, when *ng* is final in a word. In the words *length, lengthen, strength, strengthen,* however, both forms are heard in standard speech: [lɛŋθ, lɛŋkθ, strɛŋθ, strɛŋkθ].

/k/ and /g/ in Clusters

Compare the positions of the articulators in the words *key* and *cream, calf* and *question, coup* and *cute*. In each of the first words of the pairs, the /k/ sound is normally made and released. In each of the second words of the pairs, two changes take place: (1) the plosive partly assumes the lip position of the following glide, and (2) the glides are devoiced due to the voiceless quality of the preceding /k/. The same influence on the formation of the plosive sound occurs when /g/ precedes the semivowels /r, w, l, j/.

When immediately followed by another plosive consonant, the /k/ and /g/ tend to omit the release part of the plosive. When they are followed by fricative sounds, the ploded quality is absorbed by the noise of the fricative sound. Thus in *act, begged*, and *cook tin*, there is no ploded release of the /k/ or /g/, and in *dogs* and *big vine*, the /g/ release is absorbed. Compare these with the /k/ and /g/ in *keel* and *get*.

Other Varieties of /k/ and /g/

In less cultivated speech, /k/ is made with either too much or no aspiration when usage dictates otherwise. Such pronunciations are usually due to the influence of a language other than English.

Final /g/, like final /d/, is a weakly ploded and partially devoiced sound. When final /g/ is fully devoiced, it is considered a foreignism.

The dropping of the /k/ in such words as *succinct* and *accessory* may be heard in careless speech. /g/ is commonly lost in *English* and *England* by some educated and many less cultivated speakers, and it is often not pronounced in *recognize, suggest, language*, and *distinguish* by the same speakers. The added /g/ in words like *singer*, and the dropping of the /g/ in words like *finger*, are discussed elsewhere (see page 109).

THE GLOTTAL STOP

The sound known as the glottal or laryngeal stop results from the compression and sudden release of air at the glottis. The sound is produced when the separating vocal bands allow the compressed air to rush through the space between them. This plosive sound is always voiceless and unaspirated. Those who speak German will recognize the common use of the glottal stop before initial stressed vowels in that language. It also exists as a standard sound in such languages as Danish, Arabic, and in the Scots dialect of English. It has no spelled form in our language. When made by English-speaking people, it is found before initially stressed vowels, sometimes between vowels when the second vowel begins a stressed syllable, and as a transition sound from a final to an initial vowel. Note the following phrases where the glottal sound may be heard:

triumphant, aorta, India office, I did.

In each of these words and phrases, the glottal sound may be found in the speech of educated speakers. Since its presence attests to a degree of laryngeal tension singers carefully avoid it. When projecting their speech across the footlights, actors may find themselves using this sound in words or phrases like the above ones quite unconsciously, but they too try to avoid it.

Used occasionally, the glottal stop attracts little notice; used frequently, it interrupts phrasing and distorts the rhythm of speech. For these reasons, it is usually counseled against.

In the instances noted below, most authorities consider the use of the glottal stop as an aspect of less cultivated English and recommend its avoidance. In the following phrases, check your own pronunciation, noting if you use a glottal stop.

Before a syllabic /l/ or /n/		*When a plosive precedes another consonant*
mutton	mountain	*let him pass*
beetle	lantern	*what one*
bottle	hospital	*not many*
kitten	subtle	*What did you say?*

REVIEW AND PRACTICE SECTION

1. In order to indicate some of the narrow or small differences between similar sounds, phoneticians may make use of diacritic marks when they desire to represent some of the small, nonphonemic, differences we have been discussing. To describe these differences, you will find the following symbols useful:

> [pʰ]—a fully aspirated /p/ before a stressed vowel, as in *pen*.
> [p‘]—a lesser or slightly aspirated sound when before an unstressed vowel, or sometimes finally, as in *pajamas* or *hip*.
> [p']—the unaspirated plosive sound, commonly after *s*, as in *spend*.
> [p⁻]—an unreleased plosive as in *hip boot*, and sometimes finally as in *map*.

   Using the above symbols, indicate the appropriate transcription for each of the following:

slippery	kept	attempt	tempo
penny	cheap	depose	trick
people	splatter	whisper	sky
patent	scanty	pulse	determine

2. Indicate a key word for each of the above symbols when added to the /t/ or /k/ sounds:

3. Indicate which words are nasally ploded, laterally ploded, or normally ploded:

platter	topmost	ladle	beaten
batting	tenting	fiddle	button

4. Arrange the following into two columns, placing those with fully aspirated plosives into one column, and all others into another column.

apart	what time	terrace	liquor	flapping
atom	seventy	acclimate	accord	spear
emperor	sit over there	liked	account	cheap
suppose	button	matter	torque	atomic

5. Comment on the nature of the plosive sounds in each of the following words or phrases: *cupful, obvious, breadth, mob violence, hit the ball.*

6. Which, if any, plosives exist in your pronunciation of the following?

one side	lanes	prince	center
altogether	wonderful	mitten	singer
lengthen	aorta	seventy	twenty
anxious			

7. Do you use a glottal stop when you pronounce the following?

   oh!   Don't *ever* do that!   triumphant   my own   let him pass

8. Say the following sentences aloud and transcribe your pronunciation. Comment on the nature of the plosives.

   > Grace and Gus took their bikes to school.
   > Do you place the /t/ and /d/ on the teeth?
   > Depend on practice and your performance will improve.
   > The fungus resulted in a gangrenous condition.
   > Tetanus shots are preventive measures.

9. Transcribe the following passage from the Taoist Scriptures.

   > Attain to the goal of absolute vacuity;
   > Keep to the state of perfect peace.
   > All things come into existence,
   > And thence we see them return.
   > Look at the things that have been flourishing;
   > Each goes back to its origin.
   > Going back to the origin is called peace;
   > It means reversion to destiny.

CHAPTER 5

The Fricative Sounds

INTRODUCTION

A FRICATIVE SOUND is one in which the breath stream is continually emitted between two closely posed articulators. The term is an acoustic one, meaning "friction-like." It is used to describe all open continuant consonants except those that are labeled glides, semi-vowels, or nasals. In actuality, all continuant consonants are fricative, for they all possess some degree of friction, however slight; but those consonants that tend toward noticeably open or vowel-like sounds are commonly excluded from the fricative classification.

There are ten fricative sounds in the English language. They appear as the initial sounds in the words *fee, veal, thin, then, see, zoo, she, he* and *when;* and the medial *z* of *azure.* The "wh" in *when* is not used consistently by all speakers of American English. Many speakers never use this sound. They substitute the *w* of *we* in such *wh* words as *when* and *where* (see Figure 11).

Voiced fricatives are normally partially devoiced when they appear initially or finally in a sentence or phrase, and when they precede voiceless consonants. This partial devoicing can be noticed in the following sentences:

82

*Z*ebras are found in zoo*s*.   ⎫ Beginning and end of phrase
*Th*ere are fi*v*e.   ⎭

He has fi*v*e cents.   ⎫ Immediately preceding a voiceless
He folded his clothe*s* poorly.   ⎭   consonant

Complete devoicing of a voiced fricative, especially when the fricative sound is in final position, is considered a fault of careless usage.

THE FRICATIVE CONSONANTS /f/ AND /v/

The fricative continuant sounds /f/ and /v/ are made with the lower lip in contact with the upper teeth. Both sounds are emitted orally. /f/ is the voiceless cognate of /v/. Both sounds are found in the initial, medial, and final positions of words: *feel, safely, knife, veal, living, live.* /v/ tends to be made with less constriction (or pressure of the teeth against the lip) than the /f/. It is more *lenis* than /f/.

When immediately followed by a voiceless consonant, and when at the beginning or end of a sentence or breath group, /v/ is normally partially devoiced:

Gi*v*e *S*usan her book.
I ha*v*e *f*ive *c*ents worth.
She will ha*v*e *t*o call.
*V*ery many of the fish were ali*v*e.

Other Varieties of /f/ and /v/

1. When in cluster position with the bilabial sounds /p/, /b/, and /m/, the /f/ and /v/ sounds may be deleted. In their place a bilabial fricative sound (a sound made with both lips creating a long narrow passageway for the breath stream) is heard in the speech of many speakers. In the following words the bilabial fricatives [ɸ] and [β], sounds made with the lower lip and upper teeth, may be heard in place of /f/ and /v/ (see page 72).

obvious   [ɑbvɪəs] > [ɑβɪəs]
cupful   [kʌpfʊl] > [kʌɸʊl]
same voice [seɪm vɔɪs] > [seɪmβɔɪs]
comfort   [kʌmfɚt] > [kʌmɸɚt]

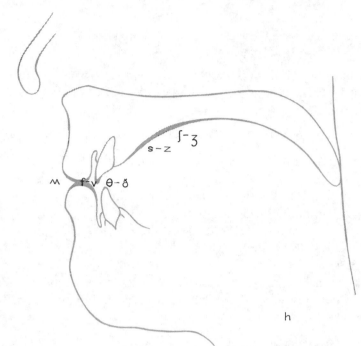

FIG. 11. The articulators that act as obstructors to the breath stream to form the fricatives. /ʍ/: both lips; /f—v/: lip and teeth; /θ—ð/: tongue and teeth; /s—z—ʃ—ʒ/: blade of tongue and hard palate; /h/: vocal bands.

2. /v/ is sometimes omitted in the unstressed words *of* and *have* and in the word *five*. This is heard in such expressions as:

The cover of the book   [ðə kʌvə(r) ə ðə bʊk]
He should have walked   [hi ʃʊd ə wɔkt]
I've five dollars   [aɪv faɪ dɑləz]

3. Those with language backgrounds other than English may completely devoice the final /v/, as in *five* > [faɪv̥], *live* > [lɪv̥], and *save* > [seɪv̥]; or, especially if German or Spanish, may substitute [β] and /b/ for /v/, and [ɸ] or /p/ for /f/.

THE FRICATIVE CONSONANTS /θ/ AND /ð/

The fricative continuant *th* sounds are tip of tongue-teeth sounds, emitted orally. They are made with the tongue-tip in contact with the inner surface of the upper teeth, or with the tongue-tip between the upper and lower incisors. /θ/ is the voiceless cognate of /ð/. Both sounds are found in initial, medial, and final positions as in *thin, frothy,* and *cloth, then, writhing,* and *bathe.*

Like other voiced fricative sounds, the /ð/ is partially devoiced when it is initial or final in a phrase, or when it immediately precedes a voiceless consonant:

*Th*eir father decided to ba*the T*ommy.
She tried to clo*the S*usan's doll.

Other Varieties of /θ/ and /ð/

The mass media (radio, television, movies, and newspapers) often represent the speaker of uncultivated English as substituting an alveolar or dental stop (/t/, /d/) for either *th* sound. Thus *dese, dem, dose, nuttin',* and *tin* for *these, them, those, nothing,* and *thin* have come to personify the uneducated speaker. Excessively rapid and careless speech will show a similar substitution. At such times, the speaker will place the tongue in the position for the *th* sound, but, in his hurry, will fail to allow time for the making of a continuant *th* sound, resulting in a dentally made /t/ or /d/ sound: [t̪], [d̪].

The above substitution, or the actual deletion of the *th* sound, occurs in certain difficult clusters. The words *fifths, sixths,* and *months* may sometimes be enunciated as [fɪfs] or [fɪfts], [sɪks] or [sɪkts], [mʌns] or [mʌnts]. A common pronunciation without *th* is found in such expressions as "Who's there," "Who's that," and "What's this," in which the previous /z/ or /s/ sound is lengthened and substituted for the *th* sound: [huz:ɛɚ], [huz:æt], [wɑts:ɪs].

Complete devoicing of final /ð/ or the substitution of /θ/ for /ð/ may be heard in the speech of non-native speakers: *bathe* ⌐ [beɪθ]; *either* > [iθɚ].

THE FRICATIVE CONSONANTS /s/ AND /z/

The hissing or sibilant-fricative sounds /s/ and /z/ are found in all positions of words. They are normally made with the apex of the tongue held near or just in front of the alveolar ridge of the hard palate. The breath stream is forced through a narrow groove of the tongue against the hard palate. It is then deflected over the upper edges of the lower incisor teeth. The lips are normally in spread position.

The high frequency characteristics of our English sibilant sounds deserve a note in passing. Sibilant sounds possess higher frequency ranges than do any other sounds in our language. This statement may be more meaningful if we compare the frequency characteristics of these sounds with certain other sounds. A note sung to coincide with middle C on your piano results from the vibration of the vocal bands at a rate of approximately 250 cycles per second (cps). The sound of the highest note on your piano (the C of the fourth octave above middle C) results from vibrations in the area of approximately 4,000 cycles per second. The characteristic frequency ranges for the /s/ or /z/ friction noise extends from 3,000 to 7,500 cps, that for /ʃ/ from 2,000 to 4,500 cps.

The ranges or regions of characteristic frequency are known as *formants* to the linguist who studies the acoustic nature of speech sounds. Investigations by acoustic researchers have demonstrated that the English fricative sounds are identified by a generally high, single frequency range, while the identification of vowels depends on a minimum of two ranges, or formants, both fairly low, somewhere between 300 and 2,400 cps. Frequency ranges above the two lower formants help identify what we know as "voice quality" in contradistinction to the identification of the sound as a linguistic unit.[1] The typical two lower ranges that identify /u/ are 300 and 800 cps. 300 and 2,400 cps are the two lower formants that identify

[1] See, for example, Pierre Delattre, Alvin M. Liberman, Franklin S. Cooper, and Louis J. Gerstman, "An Experimental Study of the Acoustic Determinants of Vowel Color: Observations on One- and Two-Formant Vowels Synthesized from Spectographic Patterns," *Word*, Vol. 8 (December, 1952), pp. 195–210.

/i/, while 800 and 1,200 cps result in our identification of /ɑ/, all as voiced by an adult, male baritone voice.

As you can see now, the typical frequency for the friction-sibilant sounds is quite high. Their intelligibility is, therefore, seriously affected when a speech recording of these sounds is reproduced through a system which can filter out the higher frequencies. Eliminating frequencies above 3,000 interferes with the intelligibility of /s, z, ʃ, ʒ/, especially when they are not in the context of speech. Vowel sounds are negligibly affected by eliminating such high frequencies, since the highest formant frequency that is related to linguistic intelligibility for any of the English vowels does not exceed 2,400 cps.

The exact place of articulation varies with the height of the palatal arch. Generally, the tongue-tip is set some place between the gum line of the upper incisors and the alveolar ridges of the palate. Many speakers, however, place the tongue-tip immediately behind the lower incisor teeth. In this position, the blade of the tongue is arched and grooved toward the alveolar ridge. This position normally results in a sound of slightly lower acoustic frequency. When making the /s/ or /z/ sounds, the sides of the tongue are in contact with the sides of the palatal arch or with the inner surfaces of the bicuspid and molar teeth.

Other Varieties of /s/ and /z/

A considerably lowered frequency of these sounds results from a wider groove of the tongue or from a wider aperture between the tip of the tongue and the biting surfaces of the teeth. Such sounds generally prove annoying and are best avoided. You have probably heard how annoying such sounds can be when your radio set is not tuned in just right and the announcer is speaking. His speech sounds as though it is "full of s sounds." As in the failure to tune in the radio speaker, distorted sibilant sounds often result from the failure to adjust the articulators involved. Adjustments are made by motion of the tongue and the lower jaw. If the bite is normal, you can note a slight overlapping, or overbite, of the upper incisors over the

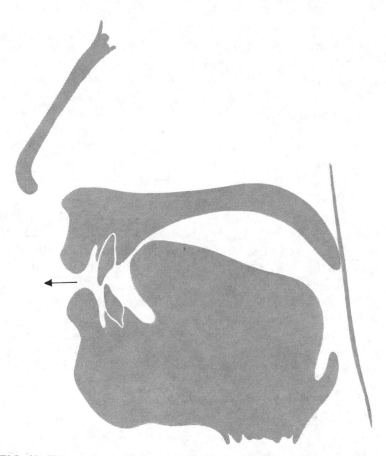

FIG. 12. The articulation of /s/ and /z/ with tip of tongue raised:
[sˑ, zˑ].

lower, when the molars are in contact. An excessive overbite (or underbite, or spaces between the teeth, or failure to keep the lips from interfering with the sound) tends to obstruct or distort the breath stream and results in noticeable sibilant sounds. In such instances, the speaker must adjust the articulators so that the sound approaches a higher-pitched sound.

The /z/ sound may be completely unvoiced in careless speech

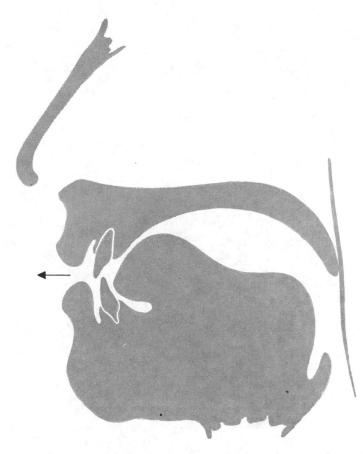

FIG. 13. The articulation of /s/ and /z/ with tip of tongue lowered: [sᴛ, zᴛ].

when it is found in the final position of a phrase or sentence. *Gaze* may become [geɪz̥] in the sentence "She met his gaze."

An acoustic distortion of the /s/ and /z/ sounds results when the sounds are made while the tongue-tip is in contact with the teeth (known as a dental lisp), when it protrudes between the teeth (known as a protrusion lisp), or when it permits the air to escape over the sides of the tongue (known as a lateral lisp).

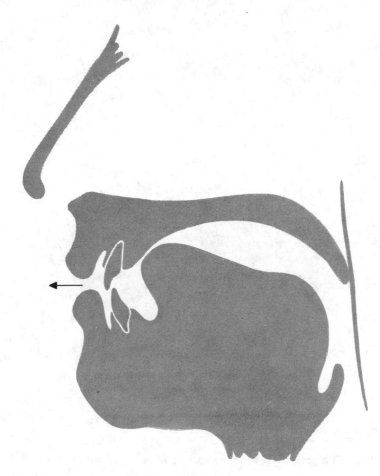

FIG. 14. The position of the tongue for /s/. Compare with Figure 15.

THE FRICATIVE CONSONANTS /ʃ/ AND /ʒ/

These sibilant-fricative sounds are made in the alveolo-palatal area of the mouth. A slightly broader surface of the blade of the tongue is used in making these sounds than is used for the /s/ and /z/ sounds. The whole tongue is farther back in the mouth and the groove of the tongue is wider, directing a wider stream of air forward

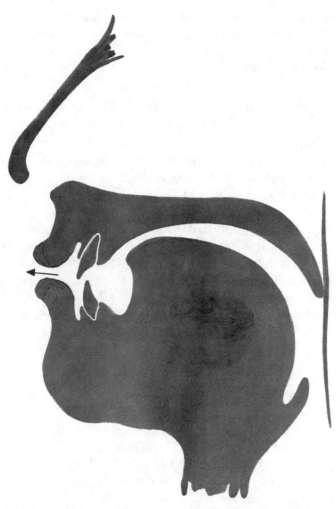

FIG. 15. The position of the tongue for /ʃ/. Compare with Figure 14.

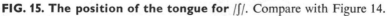

toward the teeth than when forming the /s/ and /z/ sounds. The tip of the tongue is again high in the mouth. Many speakers, however, place the tip of the tongue behind the lower incisor teeth and manage to emit an acceptable /ʃ/ or /ʒ/ sound. A slight protrusion of the lips normally accompanies these sounds when formed. The /ʃ/ sound is found in all positions of words. The /ʒ/ sound is never found initially in English. It exists only in medial and final positions, in such words as *measure* and *garage*. /ʃ/ is the voiceless cognate of /ʒ/.

Other Varieties of /ʃ/ and /ʒ/

Complete devoicing of the /ʒ/ sound, when in final position of a phrase, is considered substandard (for example, *garage* > [gərɑʒ] or [gərɑʃ]).

A faulty /ʃ/ or /ʒ/ sound will result if the breath stream is directed over one or both sides of the tongue. Such an emission of the breath stream is known as a lateral lisp, phonetically transcribed as a voiceless *l*, [ḷ].

Like the sibilants /s/ and /z/, the /ʃ/ and /ʒ/ are acoustically distorted if the articulators are not appropriately adjusted to each other. An acoustically annoying sound will result if the tongue is in contact with the incisor teeth, if the teeth are not appropriately occluded, or if the tongue protrudes while making the sound. Speakers possessing such defects of speech need the special assistance of a qualified speech therapist.

THE AFFRICATES /tʃ/ AND /dʒ/

Sounds which are combinations or compounds of a stop and a fricative are called *affricates*. An affricate results from the slow and nonimpulsive release of the stop sound into a fricative sound made in the same area of the mouth. The affricate is treated as a separate entity in the language, a phoneme in its own right. Despite the transcription of an affricate with two phonetic symbols, it is recognized as a single phoneme.

There are two affricates in the English language, the /tʃ/ and /dʒ/ in *church* and *judge*. These are the only recognized affricates in the standard pattern of English. The /ts/ and /dz/ in *hats* and *bids* are recognized as two distinctive sounds in each cluster, rather than as single phonemic entities, for the plosives /t/ and /d/ are separable, in each instance, from the following fricative sounds /s/ and /z/.

/ts/ and /dz/ are therefore clusters of two separable phonemes, while the /tʃ/ of *cheese* and *catch* and the /dʒ/ of *jury* and *huge* are single phonemic entities.

The words in each of the pairs *sheer—cheer, cashing—catching, hush—hutch* differ from each other in that they each contain the different phonemes /ʃ/ and /tʃ/. The words in each of the pairs *less—lets, guess—gets, place—plates* differ from each other in that the first word contains one phoneme less than the second of each pair. *Less—let, guess—get, place—plate* contain different terminal phonemes as do *hush—hutch, mush—much.* Much recent linguistic writing identifies these affricates with special single phonemic symbols /č/ and /ǰ/, for our ligatured /tʃ/ and /dʒ/, to avoid any possible confusion about the single phoneme concept. However, all recognize that these affricate sounds combine a momentary stop and fricative effect in close conjunction, and that a syllable break cannot fall between the stop and fricative parts as it can between the /t/ and /ʃ/ in "cat shop," "light ship," and "flat shape." The /t/ and /ʃ/ in each of these phrases is separable. The affricate /tʃ/ in *catching* and *fetch* contains the phonetically identifiable characteristics of /t/ and /ʃ/, but their use in these words is as single entities rather than as separable stop and fricative sounds. The impression of affricates as single sounds is not hindered by recognizing that each begins as a stop and culminates in a momentary fricative sound.

The /ts/ cluster does exist as a phonemic entity in certain other languages, as in Hebrew *ets* [ets], meaning "tree," or German *Zeit* [tsaɪt], meaning "time." And when we borrow words containing such sounds from other languages, we may, quite normally, conceive of them as single phonemic entities, rather than as clusters: the /ts/ in Russian *Tsar*, in Bantu *Tsetse*, or in Italian *pizza*.

Both affricates are made in pre-palatal (or post-alveolar) position, with the tip and blade of the tongue directly behind the alveolar ridge.

Other Varieties of /tʃ/ and /dʒ/

There are two common substandard varieties. The first occurs when the tip of the tongue is placed in contact with the lower teeth, while the blade of the tongue remains close to the palatal area. The resulting acoustic value of this dentally made sound is lower in frequency than normally expected. The other results from a complete devoicing of the /dʒ/ when in the final position of a phrase: "Which college?" > [ʍɪtʃ kɑlɪdʒ̥]. Such devoicing is found in the speech of many non-native speakers.

The /t/ component of the affricate is sometimes lost in cultivated British speech in such words as *wrench, gulch, inch,* and *belch:* [rɛnʃ, gʌlʃ, ɪnʃ, bɛlʃ]. Such loss is uncommon in cultivated American speech.

THE GLOTTAL FRICATIVE CONSONANT /h/

The fricative /h/ occurs as the breath stream passes through the glottis. The vocal bands obstruct the stream sufficiently to produce a slight degree of friction. This whispered sound is therefore known as the glottal fricative sound.

When pronouncing the /h/ sound, the articulators are in the position of the following vowel sound. Compare your pronunciations of *he, who,* and *hat.* You will note that both the lips and the tongue assume the /i/, /u/, or /æ/ positions before the word is initiated. There are as many positions for the formation of the glottal fricative sound as there are positions for sounds that can follow the /h/ sound.

When the /h/ sound is in intervocalic position (between two vowels), as in *behest* or *perhaps,* the /h/ is frequently voiced. The IPA symbol for the voiced allophone is [ɦ].

There are no common uncultivated /h/ forms in American English. In the words and phrases listed below, note the various forms we use for /h/. Unless your speech is of foreign origin (or of a dialect such as Cockney, where the initial /h/ before stressed vowels is commonly deleted) your pronunciation will agree with the forms as listed:

1. *Initial* /h/ *before stressed syllables*

> *he*—He gave John the bat.
> *whose*—Whose book is there?

hair—His hair is black.
high—They found a high shelf.
whole—The whole group came.

2. /h/ *frequently voiced to* [ɦ]

    perhaps, behind, prohibit, apprehend, behold, behave, rehearse, behest, rehearsal, rehash

3. *Commonly deleted* /h/ *when before unstressed vowels*

    prohibition, philharmonic, annihilate, vehement, vehicle, unhistoric, rehabilitate

4. *Loss of initial* /h/ *in the following words when used as weak (unstressed) forms in a phrase*

    has—Where has he gone?
    have—I have gone to the store.
    had—He had twenty of them.
    his—I saw his car.
    he—Did you see how he ran?
    him—He gave him his books.
    her—We watched her go.

5. *A commonly omitted* /h/ *in a stressed word:* Come here! [kəmːɪɚ]

THE FRICATIVE CONSONANT /hw/

The *wh* spelling 'is represented by the [hw] or [ʍ] transcription, either symbol representing the common pronunciation for the *when* and *where* words in American English. The difference between the two forms is essentially the degree of aspiration with which the sound begins. They are variants of each other, the [hw] representing an aspirate onglide to the /w/ sound, the /ʍ/ representing a voiceless fricative labiovelar sound, or a voiceless /w/, [w̥]. Either of these sounds is the normal American pronunciation for all *wh* words, except *who, whom, whose, whole, whore, whoop,* and their derivatives.

Most American speakers make a clear distinction between *wh* and *w* words, so that *where—ware, whey—way,* and *which—witch* are pronounced with different initial consonants. The voiceless [ʍ], or the cluster sound [hw], is not regularly used, however, in the speech of most in New York City and in certain other sections of the East.[2] /hw/ is actually the older and still predominant form in most of the country. /w/ seems to be gaining in popularity, particularly in urban areas and among younger people.

In those parts of this country, and in England too, where /w/ for *when* and *where* words is the prevalent form, the use of /hw/ may be heard sporadically in educated speech. Hubbell reports in his previously cited *The Pronunciation of English in New York City*,[3] that those New Yorkers who consistently use /hw/ are rather rare, and that those who do, seem to have consciously adopted the sound. The /hw/ is usual in Scotland, Ireland, and the north of England, while the /w/ is the more usual pronunciation in southern England. Daniel Jones notes in his *Outline of English Phonetics*,[4] that /hw/ is taught in many schools in southern England. In 1950, Jones wrote in his *The Pronunciation of English*,[5] that the /hw/ pronunciation was adopted by many speakers in the South, but that /w/ was the common educated pronunciation. In the 1956 edition of his *English Pronouncing Dictionary*, all but a few *wh* words[6] are listed with the /w/ entry, followed with an /hw/ variant. American dictionaries list /hw/ for all the words under consideration and do not include the /w/ forms even as variant entries. Kenyon and Knott, in their *Pronouncing Dictionary of American English*, do make a special entry before the first *wh* word, noting that, although only /hw/ is shown for the *wh* words, many speakers of American English replace /hw/ with /w/.

The evidence for the use of both /w/ and /hw/ for these words is overwhelming and it is a false notion that the use of /w/ represents

---

[2] The *Linguistic Atlas* studies found /w/ regularly used in New York City, the Hudson Valley, eastern Pennsylvania, and the South Carolina-Georgia Low-Country for such words as *wheelbarrow* and *whip*. See Raven I. McDavid, Jr., "American English Dialects," in W. Nelson Francis, *The Structure of American English* (New York, Ronald, 1958), Ch. 9, pp. 513–527.

[3] (New York, Kings Crown Press, 1950), p. 52.

[4] (Cambridge, Eng., Cambridge University Press, 1940), 6th ed., p. 193.

[5] (Cambridge, Eng., Cambridge University Press, 1950), p. 115.

[6] *Whoa, whoopee, Wheatstone*, and *whelk* are the only words listed with /w/ and no alternative /hw/.

a careless or substandard pronunciation. Its use is actually less common in most of the country, rather than "uncultivated." In some sections of the country, almost all educated speakers use only /w/. In others, too many educated speakers pronounce such *wh* words with /w/, or at least are inconsistent enough in the use of /hw/ to label the variant /w/ pronunciation "substandard."

REVIEW AND PRACTICE SECTION

1. Describe the initial sound in each of the following words: *four, think, cheese, shoe.* (For example, the *v* in *veal* is a voiced, labio-dental fricative continuant.)
2. Why do the bilabial fricative sounds appear in such words as *cupful* and *obvious?* Why are they not phonemes in the English language?
3. Transcribe a common substandard pronunciation of each of the following words or phrases, and place the colloquial educated form next to each.

   sixths   fifths   five dollars   who's that
   You should have come.

4. Arrange the following words containing voiceless fricatives in one column and those containing voiced fricatives in another.

wroth	writhe	teethe	teeth	ether	either
bath	bathe	pithy	breathing	theology	nether
these	Philip	clothes	safely	never	

5. Describe the differentiating sounds in each pair of words.

safes—saves	writing—writhing	pitcher—picture
breadth—breath	eight—eighth	crush—crutch
never—nether	sheep—cheap	mad—Madge
tank—thank	bays—beige	seep—cheap

6. The following clusters often lead to mispronunciations. Can you say these words rapidly?

   sks—asks, desks, discs
   pst—lapsed, collapsed
   θs—fifths, hundredths, tenths
   $\eth z$—loathes, teethes, breathes

   sts—ghosts, crusts, tastes, waists
   θw—thwack, thwart
   sg—disgust, Miss Gray, disguise

7. Do you make a distinction between /w/ and /hw/ in *wear* and *where*? And do you hear a voiced *h*, [ɦ], in your pronunciation of *behind* and *ahoy*? Indicate which of the following you say in each of the words below: [w, ʍ, h, ɦ].

whine   woman   hurl   whirl   height   white   wide
whole   whoa   woe   whisk   unholy   behave   inhuman
anywhere   somewhat off white high   why

8. Transcribe, as you say, the following sentences.

> She wore a beige dress and was heavily rouged.
> The church bells aroused the judge each Sunday.
> Arthur said he'd stand by his brother through thick and thin.
> *This* and *that* are the singular forms of *these* and *those*.
> Why has she come to see him?
> They whirled their hats each time the pitcher hurled the ball.

CHAPTER 6

The Frictionless

Consonants

ALL CONTINUANT sounds are either fricative or frictionless sounds. Those emitted with a relative freedom from constriction of the breath stream are the frictionless consonants. There are seven such continuant sounds in the English language. Three of them are nasal sounds—the /m/, /n/, and /ŋ/ as in *me, no,* and *sing*; three are glides —the /w/, /r/, and /j/ in *we, red,* and *you*; one of them is separately classified as the lateral sound—the /l/ as in *live*.

In certain instances, some of these frictionless consonants may function as vowels. In such words as *button, glistening,* and *kettle,* the /n/ and /l/ assume the syllabic function of vowels: [bʌtn̩, glɪsn̩ɪŋ, kɛtl̩]. Frictionless consonants, functioning as vowels (syllabic consonants), are not normally found in the initial positions of words, as are other vowels. Some, such as /w/ and /j/, never appear as syllabic sounds. The frictionless sounds are sometimes called *sonorants* or *semivowels*, the former word representing the acoustic nature of voiced sounds resulting from a generally unconstricted breath stream; the latter word recognizing both the general lack of articulatory constriction and, in part, the functioning nature of these

99

sounds. All the characteristics and functions are not shared by all of these sounds. We will find it useful, therefore, to classify them generally as *frictionless-continuant* sounds and to study them separately as *nasal*, *glide*, or *lateral* consonants.

THE NASAL CONSONANTS

The three nasal sounds are articulated like stops, but during the formation and emission of all nasals the velum or soft palate is forward. This opening of the velar valve permits the emission of sound through the nasopharynx and the nasal cavity. When producing the nasal sounds, we close the oral cavity at the point of articulation. These three points of articulation are the same as those for the three pairs of stops: /m/ is nasally emitted while the lips are closed as for the /b-p/ position; /n/ with the tongue-tip at the alveolar ridge for the /d-t/ position; /ŋ/ with the dorsum of the tongue against the velum as for the /g-k/ position. Any complete blocking of the nasal port (such as may result from a severe cold) produces the voiced oral homorganic substitute for the nasal sound intended. Such a person says [bɛd] for *men*, [do] for *no*, [kɪg] for *king* and [bɛdi bɛd kəd sɪg] for "many men can sing."

Nasals are normally voiced sounds, but when immediately following a voiceless consonant in the same syllable, they are partially devoiced. Note the devoiced variant as the nasal sound begins in *smile* and *sneeze*, when compared with the fully voiced nasal in *mile* and *neat*.

The positions of articulators for each of the nasal sounds are shown below. Note that each nasal sound is articulated as is one of the pairs of stops. /m/ and /n/ are found in initial, medial, and final positions of words. /ŋ/ is found only medially and finally, as in *sing*, *wronged*, and *singer*.

The Nasals as Syllabics

The three nasal sounds can assume a particular function of vowels, that is, they can act as unstressed syllabic sounds. Note your

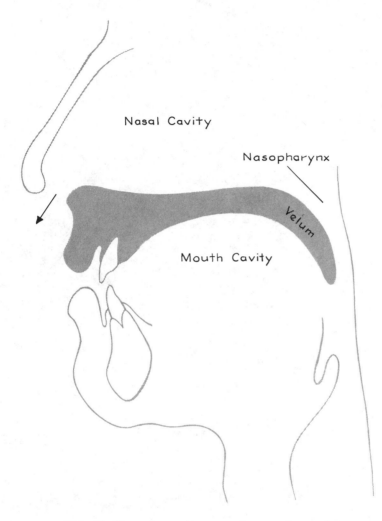

FIG. 16. The velar valve open for nasal sounds.

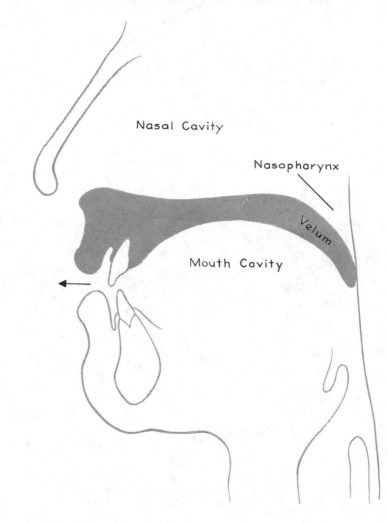

FIG. 17. The velar valve closed for non-nasal sounds.

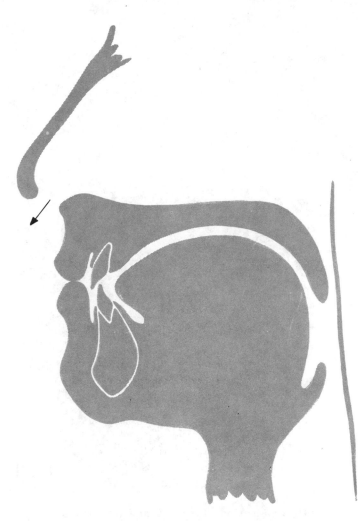

FIG. 18. Position of the articulators for /m/.

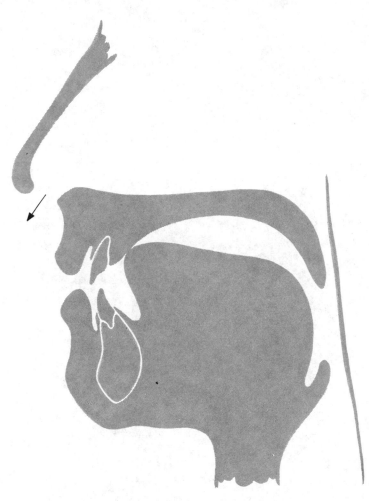

FIG. 19. Position of the articulators for /n/.

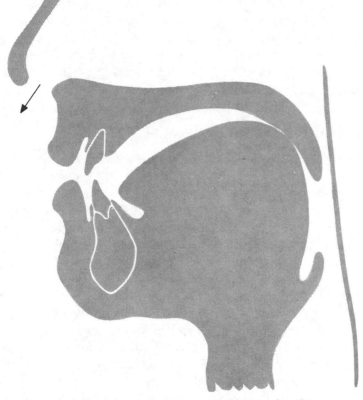

FIG. 20. Position of the articulators for /ŋ/.

dictionary respellings of the following words: *bitten*, *hidden*, *schism*, and *chasm*. In each of the first two words, the articulators are already in the position of the /n/ sound while the /t-d/ are being made. No vowel intervenes between the /t-d/ and /n/. The /m/ in the two final words is made by an immediate closing of the lips while the tongue has not quite completed the preceding /z/ sound. In all four words, the nasal sounds act as syllabics. They are transcribed [bɪtn̩, hɪdn̩, sɪzm, kæzm̩], showing no vowel between the /t/, /d/, or /z/ and the following nasal sound. Such syllabic nasals are part of the standard speech pattern. We hear and say them quite commonly in such phrases as "Get in the car," [gɛtn̩ ðə kɑɚ], "He sighed and moaned," [hi saɪdn̩ moʊnd], "Slap him," [slæpm̩], and "Tip him," [tɪpm̩]. A syllabic /ŋ/ is not as common in cultivated American English.

Modifications of the Nasal Consonants

The /m/ sound is produced, occasionally, in labiodental position when it immediately precedes an /f/ or /v/ sound. Note what occurs to the articulatory position of the /m/ sound when you say the words *comfortable* and *triumvirate* fairly quickly. This accidentally-made variation of the /m/ is represented by a special labiodental symbol in narrow phonetic transcription: [ɱ] (*comfort*—[kʌɱfɚt], *triumph*—[traɪəɱf]).

The /n/ is dentally made when it immediately precedes a *th* sound in such words and phrases as *month*, *tenth*, *in the*, and *on the*. This dental *n*, [n̪], is used by all speakers of standard English.

The /ŋ/, although commonly spelled with the two letters *n* and *g*, is a single continuant sound. It also appears for a spelled *n* in certain words, when preceding *k* or *g*, as in *sink* and *tingle*. The "ng" was formerly pronounced [ŋg] in all instances.

In early Modern English, the final /g/ of the cluster was dropped from all words ending in "ng." It is because of this earlier dropping of the final /g/ that we pronounce *sing* and *among* with /ŋ/, *single* and *hunger* with an /ŋg/ cluster today. Because of much confusion on the use of this sound, it is wise to note the following generalizations that describe its pronunciation.

1. Whenever final in a word, "ng" (or "ngue") is always pronounced /ŋ/: *sing, bring, tongue, harangue*: [sɪŋ, brɪŋ, tʌŋ, həræŋ]. Inflectional endings added to such words do not change the /ŋ/ form: *singing, bringer, tongues, harangued*: [sɪŋɪŋ, brɪŋɚ, tʌŋz, həræŋd]. Compound words possessing this sound are found in certain place names. They are pronounced as are other final /ŋ/ forms: Springfield [sprɪŋfɪld], Bingham [bɪŋəm], Binghamton [bɪŋəmtən], and Washington [waʃɪŋtən].

2. Medial "ng" sounds are pronounced /ŋg/ when they are not in compound words *(Springfield)* nor in inflected forms *(singer)*. *Mingle, finger*, and *Rangoon* are heard as [mɪŋgəl, fɪŋgɚ, ræŋgun].

3. A number of exceptional words do not fit into the generalizations described above. They are best noted separately:

   /ŋ/: gingham
   /ŋg/: the comparative and superlative forms of *long, strong, young*[1]

   longer—[lɔŋgɚ]
   longest—[lɔŋgɪst]
   stronger—[strɔŋgɚ]
   strongest—[strɔŋgɪst]
   younger—[jʌŋgɚ]
   youngest—[jʌŋgɪst]

   /ŋg/: words with the added *al, ate, ation*[1]

   diphthongal—[dɪfθɔŋgəl]
   monophthongal—[manəfθɔŋgəl]
   elongate—[ɪlɔŋgeɪt]
   prolongation—[prolɔŋgeɪʃn̩]

   /ŋ/ or /ŋg/: clangor—[klæŋɚ, klæŋgɚ]
   hangar—[hæŋɚ, hæŋgɑɚ]

   /ŋ/ or /ŋk/: length—[lɛŋθ, lɛŋkθ]
   lengthen—[lɛŋθən, lɛŋkθən]
   strength—[strɛŋθ, strɛŋkθ]
   strengthen—[strɛŋθən, strɛŋkθən]

[1] These words retain the historical /ŋg/.

Final /n/ or /ŋ/

A comment about the use of final /n/ for /ŋ/ is worth noting. For an extended period of time, educated speakers have been known to use the "-in" for the "-ing" ending in such words as *running, coming,* and *singing.* Such use is actually more widespread than most people suppose. Actually, the final /n/ was by far the more common ending in earlier Modern English. Pre-Modern English spellings like *standyn* and *holdyn* are pointed to as proof of then current [-ɪn] endings, and as noted in Appendix A, page 289, the colloquial speech of Elizabethan times followed the [ɪn] endings for these words too, a pronunciation well established by then for probably two hundred years. Evidence of its use was so common in England and America at the end of the eighteenth century, that the dictionaries and spelling books of the time made steady mention of it. Spelling pronunciation has kept the "-ing" [ɪŋ] to the fore, however, and it is normally expected in the speech of educated people.

Although preference for the [ɪŋ] seems clear, it might be kept in mind that ". . . it must not be hastily concluded that the pronunciation [-ɪn] instead of [-ɪŋ] in *coming, going,* and the like, is necessarily a mark of ignorance or lack of cultivation."[2] The [-ɪn] for [ɪŋ] is, of course, the common and normal form in less-cultivated speech. It is probably because of this practice, and the strong power of the spelled form, that [-ɪn] for [-ɪŋ] is so widely counseled against.

Other Varieties of the Nasal Sounds

1. The nasal sounds are distorted when some obstruction in the nasopharynx or the nose prevents the normal emission of the breath stream and the resonance of these frictionless sounds in the nasal cavity. And there are instances where no obstruction exists and still the speaker fails to emit the sounds properly. In both of these instances medical and speech therapeutic help should be sought. A complete blocking of the nasal passage results in the substitution

[2] John S. Kenyon, *American Pronunciation,* 10th ed. (Ann Arbor, George Wahr Publishing Co., 1951), p. 154.

of the voiced homorganic stops for the nasals: /b/ for /m/, /d/ for /n/, and /g/ for /ŋ/, as noted earlier.

2. The nasalizing of a vowel before a nasal consonant results from the lowering of the soft palate while the vowel is being spoken. *Candy*, *manner*, *man*, and *fine* would be transcribed with nasalized vowels as [kǣndi, mǣnɚ, mǣn, fãɪn]. Actually *some* nasalization of a vowel preceding a nasal consonant is unavoidable. The assimilative tendency (see Chapter 11) to nasalize partially the vowels in *man* or *sing* results from the slight lowering of the velar valve while the vowel is still being emitted. Such slight nasalization is hardly noticed and the probability is good that all speakers, even educated ones, use some nasalization in such instances. As such, it can hardly be considered a fault of usage. Only if the vowel is completely nasalized do listeners object and place the pronunciation used in the less-cultivated category.

3. /m, n/ may be omitted when it is adjacent to /f/ or /v/, in careless speech, in such phrases as *some vines*, *come further*, and *one fine day*. In such instances the nasal sound is dropped and the preceding vowel is nasalized: [sÃvaɪnz, kÃfɝðɚ, wÃ fãɪ deɪ].

4. The use of an excrescent /p/ following a final /m/ of a word may be heard, in careless speech, when the following sound is voiceless, as in *come closer* or *some time*. It can be avoided by simply continuing the nasal resonance and emission throughout the /m/ sound.

5. A dental *n*, [n̪], may be heard in the speech of many who do not speak English as a native tongue, as well as in less-cultivated speech. This dental sound is made with the tip of the tongue placed against the upper or lower teeth. The blade of the tongue is in contact with the hard palate. Those whose native tongues are Spanish, Yiddish, or Italian are among those likely to use this pronunciation.

6. The /ŋ/ presents particular difficulty to those whose native language possesses either /ŋ/ or /ŋg/, but not both. Native English speakers do not ordinarily demonstrate the same confusion. Speakers of German tend to pronounce all /ŋg/ words with /ŋ/: *finger* as [fɪŋɚ], *hunger* as [hʌŋɚ]. Central European language speakers tend

to pronounce all /ŋ/ words with [ŋg] or [ŋk]: *singer* as [sɪŋgɚ], *sing* as [sɪŋk], *bringing* as [brɪŋgɪŋg] or [brɪŋgɪŋk].

7. Occasional substitution of syllabic [ŋ̩] for [n̩] or [ən] may be heard when a vowel plus /n/ follows the velar /k/. This substitution may be heard in such words as *taken, sicken,* and *chicken* when pronounced as [teɪkŋ̩, sɪkŋ̩, tʃɪkŋ̩].

Although the syllabic [ŋ̩] is uncommon in cultivated American English speech, some such occurrences have been noted, like the variants [beɪkŋ̩] for *bacon,* [aɪ kŋ̩ goʊ] for *I can go,* [bæg ŋ̩ bæɡɪdʒ] for *bag and baggage,* [broʊkŋ̩ glæs] for *broken glass* and [dʒækŋ̩ keɪt] for *Jack and Kate.*[3]

Such syllabic [ŋ̩] forms are not listed in our current dictionaries with the exception of the Kenyon and Knott dictionary cited in the footnote. Although as educated speakers we tend to avoid such usages, undoubtedly due to the imposing influence of the spelled form, most of us probably say [aɪ kŋ̩ goʊ] and the like in informal situations in rapid speech. Despite the failure of our dictionaries to report this aspect of our speech, the occasional existence of syllabic [ŋ̩] in educated speech is not to be denied.

8. A fronted palatal-nasal sound, made by placing the blade of the tongue against the palate, is found as a regular sound in the speech of the Gullah dialect of the South Carolina and Georgia coast, where *new* and *young* may be heard as [ɲu] and [ɲoŋ]. This sound, [ɲ], is found also, in the careful pronunciation of certain French and Spanish loan words or place names, such as *señor* and *Avignon.* Most of us use [nj] in the pronunciation of such words as the closest English equivalent: [sɛnjɔř] and [ɑvinjɔ̃].

9. [n] and [ŋ] vary freely as alternative pronunciations of orthographic *n* plus *c, g,* or *q* in many words. There seems to be a preference for retaining the spelled *n* sound in American English instead of an assimilated [ŋ], which seems to be more common in

---

[3] See the listing for *can* and *bacon* in the *Pronouncing Dictionary of American English,* in John S. Kenyon, "Syllabic Consonants in Dictionaries," *American Speech,* Vol. 31 (December, 1956), pp. 243, 250, and Stuart Robertson, *The Development of Modern English,* rev. by Frederick G. Cassidy (Englewood Cliffs, N. J., Prentice-Hall, Inc., 1954), p. 352.

RP British English. A number of such words are noted below, and for comparison, the British RP forms, as listed in Daniel Jones, *English Pronouncing Dictionary*,[4] are noted also.

a. Both [n] and [ŋ] are used in American and British speech in the following words:

concord	concourse	concrete
concubine	income	pancake

b. Americans use [n] for the following words while British speakers use both [n] and [ŋ]:

concave	conclude	conglomeration
congratulate	enclose	encompass
encourage	encrust	engraft
engrave	engulf	enquire
incapable	incapacitate	incarnate
inchoate	inclement	incline
incognito	inglorious	ingratitude
nonconformist	panchromatic	synchronic

c. Americans use both [n] and [ŋ] while the British preference is [ŋ] in the following words:

Congreve	congruence	conquest
idiosyncrasy	synchronize	syncopate
syncope		

THE GLIDES

Three frictionless American English sounds are formed as the articulators involved move from one position to another. These sounds are called *glides*, and are recognized as they go through such articulatory motion. Each of these glide sounds, /w/, /r/, and /j/, is closely associated with a specific vowel, the initial area of its formation. /w/ begins at or near the [ʊ – u] position, /r/ at or near the [ɚ – ɜ] position, and /j/ at or near the [ɪ – i] position. Note that as you begin to say the /w/ in *we*, the lips and tongue are approximately in the [u] position. And as you begin the words *red* and *yes*, the lips

---

[4] (New York, Dutton, 1956.)

and tongue approximate the [ɝ] and [i] positions. They assume their identity as the articulators move rapidly from the initial vowel positions just mentioned to the following vowels in the words.

It is really more accurate to say that these glide symbols do not represent absolutely identical initiating positions before all vowels. If you compare the initial sounds in *year* and *yard*, you will notice that the /j/ of the first word begins with the front of the tongue higher and more advanced than the /j/ of *yard*. It is useful to keep in mind during our discussion of these glides that for /j/ the tongue is always higher and more advanced than for the following vowel; that for /w/ the tongue is always higher and more retracted and the lips more rounded than for the following vowel; and that for /r/ the tongue is always in a more central position and with more "r–coloring" than for the following vowel.

Following the description for the glides noted above, you will realize that the glides appear only in prevocal (before vowels) positions. Other consonants appear in prevocal and preconsonantal positions, still retaining their identifying characteristics. As we have defined the glides, they cannot appear in preconsonantal or final positions as off-glides: [jɛs, rɛd] and [wɛd] show the glides prevocalically as on-glide sounds; [haʊ, haɪ] and [fɪɚ] show what has been described above as the initiating position of the glides, but as vowel sounds in final, off-glide, position.

Much disagreement appears in the literature about the method of transcribing these glide sounds. Some phoneticians do not include /r/ with the other glides. Others transcribe the glides in both prevocal and postvocal positions. Still others transcribe the /r/ in such a way as to permit it to assume its place as a normal vowel in American English, with stressed and unstressed vowel forms, as exemplified in the pronunciations [θr̩d] and [bɛtr̩] for *third* and *better*— the /r/ functioning in both words as the syllabic nucleus. The use of /r/ for prevocalic, postvocalic, stressed, and unstressed forms as in *red, far, third,* and *better* is more commonly associated with phonemic, rather than with phonetic, transcription. (See page 120 and following.)

THE BILABIAL-VELAR GLIDE /w/

The bilabial glide /w/ exists before vowels in such words as *we* and *away*. The glide has both a lip and a tongue position. The lips are rounded and protruded, while the dorsum of the tongue is raised toward the velum of the mouth, as for the [υ – u] positions. It is thus accurately described as a bilabial-velar glide. The degree of lip-rounding and the height of the tongue varies with the nature of the vowel following the /w/ sound. Greater degrees of lip rounding and tongue height exist before the rounded vowels in such words as *woo* and *womb*, *woof* and *wool*, than before the unrounded vowels in such words as *wash*, *wet*, and *we*. The sound is recognized only as the lips and tongue move quickly to the following vowel position, even though it is slightly differently formed before different succeeding vowels.

Modifications of the /w/ Sound

A devoiced form of this glide may occur when it follows a voiceless consonant. In the words *sweet*, *quick* and *twenty*, the glide form is heard as [sw̥it, kw̥ɪk tw̥ɛnti. The above forms may be transcribed, also, as [sʍit, kʍɪk, tʍɛnti.

/w/ and /hw/ vary freely in American speech for the *wh* words as in *when* and *where*, as discussed earlier (see pages 95–97). Both sounds are heard in educated American speech for words of this type.

An "added *w*" may be inserted between a syllable or word ending in /o/, /u/, or /υ/ and another beginning with a vowel. The use of the glide in such phrases or words as *you are*, *go on*, *you eat*, and *sowing* occurs in educated speech, although not consistently. Consistent use of this added or intruded glide as in [juwɑɚ, gouwɑn, juwit, souwɪŋ] is considered an aspect of less-cultivated speech, and as such is avoided in the speech of careful speakers of standard English.

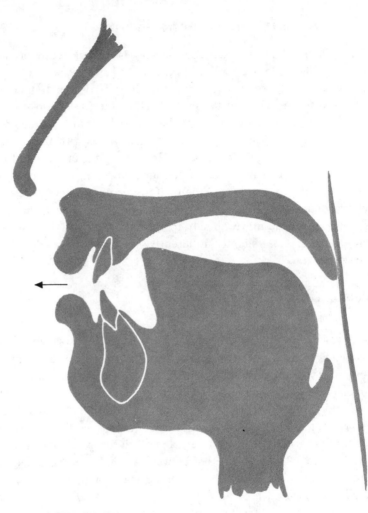

FIG. 21. Tongue position for postalveolar /r/.

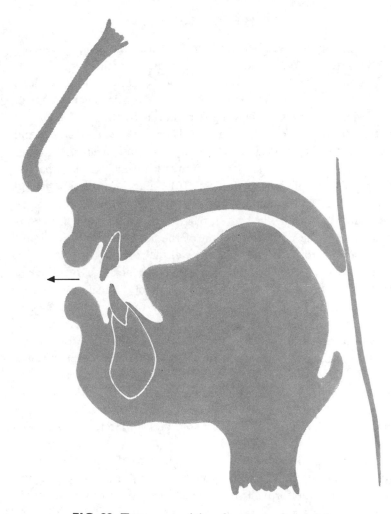

FIG. 22. Tongue position for postpalatal /r/.

THE GLIDE /r/

The glide is variously formed in American English, possessing slightly different tongue positions. Individuals in different sections of the country, and often those speaking the same regional dialect, may form this sound with somewhat varied acoustic effect as a result of the small changes in the tongue position. In the most common position for /r/ before stressed vowels, as in *red* and *erupt*, and initially before unstressed vowels, as in *refer* and *rheumatic*, the tip and blade of the tongue are turned upward, toward the hard palate, the tip pointing to (but not touching) the area immediately behind the alveolar ridges. In another common formation of /r/, the tongue tip remains low, while the central part of the tongue bunches and is raised toward the posterior section of the hard palate. When inter-vocalic and before an unstressed vowel, as in *very* or *parent*, the tongue moves rapidly to and from the first position mentioned, although quite commonly the tongue merely bunches centrally toward the second position and then very rapidly moves toward the position of the unstressed vowel. The resulting /r/ is of very short duration. Other forms of prevocalic /r/ result from some slight variation of the two positions mentioned—either greater retroflexion of the tongue tip, even to the point of making contact behind the alveolar ridges or retracting and raising the back of the tongue toward the velum of the mouth. In all formations of /r/, the sides of the tongue are in contact with the bicuspid and molar teeth, as for /n/ or /d/.

The initial position of the glide is close to the position of the stressed vowel of *earn* [ɜn]. As you say [ɚ-ɛd] and [ɚ-id], you will find that you glide through the /r/ position, pronouncing the words *red* and *reed*. If you attempt to pronounce just the initial sound of these words, a sound approximating the initial sound of *earn*, [ɚ], will result. This sound exists only before vowels. It is not found before consonants, nor in the final position of a phrase. The /r/ in American English is usually accompanied by some slight protrusion of the lips.

Modifications of the /r/

The /r/ is probably the most variable of all the consonants in our language. The history of its development accounts for the many variations we find. Earlier /r/ was a trilled sound, then a fricative sound, both clearly consonantal in acoustic value. During the seventeenth century, the consonantal aspects of the sound seem to have weakened and the sound became more and more vocalic, so that today it closely approximates a vowel. In certain parts of the English speaking world, the trilled r, [ř], is still the common form. This is the sound heard in Scottish and Irish speech. Southern British speakers possess a fricative r, IPA symbol [ɹ], made in the post-alveolar position. (The fricative quality results from the force of the breath stream through the narrow aperture between the tongue tip and the hard palate.) They also use a frictionless /r/, made with a wider aperture between the tongue and the palate. A friction type of r, [ɹ], may be heard in the speech of many Americans after /t/ and /d/—voiceless after the /t/ of *tree*, [tɹi], voiced after the /d/ as in *dream*, [dɹim].[5]

The frictionless r is the common form heard in American and Canadian English. Our speech has lost the fricative r, except in a few isolated instances such as when immediately following the /t/ or /d/. Before vowels, /r/ is a vowel-like glide. In postvocalic position we substitute either a vowel for the r, or delete it entirely. In some instances, this loss of r is manifested by a lengthening of the previous vowel. *Farm* may be heard in American English as [fɑ:m], fɑəm], and [fɑɚm].

A voiceless or partially devoiced r, [r̥], may be heard after the voiceless stops /p, t, k/, as in *pray*, *tray*, and *cream* (but not when they in turn are preceded by s, as in *spray*, *stray*, and *scream*):[pr̥eɪ, tr̥eɪ, kr̥im] but [spreɪ, streɪ, skrim]. Some unvoicing of the glide may

---

[5] A variation of the trilled r is retained in the speech of many Southern British speakers. This r is called a single-tap r, [ɾ], and is used only in intervocalic position. It appears in such words as *worry* and *merry*, and in such phrases as *far away*, *there are*, and *more of them*, [wʌɾɪ, mɛɾɪ, fɑɾəweɪ, ðɛəɾɑ:, mɔɾəv ðəm].

be heard, also, when it follows the voiceless sounds /θ, f, ʃ/ as in *thrust, free,* and *shriek*.

All of these forms are represented by the symbol [r] in broad

[ɾ]—for the flapped alveolar sound, as in British *worry;*
[ɹ]—for the fricative sound in American *dream,* or the prevocal British *r* in *red;* (Southern British loses all final and preconsonantal *r* sounds.)
[r̃]—for the trilled sound, as in Irish speech.

Linking *r*. People who live in Eastern New England, New York City and its environs, and the South live in what is known dialectally as "*r*-less territory." Speakers in these areas may delete the final *r* in *far, fear,* and *pour,* but will reinsert the *r* when the word is followed by another with an initial vowel. Such "*r*-less people" will pronounce *tour, far,* and *their* as [tʊə], [fɑ:] or [fɑə], [ðɛə], but will say [tʊrəraʊnd, fɑrəweɪ, ðɛəroʊn] for *tour around, far away,* and *their own.*

This *r* is a "linking" or "liaison *r*." It is a part of the standard pattern of speech in the "*r*-less" sections of the country except for speakers in the South who seem to avoid it easily.

Final and preconsonantal *r*. Our previous discussion has been concerned with the /r/ when it exists before a vowel. As such, it is a nonsyllabic sound, functioning as do other consonants in the language. Spelled *r*, when in final or preconsonantal position of a word or phrase, takes a somewhat different form. It no longer functions as the glide sound previously discussed.

In the words *far, farm, first,* and *third,* our American English *r* loses its consonantal as well as its characteristic glide form. In certain sections of the country, the sound may be lost completely. In such "*r*-less territory" these words might be pronounced as [fɑ:, fɑə, fɑ:m, fɑəm, fɝ·st, θɜ:d]. You will note that in these words, the spelled *r* is replaced by either a lengthened form of the previous vowel, or by the addition of the weak vowel, [ə], which acts as an offglide to the stressed vowel of the syllable, creating a diphthong.

Most speakers in Eastern New England, New York City, and the coastal regions of the South delete final and preconsonantal *r*, although not all persons in these sections of the country are "*r*-less." We hear increasing numbers of native New Yorkers with post-vocalic *r*, and C. M. Wise reports, "... in many parts of the South, especially in urban centers, the pronunciation of *r* ... in final and preconsonantal positions is increasing."[6]

In the remainder of the country, spelled *r* in final and preconsonantal positions may assume either a syllabic or nonsyllabic quality. The symbol [ɚ] represents a sound very similar to [r], except that [ɚ] is not a glide but a vowel. It is discussed with the other vowels in the next section, since it functions as a vowel. This "*r*-colored vowel" however, is an allophone of the phoneme–class /r/, appearing only in unstressed positions. As an allophone of /r/ it deserves mention here.

[ɚ] may be used for syllabic *r*, the sound of the second syllable in *father* and *neighbor*, whenever *r* is not lost in the pattern of speech [ɚ] varies with the [ə] of "*r*-less speakers," in such words (Middle Atlantic [fɑðɚ], Eastern New England [fɑðə]; Middle Atlantic [neɪbɚ], Eastern New England [neɪbə]). [ɚ] may also represent a nonsyllabic *r* added to a previous vowel, the retroflexion of the tongue following another vowel, as in the word *farm*, [fɑɚm], or *fear*, [fɪɚ]. And finally, [ɚ] may be heard as an offglide sound added to a previous vowel creating a diphthong. These three forms may be transcribed as: [fɑðɚ] or [fɑðr̩] for the syllabic *r* of *father*; [fɑɚm] or [fɑrm] for the nonsyllabic *r* of *farm;* [fɪɚ] or [fɪr] for the "*r* diphthong" of *fear*.

The stressed vowel of the preconsonantal sound in *burn* and *earn* or the final sound in *burr* or *err* is another allophone of /r/ in American English, and is represented by the phonetic symbols [ɜ] or [ɝ]. Since these sounds function as vowels and not as glides, they are discussed in the chapter on vowels. [ɜ] is the sound used by "*r*-less"

[6] *Applied Phonetics* (Englewood Cliffs, N. J., Prentice-Hall, Inc., 1957), p. 209.

speakers for these words, while [ɝ] represents the same central vowel with "*r*-coloring" or retroflexion of the tongue.

Phonetic Transcription of the /r/ Allophones

The earlier comment about the transcription of these allophones of /r/ (see page 112) can now be expanded. You might well ask why it is necessary, or useful, for phoneticians to use the symbols [ɚ — ɝ] when admittedly they are merely allophonic variants of the /r/ phoneme. Would not the transcription [faðr] or [θɾd] show them both as syllabics in an unconfusing manner? And would not their relationship to other allophones of /r/ be made clearer if all these allophones of /r/ used the symbol [r]? The answers may not satisfy all readers. Certainly phoneticians themselves are not agreed on the most satisfactory method for transcribing the /r/ allophones in American English.[7] In such a system of phonetic transcription the pairs of words *yes—say*, *wan—now*, and *rip—peer* would appear as [jɛs—sej, wɑn—naw, rɪp—pɪr], rather than as [jɛs—seɪ, wɑn—naʊ, rɪp—pɪɚ] as is done in this and many other phonetic texts. The major reasons for using [ɚ] and [ɝ] for the unstressed and stressed "*r*-vowels" are:

1. /j/, /w/, and /r/ are the symbols used for the glide sounds in such words as *yes*, *we*, and *red*. As glides, they appear in prevocal positions only. Using a postvocalic [r] symbol would call for the use of postvocalic [j] and [w] too. Such is not common phonetic practice, nor is it too helpful in establishing certain phonetic concepts. If anything, it tends to be somewhat confusing.
2. Stressed [ɝ] and unstressed [ɚ] are the variant forms of [ɜ] and [ə] in such words as *murmur*, *shirker*, *burner*, and *further*. Retaining the [r] symbol for one American dialect pattern and the vowel symbols [ɜ—ə] for others, would not show the appropriate relationship.
3. [ɝ] and [ɚ] are vowel symbols and can be easily recognized as such.
4. The phonetic relationship of these vowel symbols to the /r/ phoneme can be kept as clearly as by using some modifying symbol with the [r].

[7] See, for example, Allan F. Hubbell, *The Pronunciation of English in New York City* (New York, Kings Crown Press, 1950), p. 49; and Lee S. Hultzén, "Symbol for the Nonsyllabic Postvocalic R of General American," *The Quarterly Journal of Speech*, Vol. 36 (April, 1950), pp. 189–201.

The conclusion for our phonetic transcription, then, will be to use the [r] before vowels, [ɜ˞] for the stressed vowel as in *err*, [ə˞] for the unstressed vowel of *father*, and [ɜ] and [ə] for the vowels of the word *murmur* in "r-less" dialects. These four vowels are discussed, in detail, in Chapter 9.

Other Varieties of /r/

Trilled *r*. The use of a trilled *r*, [r̃], for the frictionless /r/ is due to the influence of another language in which the trilled *r* normally appears. The trill may be made either in the alveolar area, as in Scottish, Welsh, Spanish, and the Slavic languages, or in the uvular area as in French and German. The easiest way to adjust the trilled sound is to approach it as a glide through the [ɜ˞] vowel, and actually to think of it as a vowel-like sound. If *red* is initiated as [ɜ˞-ɛd], the initial sound being made with the tongue tip curled toward the palate and held there, a frictionless sound results.

Weak *r*. Excessive use of the lips is sometimes seen in the pronunciation of what is known as the "weak *r*." The acoustic value of such a sound approaches the /ʊ/ or /u/ sounds. When this "labialized *r*" (its other name) is formed, the back of the tongue is high, close to the /u/ position. A weak *r* of this type may be heard in any regional area of the country, in substandard speech.

Added *r*. The added *r* (also called the "intrusive *r*") of *law-r office* and *idea-r of* has been heard by all of us. This added *r* seems to occur predominantly in the speech of those who live in the "r-less" areas of the country, excluding the South. By analogy with the use of the linking *r*, speakers may add the *r* to those words where no historical *r* exists. Such persons hear the words *fear* and *tore* as [fɪə] and [tɔə], and a linking *r* when these words are in such phrases as *fear of* and *tore off*. By analogy, then, they add the same sound to *idea* and *saw* when in such phrases as *idea of* and *saw a man*.

When it is used, this added *r* is found most often after the /ə/, when a linking position is possible: *Ida and May, umbrella over, China office, idea of*. It is also heard after /ɔ/ and /ɑ/, as in *law office, saw a man, Utah and Wyoming, the Shah in the story*. The use of the added *r* in educated speech seems limited mostly to the position after /ə/. It is heard less commonly after /ɔ/ and /ɑ/. After spelled *o* or *ow*, it is rarely found in the speech of educated people, even when in possible linking position, in such words as *tomato, fellow, following*, and *window*. Similarly, the added *r* is not commonly found where a previous syllable possesses an *r*, as in *Clara and Jane, the orchestra is good*.

There is some disagreement as to the acceptability of this intrusive *r* in educated speech. Most authorities admit its common use among educated and cultured speakers. Kenyon notes:

> It is a very common practice among cultivated speakers in England and eastern America, but apparently less in southern America. The evidence of its universality in these regions is so overwhelming that it is mere ignorance of the facts of cultivated usage to deny it.[8]

But despite its wide spread use by many educated speakers, the intrusive *r* is still considered part of the substandard pattern by most. Speakers who use it unknowingly consciously avoid it if made aware of it. The intrusive *r* is the normal pattern of the less-educated speakers. Its widespread use in educated colloquial speech, however, cannot be disregarded, regardless of labels.

Added vowel before *r*. You occasionally hear some people add a syllabic sound before /r/. Such pronunciations as [ʌmbərɛlə] for *umbrella*, [kərim] for *cream*, [hɛnəri] for *Henry* and [dəraʊn] for *drown* are not found in educated speech.

THE LINGUA-PALATAL GLIDE /j/

The voiced palatal glide is made with the front of the tongue raised toward the hard palate. The sides of the tongue are in contact with the bicuspid and the molar teeth. The initial position of this sound is similar to that of a very high and tense /i/ sound. Its acoustic value becomes clear as the articulators move, very rapidly, to the position of the following vowel. This frictionless glide exists

[8] John S. Kenyon, *American Pronunciation*, 10th ed. (Ann Arbor, George Wahr Publishing Co., 1951), pp. 164–165.

only before vowels, in the onglide position. It is not found before consonants nor finally. The lips assume the position of the following vowel: spread before front vowels ([jist, jɛs]); relaxed and open before mid-vowels ([jʌkə flæts, jɜ˞n]); rounded before the back vowels ([juz, jɔn]).

Like other glide and semivowel sounds, the /j/ sound is somewhat devoiced when it follows the voiceless plosives /p/, /t/, and /k/ in a stressed syllable. In *pure*, *cute*, and *tune*, the glide may be heard as [pju˞, kjʊt, tjʊn]. This devoiced glide does not exist when the three voiceless plosives are in turn preceded by an /s/ sound, as in *spume*, *stew*, and *skewer* ([spjum], and the like). In such instances, the glide retains full voiced quality. After other voiceless consonants, a devoiced [j] is also present, as in *suit*, *enthuse*, and *few*.

Modifications of the /j/ Sound

The [ju] **variants as in** *tune* **and** *duty*. There is no real consistency in the use of [ju], or the variants [ɪu], [u], in words of this type. Substandard speakers are generally consistent in avoiding the use of [ju], except with the first group of words noted below:

1. All levels of speech consistently use [ju] when the spelled *u*, *iew*, *eau* follow the /p, b, f, v, m, k, h/ sounds, except in very isolated instances. *Pure*, *beauty*, *few*, *view*, *music*, *cupid*, and *human* are pronounced with [ju].

2. In all other instances, three possible pronunciations are used by educated speakers: [ju], [ɪu], or a slightly fronted [u˖] sound. *Tune*, *new*, *duty*, *suit*, and *enthuse* are pronounced by educated speakers with all three forms.

3. The [ju] variant is not heard after the consonants /r/, /ʃ/, /tʃ/, /dʒ/, or a consonant plus /l/, as in *rumor*, *shoe*, *chew*, *June*, *flew*, or *blue*. In these instances, [u] or the fronted [u˖] or [ɪu] are used by speakers of educated American English.

The /hj/ **in** *huge* **and** *human*. The /h/ approach to the /j/ glide (or its variant, a voiceless palatal fricative sound, written phonetically [ç]—the sound known in German as the *ich laut*) is the common standard form for the spelled *h* plus *u* words in both American and British speech. Substandard speech shows a reasonably consistent use of /j/ for /hj/ words of this type. Although sporadic use of /j/ for /hj/ is found among educated speakers, almost all authorities recognize the /hj/ form as the preferred form. The extent of /j/ for /hj/ in educated speech is actually not known at present. Kenyon and Knott[9] list the following words with both the [hju] and [ju] variants: *huge, human, humane, humor, humorist, humoristic,* and *humorous.* They list other *hu* words, such as the following, with the [hju] only: *hue, Hugh, Hugo, Hume, humus, humerus, humid, humidify, humidity, humidor, humiliate,* and *humility.*

Other Varieties of /j/

/j/ may be heard as an excrescent sound when a syllable ending in /i/ or /ɪ/ is followed by another syllable beginning with a vowel, as in *my own, my eye, he is, see if.* The tongue, moving from the /i/ or /ɪ/ positions, glides through the /j/ phoneme to the next vowel. This pronunciation is especially difficult to avoid when the following syllable demands some degree of stress. It is considered a fault of usage, not commonly found in educated speech.

THE LATERAL SEMIVOWEL /l/

The /l/ in English is a voiced, alveolar, vowel-like sound, made with the sides of the tongue free from contact with the teeth or gums. This laterally emitted sound is found initially, medially, and finally. Like the other glide or semivowel sounds, the /l/ is partially devoiced when it follows the voiceless plosives in a stressed syllable: *play*, [pḷeɪ], and *clean*, [kḷin]. It is also partially devoiced when following other voiceless sounds, as in *flew*, and *sly*.

Modifications of the /l/

Light and dark *l.* The /l/ in American English possesses two clearly distinguishable allophones, commonly referred to as *light* and

---

[9] *Pronouncing Dictonary of American English,* pp. 209–210.

dark l. The light [l] is the sound we make when /l/ precedes a front vowel, or when it is followed by /j/, as in *leave, lit, land,* and *value.* It possesses the quality or resonance of a front vowel. When the /l/ is in the medial position before an unstressed vowel (as in *telephone*), in final position (as in *fill*), when it precedes a back vowel (as in *lose*), or when it is syllabic (as in *beetle*) the sound is made with the back of the tongue higher in the mouth. It possesses the quality or resonance of a back vowel. This /l/ is called "dark," and is transcribed phonetically as [ɫ]. The degree of lightness or darkness is actually a relative one. In general, initial *l* sounds tend to be lighter than final or preconsonantal *l* sounds. (Compare *live* with *milk* and *sealed,* prolonging the lateral sound so you can hear its acoustic value better). As a major portion of the tongue is raised in the front of the mouth, a clearer or lighter *l* results; as the major portion of the tongue is elevated toward the velar part of the mouth, a darker *l* is formed. The drawings below show these different positions of the tongue.

Many of us who live in the "*r*-regions" of the country use a darker variety of *l* in all positions of words, while a clear or light allophone of /l/ is common, postvocalically, in the South Atlantic regions of the country.

Palatalized *l.* A palatalized variety of this sound, transcribed [lʲ], is found when the light *l* immediately precedes the /j/ sound, in such words or phrases as *million, will you come.* In these instances, the front part of the tongue is still in contact with the alveolar ridge, but the blade of the tongue rises toward the palatal section untilthe /j/ sound is formed. This resulting [lʲ] has a slightly different acoustic effect from either of the *l* sounds described previously.

Dental *l.* The *l* is dentally made when it precedes either *th* sound as in *health, wealth,* and *fill the cup*: [hɛl̪θ, wɛl̪θ, fɪl̪ ðə kʌp].

Syllabic *l.* Like the nasals and /r/, the /l/ may assume the function of a vowel and act as an unstressed syllabic sound, especially after /t, d, n/, as in *ladle, beetle,* and *funnel*: [leɪdl̩, bitl̩, fʌnl̩]. Syllabic *l*, [l̩], may also be heard after the sibilant and affricate sounds /s, z, ʃ, tʃ, dʒ/, as in *missile, sizzle, bushel, satchel,* and *vigil*: [mɪsl̩, sɪzl̩, buʃl̩, sætʃl̩, vɪdʒl̩].

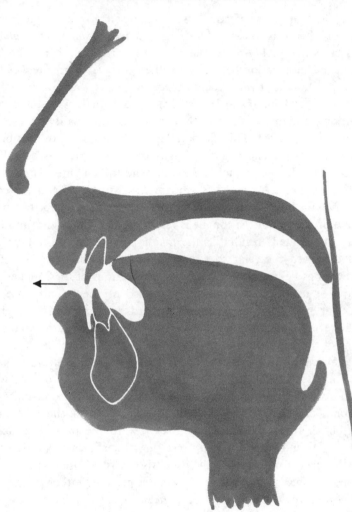

FIG. 23. Tongue position for clear /l/.

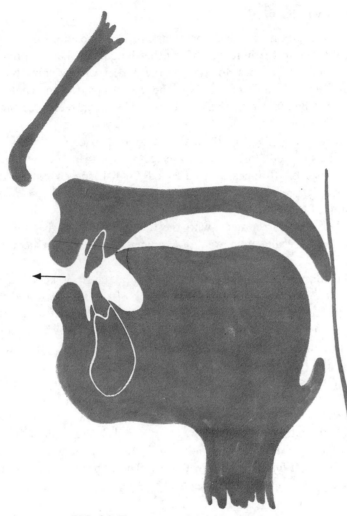

FIG. 24. Tongue position for dark /l/.

Other Varieties of /l/

The substitution of a clear for a dark /l/ in all positions of words is usually due to the influence of another language (such as French or German) which does not possess the darker variety common to our language. The difference in both the tongue position and acoustic value must be made clear before such speakers can recognize these two allophones of /l/.

A dentalized /l/, [l̪], made with the tongue in contact with the upper incisor teeth, or between the teeth, is also associated with foreign speech. [l̪] appears in educated English speech only when immediately preceding /θ/ or /ð/, as in *wealth* or *call the name*, [wɛl̪θ], [kɔl̪ ðə neɪm].

A blade-alveolar contact, with the tip of the tongue behind the lower teeth, results in a weak /l/, somewhat darker in acoustic value.

A labialized /l/, [lʷ], is heard when the tongue tip is kept low in the front of the mouth and with the back of the tongue raised toward the velum, and with no part of the tongue in contact with the palate. The lips are protruded as for /u/. [lʷ] is usually associated with infantile speech, almost approximating the pronunciations [mɪʊk] and [ʃɛʊ] for the words *milk* and *shell*.

A "careless" articulation of the dark /l/ may result in the vowelizing (vocalizing) of the /l/, especially when it precedes another consonant. This seems to be quite common in the South, especially before labial consonants, although this faulty variation is heard elsewhere in the country too. The words *help*, *shelve*, *milk*, and *film* sound like [hɛᵁp, ʃɛᵁv, mɪᵁk, fɪᵁm] in such instances. These pronunciations are associated with substandard speech.

REVIEW AND PRACTICE SECTION

1. On what basis could you classify the nasals as semivowels? Why do the glides appear only in prevocal position?
2. What variation of the nasal, glide, or lateral sound may take place in each of the following words?

smile	comfortable	tenth	length
walking	pure	parcel	health
button	twenty	million	quip

3. Transcribe your pronunciation of each of the following, noting which combination you use:

[m + p and/or f] or [ɱ + f] or [m + ɸ]?
camphor   comfort   symphony   triumph

4. Which words possess dental [n̪] or [l̪] sounds?

on the   on time   monthly   thin thrust   wealth   felt

5. What inserted sounds may appear in each of the following?

how are you	ancient	why are they	the idea is
stay over	strengthen	Shah of Iran	come closer
prancing	fence	Samson	go away

6. Indicate two alternative pronunciations for each of the following words and indicate their acceptability in standard American English. Use a reputable dictionary as a guide. (For example, *England*—[ɪŋglənd] and sometimes, regarded as careless, [ɪŋlənd]; *length*—[lɛŋkθ] and [lɛŋθ], both common in educated American speech.)

Lancaster	longer	concrete	Sinclair	ancestor
chasm	comfortable	clangor	hangar	waking

7. Do your pronunciations follow those listed below? Which do not?

Syllabic Nasal Sounds		[nk]	[ŋk]
hidden	buttoned	unclean	ink
schism	beaten	incubate	drunken
opened	Tom and Nancy	inquest	conquer
		incriminate	banquet
		inquire	monkey

8. Which words with [ŋ]? Which with [ŋg]? Which with [ng]?

wronged	Bingham	ingrown	ungodly
twangy	ingrate	single	elongate
fishmonger	kingly	anger	songster
ingot	gingham	engage	distinguish
longer	fungus	English	hanger

9. How many sounds do you pronunce in each of the following words?

singer	your own	following	humane
tune	far over	saying	eastward
third	scarred	dreamt	pardon
farm	burr	blue	fir

10. Place those words said only with [ju] in one column, those with either [ɪu, u] or [ju] in another, and those with only [u] or [ɪu] in a third column.

stupid	Tulane	lucid	stew	dune	screw
eulogy	spurious	truant	amuse	beauty	Lucy
enthuse	tumult	juniper	enumerate	futile	Jewish
putrid	few	ruin	cupid	dew	Ruth
superb	platitude	clue	tuba	durable	Lubec

11. Transcribe each of the following sentences as you speak them.

"Live and let live," is an old motto.
The runner-up tried hard to equal the champion's record.
"My own car is blue too," he answered.
He harangued the crowd after she sang her song at the banquet.
Diphthongal sounds may be easily prolonged.
It was pleasant to listen to the newly-composed songs.

CHAPTER 7

The Vowels of American

English

INTRODUCTION

1. [_ə _æ_ ou_ə_ _ _ə _ɑ_ _].
2. [_ə _ɪ_ _ɝ_ _u_ _ə _ɑ_].
3. [_ʌ_ _ə _ə _ɑɚ_].
4. [_ _i_ _ə _ _i_ _ aɪ _ _eɪ _u].
5. [ə _ou_ɪ_ _ _ou_ _æ _ɚ_ _ou _ɔ_].

THESE ARE THE vowels of five different sentences. Unless you possess a legendary sixth sense, your saying them aloud will not signify any meaning to you nor to anyone else. You do hear the number of syllables spoken in these sentences, and of course your voice has been "shaped" by the various articulators to make these different vowels. A number of possible sentences could use these vowels in the same order.

If, however, we take the same five sentences, and pronounce only the consonants, your possible guesses are so reduced that the chances are good you may guess all of them. You will not know the number of syllables unless you insert a vowel in the indicated spaces.

1. [ð_ m_n __pŋd ð_ b_ks].
2. [ð_ b_g g_l ʃ _k h_ d_l].
3. [k_m t_ ð_ f_ _m].
4. [sp_k ð_ sp_tʃ _ _ pr_ _ j_].
5. [_ r_ _l_ŋ st_ _n g_ð_z n_ _ m_s].

Now put the vowels and the consonants together, and meaningful language takes shape. Is it necessary to write out the five sentences, or have you figured them out?

1. The man opened the box.
2. The big girl shook her doll.
3. Come to the farm.
4. Speak the speech I pray you.
5. A rolling stone gathers no moss.

From this simple experiment, you can note four points:

1. Language intelligibility is much more dependent on the consonants of a language than it is on vowels.
2. Consonants may be either voiced or voiceless sounds, stopped or continuant sounds. Vowels are always voiced continuant sounds.
3. Although each vowel differs from another vowel, it never seems to differ as radically as does one consonant from another.
4. The vowel is the vehicle of the voice we use. The articulators and resonators modify the voice as it is emitted. These modifications result in the vowels of our language.

The Functions of Vowels

Vowels have specific functions in a language. As already noted, they are the syllable carriers of speech. Each syllable in a word or phrase contains either a vowel, a diphthong, or a vowel-like consonant, which acts as the nucleus of the syllable. There are eight vowels (or diphthongs) and eight syllables in the sentence "A rolling stone gathers no moss." Six vowels (or diphthongs) and six syllables are spoken in the sentence "Take John's coat off the bed."

The vowels are the carriers of the voices you hear as people speak. Vocal resonance, quality, intensity, and pitch are all heard through the vowels of the language. You can speed or retard the rate of speech you use by shortening or lengthening the vowels. Your speech sounds are clipped, drawled, staccato, or jerky, depending on the way you say the vowels. The vowels carry the major load of inflectional or pitch variation. Through them, you signify doubts, questions, complete or incomplete thoughts, or the melodic patterns of a language different from your own. As such, they are the primary keys to the dialectal differences in a language.

Vowels and voice cannot be truly separated. *The vowel is the voice of language.*

The Formation of Vowels

Except in whispered speech, vowels are voiced sounds. The breath stream passes through the larynx, activating the vocal folds. The soft palate moves back and the pharyngeal wall draws forward closing off the nasopharynx, so that the sound of all our vowels is emitted through the mouth. The pharyngeal cavity may be changed by the position of the larynx (which may be raised, lowered, retracted, or protracted), by the epiglottis (which may be moved back and forth), by the tongue (which controls the position of the front wall of the pharynx), and by the velum (which may shut off the nasopharynx). Comparatively free from obstruction as it is emitted from the pharynx, each vowel is modified in the oral cavity by the position and shape of the lips, the tongue, and the aperture of the mouth. The mouth opens or closes, the lips move into a spread, neutral, or rounded position, and the tongue is elevated toward the front, central, or back part of the palate to produce all the vowel sounds of American English.

The exact movements and positions of the articulators are difficult to describe. Despite the use of reasonably exact measuring devices, we describe the formations and acoustic values of the vowels in general and relative terms—descriptive of mouth aperture, tongue and lip positions, relative length, and tension. The positions of the articulators are so adjusted that there is a lack of articulatory constriction. During the formation of the vowels, there are no points of contact between articulators such as are felt when forming

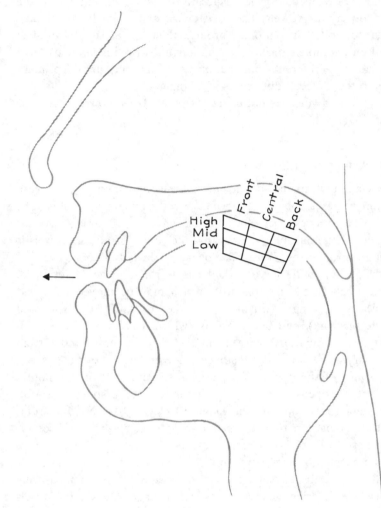

FIG. 25. The vowel areas.

the consonant sounds. Phoneticians know that vowels gradually blend into others near them, the "shades" of possible sounds between any two vowels being infinite in number. Since vowels "shade" or "blend" into each other, their differences are established by the designation and recognition of specific points or places along the line of articulatory modification of this continuous stream of vocal sound. We can see that such a concept as a "fixed articulatory position" for any vowel would be an inexact statement of the facts.

THE CLASSIFICATION OF VOWELS

Vowels can be diagrammed and charted in many and various ways. X-ray studies of the speech process, the instrumental-acoustic analyses of the vowels, and the careful observations of the involved muscle motions of speech[1] have led to and confirmed the adoption of a conventionalized method of diagramming or charting the articulatory positions of the jaw, tongue, and lips during the formation of the vowels of American English. Some of these conventionalized diagrams appear below.

[1] Such as those reported by G. Oscar Russell, *The Vowel* (Columbus, Ohio State University Press, 1928); S. N. Trevino and C. E. Parmenter, "Vowel Positions as Shown by X-Ray," *The Quarterly Journal of Speech*, Vol. 18 (June, 1932), pp. 351–369; R. K. Potter and J. C. Steinberg, "Towards the Specification of Speech," *Journal of the Acoustical Society of America*, Vol. 22 (November, 1950), pp. 807–820; P. Delattre, A. M. Liberman, F. S. Cooper, and L. J. Gerstman, "The Acoustic Determinants of Vowel Color," *Word*, Vol. 8 (December, 1952), pp. 195–210; Daniel Jones, *Outline of English Phonetics*, 8th ed. (New York, Dutton, 1956); John S. Kenyon, *American Pronunciation*, 10th ed. (Ann Arbor, George Wahr Publishing Co., 1951); Sir Richard Paget, *Human Speech* (New York, Harcourt, 1930); Dayton C. Miller, *The Science of Musical Sounds*, 2nd ed, (New York, Macmillan, 1937); Ralph K. Potter, George A. Kopp, and Harriet C. Green, *Visible Speech* (New York, Van Nostrand, 1947). An excellent treatment of the subject may be found in Martin Joos, *Acoustic Phonetics*, *Language Monograph No. 23* (Baltimore, Linguistic Society of America, 1948). A very fine review of the work done in acoustic phonetics may be had by consulting Bruce P. Bogert and Gordon E. Peterson, "The Acoustics of Speech," in Lee Edward Travis, ed., *Handbook of Speech Pathology* (New York, Appleton-Century-Crofts, Inc., 1957), Ch. 5, pp. 109–173.

The Vowels Charted

The tongue positions for the vowels are arbitrarily and conventionally divided into nine areas, as in the diagram below. Running from the front of the mouth to the back, the areas are known as *front, central,* and *back.* The layered areas, going from top to bottom, are known as *high, mid,* and *low.* All of the diagrams below are concerned with tongue placement. They do not indicate the mouth opening or the position of the lips.

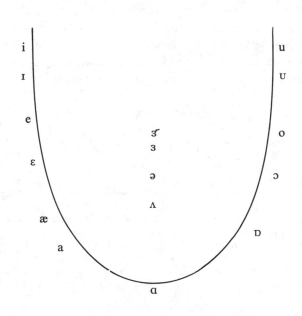

FIG. 26. The relative tongue positions of the vowels. (Adapted from Claude E. Kantner and Robert West, *Phonetics* (New York, Harper, 1941), Fig. 13, p. 71.) Kantner and West show no definite position for [ə]. It is arbitrarily placed as shown, indicating its central position.

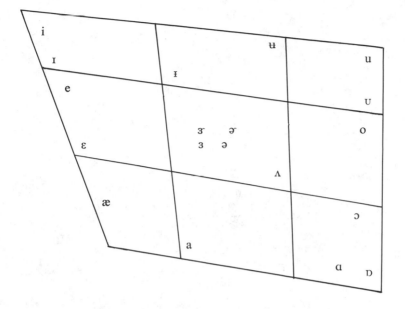

FIG. 27. The tongue positions of the vowels. (Adapted from John S. Kenyon, *American Pronunciation*, 10th ed. (Ann Arbor, George Wahr Publishing Co., 1951), Fig. 9, p. 61.)

None of the preceding diagrams and charts accounts for the general position of the tongue during the formation of the vowels. Rather they indicate in which area of the mouth the highest part of the tongue will be found. The following diagrams approximate the usual "tongue curves" during the formation of the vowels. As for all the diagrams and charts, you are again reminded that these positions are relative and approximate. Again, the different positions of the lips and the different apertures of the mouth for the different vowels are not indicated.

The above diagrams provide no means of indicating the factors of tension and lip position, without excessively complicating the drawings. Figure 31 will prove helpful in this regard.

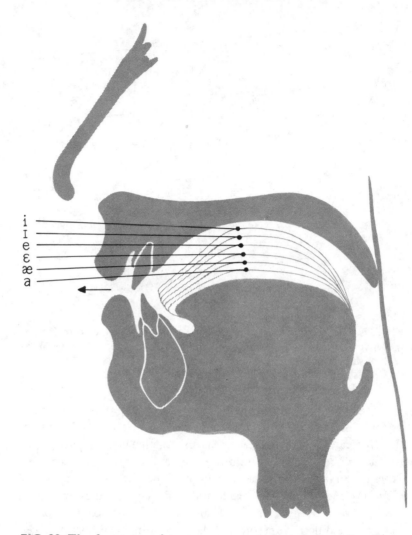

FIG. 28. The front vowel tongue curves. (Adapted from Jon Eisenson, *Basic Speech* (New York, The Macmillan Company, 1950), Fig. 21, p. 83.)

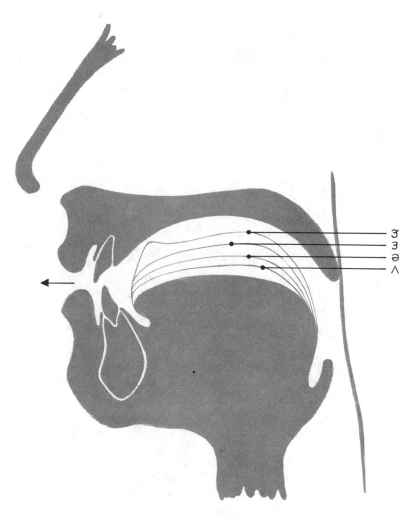

FIG. 29. The central vowel tongue curves. (Adapted from Jon Eisenson, *Basic Speech* (New York, The Macmillan Company, 1950), Fig. 22, p. 84.)

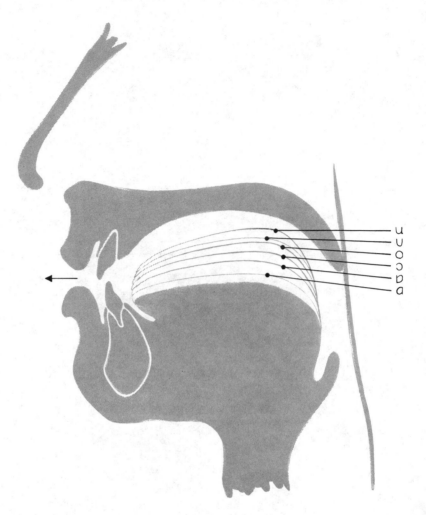

FIG. 30. The back vowel tongue curves. (Adapted from Jon Eisenson, *Basic Speech* (New York, The Macmillan Company, 1950), Fig. 23, p. 85.)

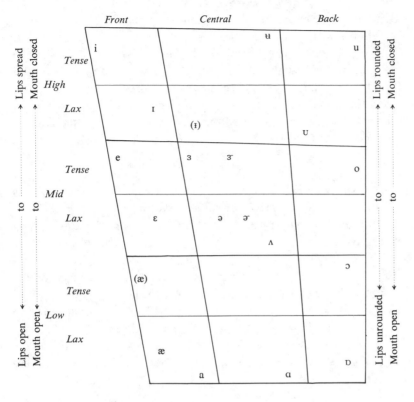

FIG. 31. The tongue and lip positions of the American English vowels.

The Tongue and Lip Positions of American Vowels

With an understanding of the charts and diagrams shown above, it is now somewhat easier to generalize about the articulatory positions of the vowels. The tongue position can always be described as either high, mid, or low, in the front, central, or back part of the mouth. The mouth moves from a closed position for the higher vowels [i] and [u] to an open position for the lower vowels [a] and [ɑ].

Similarly, the lips are more or less spread for all the front vowels [i]
—[æ], while they are more or less rounded for the back vowels
[u]—[ɒ]. For the central vowels the lips are neutral, the tongue
moving from the slightly back position of [ʌ] to the mid-high position for [ɜ]. The [ə] position can hardly be diagrammed with accuracy, for it may be posited almost anywhere in the central portion
of the mouth, approaching all the vowel positions. For the two "r-
colored" vowels, [ɜ] and [ɚ], the tongue-tip is normally turned up
toward the position of the glide /r/.

The positions of the mouth and lips can be seen easily, if you say
the vowels while watching yourself in a mirror. Note what happens
as you say the word *meow*, making sure to prolong the word. Your
mouth and lips will go through all the positions of the front and
back vowels.

Tongue positions for the vowels are not seen as easily, however.
With the tip of the tongue near the lower teeth, the blade of the
tongue is high, near the position of /j/, for the highest front vowel [i].
As you pronounce the front vowels from [i] to [a], the blade of the
tongue moves down slightly for each succeeding sound. And as you
move from the lowest back vowel [ɑ] up to [u], the back of the
tongue rises toward the soft palate for each succeeding sound. (See
Figures 28, 29, 30.)

The articulators compensate for each other too. Slight variations
from the described positions can be compensated for by adjustments
in the other articulators, resulting in the same phoneme. Thus,
our recognition of a vowel sound is dependent not so much on a
fixed position of an articulator, as it is on the complex adjustment
of all the articulators to produce the vowels of the language.

Tense and Lax Vowels

The tongue muscles are either tense or lax as we produce each
vowel sound. As you move from [i] to [ɪ], [e] to [ɛ], and so forth, you
can feel the difference in the tension of the tongue, accompanied by
similar tension of other muscles in the area. Place your fingers along
the muscles behind the chin and along the jaw of the mouth. You

will feel more tension in these muscles as you say the tense vowels. (They more readily lengthen and diphthongize too.)

The Duration of Vowels

To the classification of vowels by tension, lip rounding, and articulatory positions, we must add one final category: the relative length or duration of vowels. We can hear that the same vowel is longer when stressed than when not stressed. Thus the *o* in *obey* is shorter than the *o* in *go*, and the vowel in *see* is longer in the sentence "I *see* it," than it is in the sentence "I *did* see it."

Stressed vowels differ in duration when they appear in different parts of words or phrases. In general they tend to be longer:

1. when they appear before voiced consonants than when they appear before voiceless consonants: compare *seed* vs. *seat*, *goad* vs. *goat;*
2. when final in a phrase: compare "He should *go*." with "He should *go home*.";
3. when final, or before a final consonant, than they are before unaccented syllables: compare *see* vs. *seeing*, *stay* vs. *staying*, "I took his *coat*," vs. "I took his *coat* into the house.";
4. when followed by the sounds /m/, /n/, /ŋ/, /l/ and a voiced consonant than when they are followed by one of these and a voiceless consonant: compare *crumble* vs. *crumple*, *one* vs. *once*, *songs* vs. *songstress*, *killed* vs. *kilt*.

Although the above generalizations describe some of the major differences of vowel length, it is wise to keep in mind that such lengthening is merely a likelihood. As you can see, there are many variable factors involved. These are tension, position in the word or phrase, the number and kind of following sounds, and the degree of stress. Since variation in length is more subtle than a transcription system can indicate, and since the concept of length is merely a relative one anyway, a narrow transcription system shows these relative lengths as short (unmarked), half long [ˑ], or long [ː]—[sɛt], [siˑt], [siːd]. Normal (broad) transcription avoids the use of these relative marks. They are used only when it is necessary to draw comparisons, or to point up differences to a person to whom English is not native.

The Phonemic Classification of American English Vowels

The previous chartings of the vowels follow the common phonetic practice today. These symbols provide us with the working basis needed to describe the pronunciations commonly found in American English, in one dialect or another. With these symbols, and the diacritic modifiers for rounding [']', centralizing [-] or [··], raising [ᴗ], lowering [ᴠ], fronting [ᴠ], retracting [ᴞ], lengthening [·], [:], and nasalizing [~], we can represent the generally known pronunciation characteristics of the vowels in most, if not all, dialects of American English.

The classification of the phonetic data into a generally accepted phonemic system has, as yet, not occurred. As in other areas of study, neither your teachers, nor theirs, have all the answers, and this is one area, among many others, where the analysis of the evidence is not, as yet, conclusive. There is comparatively little disagreement as to the nature and number of consonant phonemes in our language. But there is much seeking and scholarly questioning about the vowel phonemes in our language.

The vowels show great variation from dialect to dialect. In some regional dialects certain sounds that appear as simple vowels may appear as diphthongs in other dialects. Certain dialects do not possess the same vowels in given key words found in other dialects. And not all the dialects possess either the same vowel phonemes nor the same total number of simple or complex syllabic nuclei. If the problem were the phonemic analysis of one regional dialect of the language, the solution would be comparatively simple. But the problem is to attempt an analysis of the vowel phonemes of American English, and the significant phonemes of any one dialect may, and probably do, vary from those of any other. The result has been to attempt to analyze and systematize the known values of the vowels in certain specific dialects, and to structure the vocalic system based on such data in a reasonable and symmetrical manner. No phonemic system has been presented in which all the data collected by American dialect geographers can be presented comfortably.

Field workers collecting such data find it convenient, if not necessary, to present certain available evidence phonetically, being reluctant to accept any phonemic conclusions for an over-all American English pattern that do not permit the accurate representation of known pronunciation features of certain regional dialects.[2]

In the discussion of the vowels and diphthongs that follows, the data will be presented without any attempt to prove a preference for any one phonemic system of American English. Where the evidence will permit the drawing of phonemic conclusions for any given dialect, or for most or all of our dialects, we shall, of course, do so. Both slant lines and brackets will be used to designate phonemic and phonetic concepts, as was done with the discussions on consonants. Certain concepts should be kept in mind throughout these discussions:

1. No symbolization for a phonemic system of American English is presently available which seems to satisfy all scholars in the field. The IPA symbolization followed here is the system most widely known to phoneticians. Other systems are used, however, and some are noted in the Appendix for your use and study.

2. You will note that some vowel nuclei are simple and that some are complex. If in one dialect the syllabic nucleus in a given word is simple, while in another dialect the pronunciation of the same word will normally contain a complex or diphthongal form, the phonetic symbolization will make note of this, regardless of the phonemic representation of the sound.

3. The vowel nuclei will be presented first as phonemic concepts, followed by a discussion of the variations in the use of the sound, as known. Once you have examined the phonetic data of your own dialect, you should be able to arrive at a phonemic system that will represent the vocalic structure of your own dialect. Such a system will differ from dialect to dialect. For all of us, there is a "common core" of sounds which permits our dialects to be intelligible to each

---

[2] See Raven I. McDavid, Jr., "American English Dialects," in W. Nelson Francis, *The Structure of American English* (New York, Ronald, 1958), pp. 513–527.

other. Since the dialects differ from region to region (if not from person to person) the problem is to attempt to arrive at some possible over-all pattern. Such an over-all pattern would include not only the sound features common to all our dialects, but those which are significantly different in our different dialects. No one idiolect (the speech pattern of a single person), or dialect, contains *all* the significant vowel features. And should continuing investigation turn up distinctive vowel patterns not presently accounted for, we shall have to modify our over-all pattern to include them.[3]

We are now ready to proceed with the analysis of the vowels, with a final caution to our thinking. More than the consonants, vowels are quite variable, even in a given person's speech, and even while being made in a given syllable. During the speech act, the speech organs are in almost continous motion, not only from one sound to another in a word or phrase, but while the syllable nucleus is spoken. As a result, the formation and acoustic value of any vowel is constantly shifting from the beginning to the end of the sound. A vowel may vary from hardly perceptible shifting to such easily identifiable shifts so that we recognize having heard a diphthong or vowel cluster. Therefore, descriptions of any vowel nucleus must be based on the position and acoustic values of its most essential, characteristic nature.

THE FRONT VOWELS

The Vowels /i/ and /ɪ/ in *Beet* and *Bit*

These are the two highest front vowels in the English language. /i/ is a tense vowel, made with the lips spread and the mouth almost closed. /ɪ/ is made with the tongue slightly lower in the mouth. It is a lax vowel. In American English, /i/ is commonly made as a diphthong, especially noticeable when the sound is stressed and prolonged. The diphthong glides from the lax to the tense vowel and

[3] For a good discussion of the concepts of *idiolect, dialect, language, common core,* and *over-all pattern,* see Charles F. Hockett, *A Course in Modern Linguistics* (New York, Macmillan, 1958), pp. 321–338.

to the closer position: [ɪi]. If you are a student of French or German, you can probably hear the difference between the /i/ in those languages and the English [ɪi]. French and German /i/ sounds are pure vowels, tenser than in English. Since [ɪi] does not vary phonemically from [i], the sound is commonly transcribed as the simple vowel [i].

/i/ is commonly spelled e and ee, as in be and see; less commonly ie as in *field*, i in *machine*, ea in *reach*, ei in *receive*, eo in *people*, ey in *key*, ae in *Caesar*, ay in *quay*, oe in *amoeba*, and y in *fully*. /ɪ/ spellings occur as i in *fit*, and less commonly as e in *pretty*, ee in *been*, ie in *sieve*, o in *women*, ui in *guild*, u in *busy*, and y in *myth*. Both /i/ and /ɪ/ appear in initial, medial, and final positions of words.

Modifications and Variations in Usage

1. A small number of words are pronounced with either stressed /i/ or /ɪ/. You probably can find both pronunciations current among members of your class for such words as *creek* and *breech*: [krik—krɪk], [britʃ—brɪtʃ].

2. In an initial unstressed syllable, /i/ normally weakens to /ɪ/. *Event, evade, believe, erupt, defend*, and *emotion* all show /ɪ/, less commonly /i/. When in final position, as in *pity* and *beauty*, both /i/ and /ɪ/ are heard in standard American English, most speakers using the short /i/. All of us use /i/ in such words as *settee, employee*, and *guarantee*, where the final syllable retains some stress. But when the final syllable is unstressed, as in *city* or *pity*, most speakers seem to use a shortened, lowered, and lax form of /i/, although many of us use different allophones of /ɪ/ in both syllables of *city* and *pity*. Compare your pronunciation of *taxis* and *taxes*, *candied* and *candid*, *posies* and *poses*, *Rosie's* and *Rose's*. Do you hear /ɪ/ in the final syllable of each word? If you use /i/ in the final syllable of the first word of each pair, it is probably a simple [i] rather than the complex [ɪi] found in stressed syllables. It is also probably a lowered form of /i/: [kændi˞d, tæksi˞z, pouzi˞z, rouzi˞z]. Final unstressed /ɪ/ is more common in the South than elsewhere in the country, although many speakers in Eastern New England and New York City use it.

3. Most speakers use unstressed /i/ rather than /ɪ/ when the sound is a medial one before another syllable beginning with a vowel. Note your own pronunciation of such words as *react, reality, worrying, holier, audience,* and *fortieth.* In the medial position before a syllable beginning with a consonant, /ɪ/ is the normal sound, as in *happiness* and *handicap.* But in some words (for example, *medicine, Tennyson*), and especially before the suffixes -*ly,* -*ful,* -*cal,* spelled *i* is pronounced either /ɪ/ or /ə/, as in *easily, beautiful,* and *historical.* /i/ is never heard in these words in educated speech.

Those words that use unstressed [i] or [ɪ] as the final sound (*pity, hurry,* and *baggy*) retain the same unstressed forms when an added suffix begins with a vowel. The [ɪ], if used, may be raised to make the adjacent vowels more distinct: *pitying* [pɪtiɪŋ, pɪtɪˑɪŋ], *hurrying* [hʌriɪŋ, hʌrɪˑɪŋ], *baggier* [bægiɚ, bægɪˑə]. Unstressed [i] or [ɪ] are also retained when the -*ed* or -*es* suffixes are added: *pitied* [pɪtid, pɪtɪd], *hurried* [hʌrid, hʌrɪd], *pities* [pɪtiz, pɪtɪz], *hurries* [hʌriz, hʌrɪz]. (As already noted, preference for [i] rather than [ɪ] for these unstressed final sounds is noted for most of the country except the South.) Added suffixes beginning with consonants, however, are usually preceded by [ə], as in *citified, citizen, pitiful, happily* [sɪtəfaɪd, sɪtəzən, pɪtəfəl, hæpəli], although [i] or [ɪ] are normally retained before -*ness* and -*less,* as in *happiness, penniless, roominess, weariness* [hæpinɪs, hæpɪnɪs], and the like.

4. The /i/ of earlier English times is lowered to /ɪ/ when it appears before /r/ in the same syllable. We normally use /ɪ/ in *fierce, sheer,* and *clear. Experience, spirit, miracle,* and *hero* are commonly pronounced with /ɪ/, the *r* sound closing the first syllable. A tendency to use /i/ is present if the speaker ends the first syllable with the open vowel: [spi-rɪt, hi-ro], and the like.

5. A central, high vowel, [ɨ], made with the middle of the tongue high and the lips in neutral, rather than in spread, position, is another commonly heard variant of this sound. It can be heard in such words as *sister, thing, fist, fish,* and *chips,* when the /ɪ/ sound is centralized and the lips kept in neutral position. Actually this central high sound is not easily distinguished from the front vowel [ɪ] of

bin, [bɪn], except as you note its relaxed lip position and its generally centralized acoustic value. In such words as those mentioned above, it has been commonly considered "substandard" or "careless," although there is hardly sufficient evidence to so label the sound. Those speakers who try to avoid using [ɨ] can usually manage to do so in all instances. In colloquial speech, however, this sound is found in all dialects of American English and is used by well-educated as well as by lesser-educated people.

Careful analysis of the phonetic incidence of this sound and the phonemic evaluation of the data have convinced many that American English possesses three high vowels, /ɪ, ɨ, ʊ/, as phonemically distinct from each other as the three mid-vowels /ɛ, ʌ, o/ (see page 183). This would indicate that the "barred *i*", [ɨ], might well be a variant of /ɪ/ in certain words, but that in the speech of many it exists as a distinctly separate /ɨ/ sound. Its spelled form is usually *i*, and this may account, in large part, for our failure to recognize or hear it as different from /ɪ/. Also it is usually found in unstressed syllables, where the identification of a sound is not easy, even to experienced listeners.

Although /ɨ/ is a rarely heard sound in American English, many of us use it in both syllables of the word *children*, [tʃɨldrɪn], in the words *me* and *see*, [mɨi] and [sɨi], where it varies with the pronunciation [mɪi] and [sɪi], and as part of the glide [ɨu] in such words as *tune*, *new*, and *duty* where [u] or [ju] might be said by others. Many speakers consistently use this "barred *i*" instead of /ɪ/ in stressed syllables before /l/ plus a consonant, as in *silver*, *milk*, and *build*. The small words *in*, *his*, *with*, *its*, *if*, *this*, and *is* are heard, quite commonly, with /ɨ/ when stressed. The *Linguistic Atlas* findings note it as frequently used in the South, in such words as *pretty*, *dinner*, *sister*, and *mirror*.

The unstressed /ɨ/ may be heard more commonly in such words as *parted* and *horses*, [-ɨd, -ɨz], in the word *can* when in such a phrase as "I can do it," [- kɨn -], and in the word *just* (adverb) when in such a phrase as "just a moment," or "he just came in." The *Linguistic Atlas* records report it as common in the North and Southeastern areas in such words as *haunted* and *careless* and in the word *stomach* in the Midland area.

An interesting analysis of a field record of an older, educated, Southern informant was published by Sumner Ives in 1954.[4] The detailed phonetic analysis of the speech of this person, described by the field worker, Dr. Raven I. McDavid, Jr., as an "excellent example of natural cultured speaker of older generation (upcountry type)," indicated 38 pronunciations with unstressed [ɪ], but 55 examples with fronted and raised [ɪ], 156 with fronted [ɪ], and 28 other examples with shortened and lowered [ɪ] forms. Professor Ives recognizes the speech of this informant as "broadly typical of the speech of educated people in the southeastern corner of the country," even though noting that the number of "'nonstandard' pronunciations . . . are more common than would be expected in the speech of a younger informant or of any educated person of the locality when speaking formally."[5]

There is actually little doubt as to the use of this sound in colloquial American speech, and the evidence does not warrant placing a "careless" label on it whenever it is heard. You might try some of the following pairs of words on some of your teachers and friends to see if it is present in their speech. It is fairly easy to recognize. /ɪ/ is high and front and may be accompanied by some slight lip spreading. /ɨ/ is a centralized sound and the lips are relaxed or neutral, between the slightly spread /ɪ/ and the slightly rounded /ʊ/.

sin—pinnacle	*rinse—children*
river—rivet	*will he—Willie*
gist—jest—just (adv.)	*kin—I can do it*
—just (adj.)	*sister—resister*

Other Varieties of /i/ **and** /ɪ/

Most native speakers of American English experience no difficulty with these sounds. Foreign-born speakers readily substitute /i/ for

---

[4] "Vowel Transcriptions in a Georgia Field Record," *Tulane Studies in English*, Vol. 4 (Tulane University, New Orleans, 1954), pp. 165–166.

[5] *Ibid.*, pp. 149–150.

/ɪ/, since the differences in length, tension, and tongue positions are slight, and can be heard only after a reasonable period of ear training. "Give him his pen" may be pronounced [gɪv hɪm hɪz pɛn] by such speakers.

/ɪ/ may become /i/ before /ʃ/, in the stressed syllables of such words as *condition, Patricia, tradition, initiate, Galicia,* and *suspicion.*

THE MID-FRONT VOWELS /e/ AND /ɛ/ IN *GATE* AND *GET*

The tense mid-front vowel /e/ and the lax mid-front vowel /ɛ/ are made with the tongue blade slightly lower and retracted in the mouth than for the two high front vowels just discussed. The lips are opened a bit more and in a lesser spread position than they are for /i/ and /ɪ/. /e/ tends to be a long vowel, /ɛ/ a short vowel. The sound resulting from the tendency to diphthongize [e] into [eɪ] can be noticed by prolonging the vowel in such words as *gay* and *made.* The diphthong [eɪ] does not vary phonemically with the monophthong [e], and the sound may be transcribed either way. This breaking of the long vowel [e:] into a diphthong is more common in Southern British speech. American speech tends to retain the monophthong when the syllable is unstressed, as in the first syllable of *vacation,* as the monophthong with a slight off-glide when it appears in a stressed syllable before a voiceless consonant, as in *make* and *space*: [meᴵk, speᴵs], and as a diphthong in a stressed syllable when final or before a voiced consonant, as in *they* and *gave*: [ðeɪ, geɪv].

/e/ is commonly spelled *a* as in *gate.* Less common spellings are *ai* as in *pain, ay* as in *say,* and *ea, ei,* and *ey* as in *steak, veil,* and *obey.* Exceptional spellings for /e/ are found in the words *gauge* and *gaol.* /ɛ/ is commonly spelled *e* as in *get,* less commonly *ea, ei,* and *eo* as in *breath, heifer,* and *leopard* and *a, ae, ai, ay* as in *many, aesthetics, said, says.* Exceptional spellings of /ɛ/ appear as *u* in *bury, ie* as in *friend*, and *ue* as in *guess*. /e/ is found in all positions of words: *ache*, *make*, *they*. /ɛ/ exists only initially and medially in English words: *end* and *get*.

Modifications and Variations in Usage

1. The most obvious variation of the /e/ sound occurs as a diphthong. Both forms are part of the standard American English pattern, with a greater tendency to diphthongize found along the Atlantic seaboard. Older pure [e] is rarely a pure vowel in American English today. Some slight off-glide is usually noticeable. Comparatively speaking, it is a much laxer sound than is found in French or German: Fr. *armée*; Germ. *gehen*.

2. Unstressed /e/ becomes /ɪ/ (or /i/) in the final syllables of the days of the week: [mʌndɪ], [tjuzdɪ], and so forth. This follows the similar pattern seen in the unstressed endings of words like *solace, palace*, and *message*, where either /ɪ/ or /ə/ are heard: [sɑlɪs], [pælɪs], [mɛsɪdʒ]. The same change may be heard in certain common words with the *-ative* ending, when the *a* syllable is unstressed: *co-operative, initiative, nominative*. Speakers who retain secondary stress on these vowels retain the /e/ sound however: [koˈɑpəˌretɪv], and so forth.

3. Before /l/ or /r/ in the same syllable, /e/ tends toward the /ɛ/ sound, as in *pail* or *pale* and *pair*, although many speakers use only /e/ when the vowel precedes /l/. *Fail, mail, scale, fare, care*, and *their* may be pronounced with [ɛə], although [feɪl], [meɪl], and [skeɪl] are the more commonly heard forms.

4. Before *r* or *rr*, considerable variation seems to take place for the spelled *e* or *a* in such words as *there, stair, carry, merry, area*, and *variable*, with pronunciations varying from /e/ to /ɛ/ to /æ/. Regional tendencies seem to have developed and the use of one vowel instead of another may act as a partial clue to the regional source of the dialect. The Atlantic coastal area and the South normally pronounce such words as *marry, carrot, sparrow*, and *Harry* with /æ/, while both /æ/ and /ɛ/ are heard for these words elsewhere in the country, with a strong inclination toward /ɛ/ (or a raised [æˑ]). In other words with

intervocalic *r*, such as *variable*, *area*, *dairy*, and *Mary*, Southern speakers prefer [e] or [eɪ], although /ɛ/ (with the variants [ɛ:, ɛə]) is heard too. Most others from the Atlantic coastal areas, the northern inland, and the western sections of the country seem to prefer [ɛ] (or a lowered [ɛ̞]), plus the off-glides [ə] or [ɚ]. In such -*are*, -*air*, and -*ere* words as *care*, *declare*, *fair*, *stair*, *where*, and *there*, the prevailing Southern sound is /æ/ plus the off-glide [æɚ]. Northeastern and coastal midland speakers tend toward [ɛə] or [ɛɚ], while the remainder of the country prefers /æ/, occasionally /ɛ/. The sentence "Harry married Mary in the area of the stairs," would probably sound like:

Southern: [hærɪ mærɪd merɪ ɪn ðɪ erɪə əv ðə stæəz]
Eastern New England: [hærɪ mærɪd mɛərɪ ɪn ðɪ ɛərɪə əv ðə stɛəz]
New York City: [hæri mærɪd mɛəri ɪn ðɪ ɛərɪə əv ðə stɛəz]
Upper Ohio Valley: [hɛəri (hæri) mɛərid (mærid) mɛəri ɪn ðɪ ɛərɪə əv ðə stæɚz]

There is actually no complete consistency, either in the same regional area, nor in the speech of a given individual. Kenyon, whose speech is typical, educated Ohio speech, reports in his *American Pronunciation*[6] his own use of [æ] for *fairy*, *fair*, *chary*, *wary*, *where*, *there*, *beware*, *care*, and *pear*; [ɛ] in *vary*, *various*, *variation*, *barbarian*, *Hungarian*, *librarian*. Kenyon notes a strong trend toward [ɛ] in the midwestern section of the country. In the Sumner Ives report of the speech of an educated, older, Georgian informant (cited earlier, page 150), one notes a fairly typical, predominant use of [æ] in the *stair* and *carry* words, but instances do appear of *scary*, *anywhere*, and *stairs* with [ɛ]. New Yorkers use [ɛə] in all the words mentioned above, but both [æ] and [ɛ] are commonly heard in *barbarian*, *Sarah*, *parent*, and *various*.

Other Varieties

There are no common substandard forms of /e/ found among native American English speakers. Foreign language speaking

[6] John S. Kenyon, *American Pronunciation*, 10th ed. (Ann Arbor, George. Wahr Publishing Co., 1951), p. 226.

people may substitute a tenser and pure [e] for our somewhat more relaxed, commonly diphthongized sound.

/ɛ/ becomes /ɪ/ in less educated speech in words like *get, ten, cents*, and *many*, where /ɛ/ precedes an alveolar consonant. This pronunciation is found in all sections of the country. It is the result of anticipating the position of the alveolar sound, thus placing the blade of the tongue closer to the /ɪ/ position.

THE LOW-FRONT VOWEL /æ/ IN *HAT* AND *CAN*

The vowel /æ/ is a low, front vowel. For most Americans who do not use [a], [æ] is the lowest front vowel of American English. The tongue blade is slightly lower in the mouth and somewhat retracted from the position of /ɛ/. It is commonly considered a lax vowel, although a clearly tense variety of the sound exists in all parts of the country. /æ/ is a tenser sound in all positions where a lengthened vowel can occur (see page 143). The lips and mouth are more open than for any other front vowel. It is the sound we commonly call "short *a*."

/æ/ is almost always spelled with the letter *a*, as in *add* and *back*. Other spellings for this sound are rare: *ai* in *plaid* and *au* in *aunt* and *laugh*. /æ/ appears in initial and medial positions of words.

Modifications and Variations in Usage

1. The /æ/ before *r* in words like *marry, carry, harrow*, and *Sarah* is commonly raised toward the /ɛ/ sound in the speech of many throughout the country. In such instances, these words would be transcribed: [mɛːri], [kɛːri], [hɛːro], and [sɛːrə] or [mɛɚi], [kɛɚi] [hɛɚo], and [sɛɚə]. These pronunciations are somewhat distinctive from the short /ɛ/ of *get*, in that when used, they are longer than the short /ɛ/, or else diphthongized as [ɛɚ]. Persons in the "*r*-less" areas of our country tend to retain the /æ/ form ([mæri], and the like), while most other speakers front the sound to [æ-], [ɛː], or [ɛɚ]. Other variations of these and similar words are discussed under /e - ɛ/.

2. In certain phonetic contexts, the /æ/ sound is raised toward /ɛ/ in the speech of many persons, sometimes consistently, sometimes sporadically. This raising and fronting of /æ/ is noticed in the so-called "*ask* words" (see page 159), where the other possible variants, [ask] or [ɑsk], may be heard in certain sections of the country. This raised sound is also noticed before certain consonants, both voiced and voiceless, as noted below. This fronted, raised, tenser, and longer sound is found in all parts of the country, and phoneticians are beginning to indicate that two different forms are evolving in American speech. It may be transcribed [æ˙] or followed by an off-glide to produce [æ˙ə] or [æ˙ᵊ].

Compare your pronunciation of the words in the following lists, trying not to change your normal usage. You will probably note that the vowel sound is slightly higher, toward /ɛ/, in the words in the left column. If you try to pronounce the words in Group I with identical, open, lax vowel quality used for those in Group II, the pronunciation may sound strange and unnatural to you.

Group I			*Group II*		
last	ham	cash	hat	rat	sat
master	hand	badge	fat	nap	map
dance	bag	bad	gap	rack	back
cram	sag	bath	stack	shack	catch
handle	salve	fancy	hatch	batch	latch

The raised vowel for the words in Column I is common to educated persons throughout the country. Although no clear phonetic context has as yet resulted, it generally appears in words before final voiced stops (*bad*, *hag*, and the like), before the voiced affricate (badge), before both voiced and voiceless fricatives *(salve, laugh)*, and before the nasals /m/ and /n/ *(ham, sand)*, when these sounds are word finals, or in these same words and their suffixes. The irregular use of the raised vowel [æ˙] or [æ˙ə] may be seen when the sound is followed by the same consonants plus other sounds which are not regular suffixes. /æ/ before *f* is raised in *craft, rafter,* and *after*, like *laughter*, but is not commonly raised in *Africa, saffron, sapphire,* and *Afghanistan*. The raised or diphthongized sound appears before /s/ and /ʃ/

in *bask, basket, cash, cashier,* and *plaster,* but not before /z/ or /ʒ/, as in *hazard* and *casual.* It is raised in *math* but not in *mathematics* and *Catherine,* although *Cathy* is sometimes heard with [æ˞].

The raised sound is not normally found in the auxiliary words *have, had, can,* and the like, due to the fact that these words are generally found in unstressed syllables and hence possess short vowels. You should not assume that all educated speakers consistently use the fronted and raised sound. Many speakers never use this fronted and raised sound, and some do with no clearly consistent pattern.

A prolonged, tense, and diphthongized [ɛə] for /æ/ is associated with substandard speech and is noted below.[7]

Variations in the pronunciation of such words as *ask, fast,* and *class* (the "*ask* words") as [ask—ɑsk, fast—fɑst, klas—klɑs] are discussed in the next section.

Other Varieties of /æ/

1. A common substandard substitution for /æ/ is the consistent use of a tense, high, lengthened [ɛːᵊ] or [ɛə] in such words as those listed in Column I above. Although many educated speakers raise the vowel in words of this type, the completely consistent substitution of [ɛə] is found in less educated speech. The excessively tensed vowel is often nasalized. Correction of the sound toward a still lower [æ˕] or even [a] is a hypercorrect form and a mark of affected speech.

2. Other-language speakers normally possess considerable difficulty with this sound, for it is not commonly found in many languages. The substitutions of a short or long /e/, /ɛ/, /a/, or /ɑ/ for /æ/ are found in the speech of such persons. Learning to achieve an acceptable sound takes considerable ear training and practice. It

---

[7] A good discussion of this phenomenon may be found in Allan F. Hubbell, *The Pronunciation of English in New York City* (New York, Kings Crown Press, 1950), pp. 75–79. Other discussions of the same splitting of this sound are found in the observations of George L. Trager as published in *American Speech,* Vol. 5 (1929–30), pp. 396–400; Vol. 9 (1934), pp. 313–315; Vol. 15 (1940), pp. 255–258.

is most easily achieved by allowing the articulators to assume a position midway between /ɛ/ and /a/, making sure that they result in a lax vowel.

THE [a] VARIANT IN ASK AND PARK

[a] is the lowest front vowel in our language, made with the tongue in an almost central position. (Figure 28.) The dorsum of the tongue is almost, if not quite, flat. The lips are open with very slight spreading present, and the sound is generally long. The sound appears to many as a fronted [a˖] and to most persons in the country, it has no phonemic entity different from the /a/ sound in *calm*. It is approximately midway between the low-front /æ/ of *cat* and the low-back /ɑ/ of *ah*. It is the sound of the stressed vowel of the Italian word *acqua*, and of French *patte* and *là*. This vowel is found as a monophthong in only a small part of the country, in the eastern part of New England. It is, however, normally found as the first element of two diphthongs, /aɪ/ and /aʊ/, in *high* and *how*. As a monophthong, it is best remembered as a variant of the /æ/ of *ask* and the /ɑ/ of *park*. It has no special spelled form.

In such words as *path*, *ask*, and *last*, all three sounds [æ, a, ɑ] may be heard in Eastern New England, with a growing use of [æ]. [a] varies freely with [ɑ] in these "broad *a*" words throughout this area, different speakers using either sound. For some speakers in the Eastern New England area, however, [ɑ] is an uncommon sound. Such speakers possess [æ] in *cat*, [a] in *farm*, *ask*, and *calm*, and [ɒ] in *pot* and *sorrow*, without the [ɑ] many speakers in the rest of the country would use in *farm*, *calm*, and *pot*. Elsewhere in the country, the use of [a] for the "*ask* words" is uncommon. Speakers who adopt it do so consciously, affecting what they consider a "prestige pronunciation." Eastern New England is the only area of the country where [a] is frequently and consistently heard as a monophthongal form.

[a] may also be heard in the speech of many Southern and South Midland speakers in such words as *blind* or *five*, [bla·nd, bla·ᵊnd],

[faˑv, faˑᵊv], where the rest of the country uses the diphthongal [aɪ]. Most Southerners use the [aɪ] form too. But many distinguish the words *bland, blind,* and *blond* or *fair, fire,* and *far* from each other by the use of [aˑ] or [aˑᵊ] for the middle word of each group: [blænd, blaˑnd, blɑnd], and so on. Similarly, such speakers use [æ], [a], and [ɑ] plus length, [ɪ] or [ə], to distinguish *had, hide, hired, hard,* and *hod* from each other: [hæd], [haɪd or haˑd], [haᵊd], [hɑəd], [hɑd]. The use of a monophthongal [aˑ aː] or [aᵊ] for such words as *five, blind, time,* and *my* is considered substandard by many Southern speakers, but there is little doubt that many educated speakers use it.

/a/ may not be a separate and distinctive sound in your speech or regional dialect, as it is not for most Americans. Its use as a separate sound in some dialects, and as an allophonic variant of other sounds in other dialects, cannot be denied. For almost all of us, it is, if used, a variant of another phoneme, and, as such, it does not hold a special place in our vowel structure. For others, it seems to be quite distinct from any other sound. Its place in the phonemic structure of American English is not clear, although the evidence seems strong in favor of according it phonemic status in some dialects of American English. If doubt exists as to its phonemic entity, none exists as to its use as a sound frequently heard in New England and the South— distinctive or not.[8]

The Use of the [a] Variant

By the eighteenth century, the /ɑ/ of present-day *father* had, as yet, not entered the speech of most American speakers. At this time, /æ/ was the common form. Actually, the /ɑ/ sound was in sporadic

---

[8] Concerning the use of this vowel as a separate phoneme in the South, see Raven I. McDavid, Jr., "American English Dialects," in W. Nelson Francis, *The Structure of American English* (New York, Ronald, 1958), p. 513; and James Sledd's review of George L. Trager and Henry Lee Smith, Jr., *An Outline of English Structure* in *Language*, Vol. 31 (April–June, 1955), p. 320. An excellent review of the problem of distinguishing allophone from phoneme, particularly pertinent to this discussion, appears in Archibald A. Hill, *Introduction to Linguistic Structures* (New York, Harcourt, 1958), Ch. 4, "Phoneme and Allophone," pp. 47–61.

use, especially in nonurban areas, and undoubtedly many persons were saying *calm* and *father* as [kɑ:m] and [fɑ:ðər] even in the urban centers. (The older /æ/ is still heard in such words as *Pappy* and *Mammy* for *Papa* and *Mama*.) The change from /æ/ to /ɑ/ occurred in two large groups of words: (1) those words in which the vowel was followed by a final or a preconsonantal *r*, as in *car* or *hard;* and (2) those words in which the vowel was followed by a now vanished *l*, as in *calm* and *psalm*. For the first group of words, the shift to /ɑ/ was incomplete for many in New England and some in the New York City area, with a resultant [a] sound: [ha:d], [pa:t], [ka:d]. As noted earlier, Eastern New England today possesses both [a] and [ɑ] in these words. Elsewhere the shift to the /ɑ/ sound was complete for all speakers for these words. The shift from /æ/ to /ɑ/ was complete for all speakers in the country for the second group of words.

This intermediate [a] sound is not found in British Received Pronunciation either, where the shift to /ɑ/ was complete. Some writers credit the widely-followed, fashionable lexicographer John Walker of late eighteenth-century England, and Joseph Worcester, the equally fashionable nineteenth-century New England lexicographer, with much of the responsibility for the incomplete shift to [a] in America. Both considered the "broad *a*" "vulgar." This conclusion is somewhat tenuous, since other linguistic influences might well account for the change. But these influences too seem to have been based on the pressures of "fashionableness." This phenomenon is an excellent example of how fashion can influence the widespread use of a sound.[9]

In a third group of words, commonly known as the "*ask* words," a similar shift to [a] or [ɑ] took place, predominantly in the New England area. Some persons in the South, especially in eastern Virginia, use a "broad *a*" in these words, although fewer and fewer

---

[9] For further details on this interesting phenomenon, see George Ph. Krapp, *The English Language in America*, Vol. 2 (New York, The Century Company, 1925), pp. 74–77; and Arthur J. Bronstein, "The Vowels and Diphthongs of the Nineteenth Century," *Speech Monographs*, Vol. 16 (June, 1949), p. 32.

persons seem prone to retain it. And some New York City speakers use [a] or [ɑ] in such words, although these sounds are not indigenous to that area in these words. /æ/ is the common form for these words throughout the remainder of the United States and Canada. Stage speech uses /ɑ/ in these words, patterned on Received Pronunciation of England.

This change from /æ/ to /ɑ/, or to an incomplete change to an intermediate sound, occurs in words in which *a* precedes the voiceless fricatives /f/, /θ/, or /s/, as in *half, path,* and *pass,* or an /m/ or /n/ plus a consonant, as in *sample, aunt, demand,* and *branch.*

REVIEW AND PRACTICE SECTION

1. Does the foreign language you study possess the vowel phonemes you use in *beat, bit, bait, bet,* and *bat?* If not, what will the native speaker of that language say for the English sounds not common to his language?
2. Do you use /ɪ/ or /i/ for the unstressed beginnings or endings in *evade, erupt, defer, repent, fully, sultry, city?* Do you make any distinction in your pronunciation of the following? *roses—Rosie's, Maxie's—Max's, seer here—see rear, Willie—will he, spear it—spirit, heroes—hear 'ohs'—he rose, steer up—stirrup.*
3. Arrange the following words into three columns according to your transcription with /i/, /ɪ/, or /ɪ/. Be sure to pronounce the words naturally.

sister	William	feel	it	fitted
fish	fill 'em	build	eat	parted
city	crinkle	Easter	still	places
seating	spill	please	ink	sanded

4. Which sound do you use in each of the following—/e/, /ɛ/, or /æ/? *fail, fairy, fade, spade, spend, spare, pail, arrow, where, carry.*
5. Test an acquaintance on this sample sentence: "Where did Cary plan to carry Sarah's and Mary's carriages?" From what regional area does he come?
6. Transcribe the following sentence as it would be spoken by a Bostonian, Atlantan, or Clevelander: "Ask Harvey to park his car near the path."
7. Arrange the following words according to the indicated categories, transcribing each word as you say it: (*a*) medial stressed /i/; (*b*) medial

stressed /ɪ/; (c) unstressed syllabic /i/ or /ɪ/ before a vowel; (d) unstressed syllabic /ɪ/ or /ə/ before a consonant.

critic	machine	fleece	willow
English	Patricia	suspicious	hurrying
medicine	chemical	react	audience
sing	subpoena	Marian	comical

8. The following words contain lesser stressed /e/ and fully stressed /e/ in initial syllables. Transcribe your pronunciation ([e, eᴵ, eɪ]) for each.

crayon	aorta	famous	blatant
bailiff	vacate	placate	Shakesperian

9. Transcribe the words in the first two columns and compare them with your pronunciation of the vowel in the third and fourth columns. What is your pronunciation of the vowel in the last two columns — [æ, æ˔, or ɛə]?

bed	bat	bad	bag
egg	lack	lad	lag
stem	thank	flash	stand
merry	lariat	imagine	sad

10. Transcribe your pronunciation of the following:

He steered the ship while the chef created a delightful dinner.
Salving the arm saved him much pain.
The garish clothes worn at the marriage of Harry and Mary made it a long-remembered affair.
They ask fancy prices for the handiwork displayed in the arts and crafts shops.

CHAPTER 8

The Back Vowels

THE LOW-BACK VOWEL /ɑ/ IN *CALM* AND *JAR*

/ɑ/ IS THE LOWEST of the back vowels. The mouth is open wider for this vowel than for any other. The lips are neutral, neither spread nor rounded, and the entire tongue is low and lax. The tongue is drawn down and back. The sound is short in such words as *box*, *lock*, and *stop* and long in such words as *yard*, *calm*, and *father*. (Some speakers of American English pronounce the first group of words as [bɒks, lɒk, stɒp]. These variants are discussed in the next section.)

/ɑ/ is commonly spelled *a* as in *farm* and *father* and *o* in *lock* and *hot*. Exceptional spellings with *e*, *ea*, and *ua* appear in the words *sergeant*, *heart*, and *guard*. The sound is found initially and medially, as in *art* and *father*, and finally in a few words such as *spa*, *Shah*, *Pa*, and *Ma*, as well as in such words as far and star in the "*r*-less" sections of the country.

/ɑ/ is a comparatively recent sound. Modern English possessed no clearly established /ɑ/ form until well into the eighteenth century, /æ/ being the common form prior to that time. Its widespread use, in such words as *father*, *calm*, and *part*, was not common until the

162

end of the century, when it was recognized as common to most educated speakers of standard English.[1]

Variations and Modifications of the /ɑ/ Sound

1. The substitution of /ɒ/ for /ɑ/ in the short *o* words and those words initiating with *wa*, as in *box, stop, wander*, and *watch*, is found in the next section. The large majority of speakers in America consistently use /ɑ/ in all such words, so that no noticeable distinction exists in the quality of the stressed vowels of *father—fodder, carter—cotter, card—cod*. Any distinction that may exist is probably due to the greater length of the sound in the first pair of each word, or to the presence of an off-glide /ə/ or /r/ added to the vowel /ɑ/. /ɒ/ and /ɔ/ appear in Midwestern and Western speech for many of the *wa* words, in *water, watch*, and *wasp*, varying with /ɑ/. In Southern speech both /ɑ/ and /ɔ/ appear for these *wa* words, while in New England both /ɒ/ and /ɑ/ exist. Some in New York City use /ɒ/ for the *wa* words, but most speakers use /ɑ/: [wɑndɚ, wɑsp, wɑtʃ] but [wɔtɚ].

The short *o* before intervocalic /r/, as in *moral, tomorrow*, and *forest*, has been studied by Thomas,[2] who arrives at the conclusion that no regional preference for /ɑ/ or /ɔ/ can as yet be designated. Both forms are known to exist, however, with seeming preference for /ɑ/ in the "*r*-less" areas of New England, New York City, and the South, while /ɔ/ predominates elsewhere. A similar regional preference seems established for other short *o* words, as in *hot, cod, knob*, and *stop*: /ɑ/ or /ɒ/ in the "*r*-less" areas, with a noticeable

[1] The history of this sound is detailed in John S. Kenyon, *American Pronunciation* (Ann Arbor, George Wahr Publishing Co., 1951), pp. 174–184; in George Ph. Krapp, *The English Language in America* (New York, The Century Co., 1925), Vol. 2, pp. 36–86; in Arthur J. Bronstein, "The Vowels and Diphthongs of the Nineteenth Century," *Speech Monographs*, Vol. 16, No. 2 (1949), pp. 232–233; in Karl-Erik Lindblad, "Noah Webster's Pronunciation and Modern New England Speech," *Essays and Studies on American Language and Literature, No. 11* (Cambridge, Harvard University Press, 1954), pp. 8–17.

[2] Charles K. Thomas, "The Dialectal Significance of the Non-Phonemic Low-Back Vowel Variants before R." *Studies in Speech and Drama in Honor of Alexander M. Drummond* (Ithaca, Cornell University Press, 1944), pp. 244–254.

tendency to use the unrounded /ɑ/ sound; /ɑ/ in the remainder of the country. For spelled *o* plus a velar /k/, /g/, or /ŋ/, as in *frock*, *hog*, or *honk*, /ɑ/ predominates in Eastern New England and New York City, with occasional /ɒ/, while /ɔ/ predominates elsewhere with occasional /ɑ/ or /ɒ/.

The slightly rounded, low, back, usually short vowel heard in *pot*, *top*, and *forest*, as a variant of /ɑ/ or /ɔ/, is mentioned in the next section. For many of us who live in the Atlantic coastal regions, /ɑ/ is the normal form for these words, although we commonly hear [pɒt, tɒp, fɒrəst]. [ɒ] and [ɑ] seem to vary freely with each other as nondistinctive variants of the same phoneme in much of the speech of these areas. Many persons, however, who use no postvocalic /r/, retain clear vowel distinctions between *park—pock*, *lark—lock*, *chock—chocolate*, using [ɑ] or [ɑ:] for one, [ɒ] for the other. Both [ɒ] and [ɑ] may be heard as variants of each other (seemingly in free variation) in *cot*, *far*, and *farm* in certain sections of the Ohio valley, Iowa, Oklahoma, and elsewhere. The occasional use of this variant [ɒ] may well deserve phonemic status, however, even if only of limited occurrence. If sufficient samples of minimal contrasts are heard in the speech of such persons, /ɒ/ and /ɑ/ may exist as separate and distinctive vowel entities. For many of us, however, [ɒ] remains an allophone of /ɑ/, in the words mentioned above.

2. [a] is a common variant of [ɑ] plus *r* in the speech of many in Eastern New England, in such words as *park*, *hard*, and *cart*. Such pronunciations are distinctive to this area. They are not found in widespread use elsewhere in the country.

THE [ɒ] VARIANT IN *HOT* AND *TOSS*

[ɒ] is a low, back vowel, made with the lip opening slightly reduced and rounded from the open position of [ɑ]. It is not part of the normal vowel phonemes of the foreign languages you have studied. Like [a], it is found sporadically in American English: in the Eastern New England and New York City areas with some reasonable degree of consistency, and elsewhere in the country in special types of words. The tongue is slightly retracted from the [ɑ] position, approximately midway between the mid-back vowel /ɑ/ and the back rounded /ɔ/. The sound is normally short and lax. It is best remembered as a variant of /ɑ/ in *hot* and *stop*, and of /ɔ/ in *dog* and *cough*.

Depending on the dialect spoken, it may be represented phonemically by /ɑ/ or /ɔ/. When it varies with [ɑ], as in *pot* ([pɒt]), phonemicists will classify it with /ɑ/, while when it varies with [ɔ] in *toss*, *dog*, and *broth*, it is part of the phoneme /ɔ/.

For some of us, however, this sound is a vocalic entity of sufficient contrast with what others use in *calm* and *call*, /ɑ-ɔ/, so that it seems to deserve its own phonemic status. Present evidence places such use of /ɒ/ along the eastern seaboard areas, predominantly in Eastern New England, irregularly in New York City, and occasionally in the South. [ɒ] is not a phonemic entity to most of us who use only [ɑ] or [ɔ] in *balm*, *bomb*, *froth*, *fraud*, *hog*, and *hawk*. But a few of us do make use of three distinctive vowels: [bɑm, bɒm, frɒθ, frɔd, hɒg, hɔk]. For such persons, /ɒ/ in *collar*, *bomb*, *lot*, and *fog* is a separate phonemic entity, not to be confused with the /ɑ/ or /ɔ/ of *calm* and *balm*, *law* and *fall*.

The Use of the [ɒ] Variant

[ɒ] is one of the least stable sounds in American English. It is found in individual words throughout the country, but with no clear consistency according to regional or standard levels. Its most common and consistent use is found in the short *o* and *wa* words in the speech of many in New York City and Eastern New England. Not all speakers in these areas use this sound, most using the sounds predominant elsewhere in the country. When used, it is found most generally in words containing: (1) *o* and intervocalic *r*, or *wa* and intervocalic *r* as in *foreign*, *horrid*, *Warren*, and *warrant*, where other speakers use mostly [ɑ] or [ɔ]; (2) *o* or *wa* plus /f/, /s/, and /θ/ as in *cough*, *quaff*, *toss*, and *cloth*, where others use mostly [ɔ]; (3) *o* or *wa* plus the affricates /tʃ/ or /dʒ/ as in *crotch*, *watch*, and *lodge*, where others use mostly [ɑ]; (4) *o* or *wa* before the bilabial or alveolar stops, as in *cod, hop, knob, swab,* and *what,* where others usually use [ɑ].

In all the above instances, a variant [ɑ] or [ɔ] is found as noted, so that in the speech of many throughout the country, [ɒ], as a distinctive sound, never appears. The sound is more widely used in all parts of the country than is supposed. The exact detailing of the use of this sound must wait for the results of the studies now being made. It is clear, however, that [ɒ] is not confined to the Eastern New England area. Its use elsewhere may be more sporadic and less consistent, but its existence, at least as a variant of /ɑ/ or /ɔ/, in the speech of many educated speakers cannot be denied.

THE LOW-BACK VOWEL /ɔ/ IN *ALL* AND *SAW*

This slightly tense vowel is made with the back of the tongue higher than for the /ɑ/ sound, with the lips slightly rounded and protruded. /ɔ/ occurs initially, medially, and finally in words.

The sound is commonly spelled with an *a* or *o* as in *all* and *border.* Other spellings are *au, aw, al* in *fault, fawn,* and *halt* and *oa* and *ou* in *broad* and *brought.* Exceptional spellings are found in *toward* and *George.*

Modifications and Variations of the /ɔ/ Sound

1. The most obvious variation of this sound occurs when either [ɑ] or [ɒ] replaces the [ɔ] in the short *o* or *wa* words, as in *foreign, gone,* and *wash,* where regional preference so dictates. These variations have already been mentioned in the previous section on [ɒ].

2. Many speakers use a lower form of this sound, often approximating the [ɒ] sound. Since the variation is not phonemically distinctive, it is normally unnoticed, unless the lowering is extreme and the sound approaches /ɑ/, which sounds hypercorrect. Such pronunciations can be noticed in all /ɔ/ words, so that *fought, called,* and *Laura* approximate [fɒt], [kɒld], and [lɒrə]. This somewhat open sound has been noted in New York City and the New England

areas, and it exists in many other areas of the country—all on the upper educated level.

3. In Eastern New England, for many speakers, and in New York City, for almost all speakers, [ɔ] is the first element of the diphthong for those words with historical long *o* plus *r*, pronounced [oə], [oɚ], [oʊə], [oʊɚ] in other parts of the country. Such speakers make no distinction between *for* and *four*, *morning* and *mourning*, *border* and *boarder*. This levelling to [ɔ] for all these words seems to be on the rise throughout the country.

Other Varieties of /ɔ/

A common variation of /ɔ/ occurs when excessive rounding and protrusion of the lips, plus noticeable retraction of the back part of the tongue, takes place: [ɔ˞, ɔ']. The resulting sound is usually excessively tense. It is recognized as a clearly substandard form. Writers commonly show it as "t-aw-l," "aw-w-ful," and "d-aw-g." It is most easily overcome by retraining the excessively forward lip position, or by opening the mouth wider toward the [ɒ] or [ɑ] sounds. Resultant motion of the tongue away from the excessively retracted position will produce a more "acceptable" sound. This retraction is especially common before *l* as in *fall* and *ball*, and before velar *k* and *g* as in *talk*, *walk*, and *dog*.

THE MID-BACK VOWEL /o/ IN *OBEY* AND *COAT*

/o/ is a tense mid-back vowel, made with the tongue retracted at its base and somewhat raised toward the velum. The blade of the tongue is flat and somewhat retracted, while the lips are rounded and often protruded. In the speech of many persons, this protrusion may be negligible. Singers tend to use much greater protrusion of the lips for this sound than is normally found in informal, colloquial speech.

As /o/ is stressed and lengthened, it normally assumes a diphthongal form, acting in the same fashion as [e] and [eɪ]. Thus in an unstressed syllable, as in *obey*, the /o/ sound normally remains monophthongal. When stressed before a voiceless consonant, as in *coat*, the slight off-glide [ᵁ] normally appears: [koᵁt]. The off-glide becomes still more noticeable when the stressed /o/ is final or before a voiced consonant as in *go* and *sown*: [goᴜ], [soᴜn]. [o] and [oᴜ] are not phonemically distinctive from each other, and in broad transcription the sound may be represented with either form. /o/ is found in all positions in words.

/o/ is normally spelled *o* as in *no* and *note*. Other common spellings are *oa*, *oe*, *ou*, and *ow* in *road*, *doe*, *soul*, and *know*. Less common spellings of this sound appear in *brooch*, *sew*, *beau*, and *yeoman*.

Variations and Modifications of the /o/ Sound

1. Like /e/, the most obvious variation of /o/ is the diphthongal form [oᴜ], the nonphonemic variant of [o]. Pure monophthongal [o], found in other languages, is actually a rare form in American English. The sound usually possesses a more or less distinctive off-glide [ᴜ], most noticeable when the vowel is stressed and lengthened when in the final position of a word, as in *blow*, or before a voiced consonant, as in *tone*: [bloᴜ], [toᴜn].

2. A centralized variant of this sound, almost approaching the lower mid-vowel /ʌ/ of *cut*, seems to have been a part of the educated speech pattern in New England for an extended period of time. This variation is probably best represented as a centralized and lowered [ö̞], or as a slightly rounded [ʌº]. Thus the words *home*, *folks*, and *most* might be transcribed in this pattern, when heard, as [hö̞m], [fö̞ks], and [mö̞st]. It is a distinctive enough sound to have achieved the special name of "the New England short *o*."[3]

3. A centralized variety of this sound, not quite as tense as found in Southern British speech, where it approximates [ɜᴜ], is found in increasing use throughout the United States. The sound is made with the lips in a neutral position or slightly pursed, and the tongue approaching a mid-vowel, close to the position of [əᴜ] or [ɜᴜ]

---

[3] Compare G. Ph. Krapp, *The English Language in America*, Vol. II, pp. 132–133 and J. S. Kenyon, *American Pronunciation*, 10th ed., p. 192.

Persons who use this form in speaking, studiously avoid it in singing. This variation approaches the umlauted ö of German as in *schön*, though it is a much more lax sound. An excessively tense variety of this centralized vowel sounds affected and "British" to the American ear. There is no considered opinion that labels this variation a substandard fault. Actually, it is found more commonly among educated than among uneducated speakers, some writers describing it as a variant more commonly used by women than by men. No statistical proof is available to support this contention.

4. The variation of orthographic *o* plus *r*, as in *horse* and *hoarse*, has been mentioned in the previous section (page 167). Normal use throughout most of the country shows the retention of the historical distinction between /o/ and /ɔ/ in these words. The levelling of both sounds to /ɔ/, so that *oral* and *aural* are identically pronounced, is normal to almost all speakers in New York City, and to many in the southern regions of Eastern New England. Increasing use of /ɔ/ for both words is found in the Middle Atlantic regions of the United States, and sporadically throughout the country. The South seems most consistent in retaining the distinction. The [o], when used in these words, is always slightly lower than the [o] of *go*.

Other Varieties of /o/

1. Words with final unstressed [o], without the off-glide [ʊ], have been "troublesome" for quite a period of time. Sources and educators differ in their attitudes toward the substitution of [ʊ] or [ə] for [o] in such words as *tomato, potato, follow, fellow, window, piano, marshmallow,* and *mellow*. The desire to retain the spelled form is strong. When one of the above words is part of a phrase, as in "*tomato plant,*" "*window pane,*" "*potato mix,*" or "follow John up the hill and sit on the piano bench," the stress pattern of the language normally forces a short vowel to take the place of the final [o]. When alone however, an unstressed [ə], or a partially stressed [o], may be heard. The use of [ə] is common to the substandard and uneducated level. Although not so common to the educated level,

its use by educated speakers cannot be denied. [o] is considered the "conventially correct" form for these words however.[4]

2. The substitution of [ɚ] for final unstressed or partially stressed [o], as in *fellow* or *yellow*, [fɛlɚ, jɛlɚ], is clearly a substandard form. It is normally avoided by speakers of standard American English.

3. A "foreign variant" occurs in the speech of non-native American English speakers who substitute a pure, long, tense variety for the commonly diphthongized form. Adding the off-glide, or some semblance thereof, helps remove the foreign flavor of such pronunciations.

THE HIGH-BACK /ʊ/ AND /u/ VOWELS IN *BOOK* AND *BOOT*

The high-back lax /ʊ/ and tense /u/ are made with the tongue drawn up and back toward the velum of the mouth. The tense /u/ is formed with the back of the tongue higher than for any other vowel in the language. The lips are rounded for both vowels, and may be slightly protruded. Lip rounding is more noticeable and tense with the /u/ than it is for /ʊ/. /ʊ/ is a slightly lower and fronted sound when compared with /u/. The latter sound is actually diph-

---

[4] John S. Kenyon and Thomas A. Knott, *A Pronouncing Dictionary of American English* (Springfield, Mass., Merriam, 1944) shows both the [o] and [ə] as colloquial standard in these words. Giles W. Gray and Claude M. Wise, *Bases of Speech* (New York, Harper, 1946) list [ə] as an error of pronunciation in the General American and Southern areas on pages 214 and 221. In the third edition of their book (1959), however, they note [o] as the "regular" sound with [ə] often used colloquially in all three general areas: General American, p. 267, Southern, p. 284, and Eastern American, p. 303. John S. Kenyon notes on page 193 of his *American Pronunciation*, previously cited, that [ə] is used "... in the familiar speech of a great many Americans." Grant Fairbanks, *Voice and Articulation Drillbook* (New York, Harper, 1940), includes *yellow* and *window* in his list of final [o] words, page 41. *The American College Dictionary* (New York, Random House) respells these words with [o]. Victor A. Fields and James F. Bender, *Voice and Diction* (New York, The Macmillan Co., 1949), lists words such as these with final [o], page 222. Allan F. Hubbell indicates in his previously cited *The Pronunciation of English in New York City* that "... these words have [oʊ] in cultivated speech (in New York City) ...; in uncultivated pronunciation, such words are leveled with *soda* and *collar*, etc.," page 71.

thongal in character, especially when stressed and lengthened. As such, it moves from a slightly less-rounded /ʊ/ position to a tenser, stressed, and more closed /u/, transcribed [ʊu]. The diphthong has no phonemic identity different from its stressed part. As such, it compares with the highest front vowel /i/, which when diphthongized, assumes the form [ɪi]. Since [u] and [ʊu] do not vary phonemically in our language, we shall represent them with the /u/ symbol. The four nonphonemic diphthongs now covered in this section are the two high forms [ɪi] and [ʊu], both ending in tenser, stressed positions, and the mid-front and back [eɪ] and [oʊ], both ending in lax and unstressed forms.

/ʊ/ is normally spelled *oo* or *u* as in *book* and *full*. Other spellings are the *o* of *wolf* and the *ou* of *could*. /u/ is commonly spelled *oo* as in *ooze*. Other spellings appear in *jewel*, *canoe*, *move*, *soup*, *rune*, *maneuver*, *fruit*, and *true*. /ʊ/ appears medially, as in *took* and *cushion*. It is not found as an initial or final vowel in English (except for the variant pronunciation of *into* as [ɪntʊ]). /u/ appears in all positions: *ooze*, *move*, and *too*.

Variations and Modifications of the /ʊ/ and /u/ Sounds

1. Both sounds /ʊ/ and /u/ are variants of each other in a group of *oo* words (developed from Middle English long *o* words) which were all pronounced [u] in early Modern English times. You may have heard both forms in such words as *roof*, *room*, and *soot*. This phenomenon has been studied only slightly,[5] and as yet there is not enough information to generalize about the regional preferences for individual words, nor the sporadic variations that may exist for some of these words. Both forms /ʊ/ and /u/ do appear for many words in the same regions.

---

[5] See Charles H. Grandgent's comments in *Modern Language Notes*, Vol. 6. 458 ff. (1891). Part of this report is discussed in the more readily available John S, Kenyon, *American Pronunciation*, 10th ed., pp. 194–195. See also Raven I. McDavid, Jr., "Derivatives of Middle English [oː] in the South Atlantic Areas," *Quarterly Journal of Speech*, Vol. 35 (December, 1949), pp. 496–504; and Arthur J. Bronstein and Esther K. Sheldon, "Derivatives of Middle English ō in Eighteenth- and Nineteenth-Century Dictionaries," *American Speech*, Vol. 26 (May, 1951), pp. 81–89.

2. Before final *r* in the same syllable, former /u/ is lowered to /ʊ/, as in *poor*, *sure*, and *touring*. A similar situation occurs with /ɪ/ and /i/, previously discussed on page 148.

3. A fronted, unrounded variety of /u/ is heard in the speech of many throughout the country. The sound can be approximated by combining [ɪ] and [u], as you pronounce the vowel in *blue* or *flew*: [blɪu], [flɪu] or [blʉ], [flʉ]. This unrounded or centralized [ʉ] sound is made with the lips in a more relaxed position than is common for /u/. It is found in use all over the country, alongside the /u/ form, and often the same speakers use both forms for the same words at different times. Singers carefully avoid this sound, since the more rounded [u] provides a more resonant tone.

4. Unstressed /u/ before a vowel may weaken to /ʊ/, as in *gradual* and *fluid*: [grædʒʊəl, flʊɪd].

5. For [u-ɪu-ju] variants in *tune*, *duty*, and *enthuse*, see page 123.

Since the phoneme /ʊ/ does not appear in many foreign languages, /u/ is often substituted for /ʊ/ by non-native speakers: *took* becomes [tuk], *good* becomes [gud], and *book* becomes [buk]. The lax sound is easily formed, if the speaker will say the /ʊ/ sound as a short sound, with neutral or relaxed lips.

REVIEW AND PRACTICE SECTION

1. Do you pronounce six clearly distinctive vowel phonemes in each of the following words? *Pa, pop, Paul, pole, pull, pool.* Or does your regional dialect have a fewer number?
2. Transcribe the following pairs of words to see if you use the same stressed syllabic in each: *Carter—cotter, card—cod, part—pot, heart—hot.*
3. Arrange the following words according to the stressed vowel you use for each: /ɑ, ɒ, or ɔ/. Does your speech pattern reflect the discussion in this chapter? If not, where do you differ?

want	hot	stop	on	doll
wash	pot	Bob	gone	dissolve
swallow	odd	pocket	moral	resolve
quality	God	gong	horrible	possible
wasp	lodge	log	forest	posse

4. One sure method to check any difference in the quality between short *o* words and others with /ɑ/ or /ɔ/ is to listen to your pronunciation of the following sets of words: *hat—heart—hot—haughty; cat—cart— cot—caught; map—marble—mop—Maude; harry—hard—horrid— hoary; cad—cod—cawed; palm—pompous—paunch.*
5. What is meant by calling [ou, eɪ, ɪi, ʊu] "nonphonemic diphthongs"?
6. In the following columns of words, the first and third contain historical long *o* words. Do you say these words with the same vowel or do you make the /o-ɔ/ distinction?

oral	borne	for	boarder	coarse	horse
mourning	shored	abhor	story	hoard	sort
four	aural	born	hoarse	border	corpse
hoary	morning	short	sword	stork	horn

7. The following final *o* words are commonly pronounced with final [ɚ] in less-educated speech. Do you? Check each word in a sentence: *tomato, yellow, window, fellow, follow, swallow.*
8. We pronounce the stressed vowels in the following words with either [u, ɪu, ɨu, ju]. Which do you use, and do you use the same vowel in all?

suicide	Tuesday	new	constitution	lucid	shoe
assume	dew	numerous	platitude	lute	blue
resume	duty	nudity	solitude	plume	goose
suit	enthuse	annuity	student	fluke	noon

9. The following /ʊ-u/ words are arranged according to the type of sound following the stressed vowel. Do your friends pronounce these words with the same vowel in each?

broom	hoop	roof	spoon	root
room	whooping cough	proof	soon	soot

10. Transcribe the following sentences:

His father caught the bird on the roof during the morning.
The Cooper Union is a famed educational institution.
The note to obey the warning not to move the hot pots was posted on the far wall.

CHAPTER 9

The Central Vowels

THE STRESSED CENTRAL VOWEL /ʌ/ IN *CUT* AND *COME*

/ʌ/ IS A CENTRAL LOW unrounded vowel, made with the middle of the tongue slightly raised. The tongue position is very close to that of the low back vowels /ɒ/ and /ɔ/. The difference in acoustic value results from the more advanced or central position of the tongue, and the unrounding of the lips. The vowel /ʌ/ always possesses a reasonable degree of stress, and it is usually short in duration. When unstressed, [ʌ] may be replaced by [ə] or [ɪ] so that we transcribe the first syllables of *substance, subterfuge,* and *subsequence* with [sʌb-] and of *subsist, subscribe,* and *subside* with [səb-] or [sɪb-].

[ʌ] is represented in spelling by the *o* in *son* and *come*, the *u* in *sun*, and the *oo* in *blood*. Less common spellings are the *ou* in *touch* and *couple* and the exceptional *oe* in *does*. The four spellings *o, oo, ou,* and *u* may represent the three sounds /ʊ/, /u/, and /ʌ/. When Middle English [oː] became [u] in Modern English times, the *oo* spelling remained, but the sound shortened later in some words to /ʊ/ and in others to /ʌ/. Thus the words *food, foot,* and *flood* represent three different vowels in the English language. Similar changes in pronunciation, but not in spelling, gave us the three sounds in *glove,*

174

wolf, and *move; sun, pull,* and *true.* /ʌ/ occurs in initial and medial positions of words.

Modifications and Variations of the /ʌ/ Vowel

1. The most noticeable variation of this vowel is the use of [ɝ] instead of [ʌ] in those words containing a following intervocalic *r.* *Hurry* and *worry* would be pronounced [hʌri] and [wʌri] by speakers in New York, Boston, and Baton Rouge, while speakers from Buffalo, Dayton, and St. Helena would say either [hɜri] and [wɜri] or [hɝi] and [wɝi]. Actually many speakers in New York City and some in Eastern New England use the [hɜri] forms too.

2. Many actors, whose speech closely approximates British stage speech, use a lowered sound fairly close to our /ɑ/ in words where /ʌ/ is normal in American speech. The normal Received Pronunciation British form in such words as *cut* and *come* sounds like [kat] and [kam] or [kɑ˗t, kɑ˗m] to American ears. This same variation is reported in certain sections of Eastern New England, although it is not used as a distinctive sound for those words in this dialectal region.

3. The stressed forms with [ʌ] for the words *was, wasn't, of, from,* and *what* ([wʌz], [wʌznt], [ʌv], [frʌm], [ʍʌt]; instead of [wɑz], [wʌzn̩t], [uv], [frɑm], [ʍɑt]) commonly have been considered substandard forms. Reasonably widespread usage, however, has admitted them to colloquial standard speech. They do not seem so widely used on the more formal, educated level.[1]

Other Varieties of /ʌ/

1. The substitution of low, somewhat fronted [ɑ˗], or the low-back /ɔ/, for the central vowel /ʌ/ in *up* and *cut,* may be heard in the

[1] All these words appear in the Kenyon and Knott, *Pronouncing Dictionary of American English,* with [ʌ]. The *American College Dictionary* lists [wʌz], [ʌv], and [ʍʌt] but not [frʌm]. Kenyon does not list these restressed forms with [ʌ] as unacceptable in his 10th edition (1951), although he did consider them substandard in earlier editions of his *American Pronunciation.* The G. and C. Merriam Co., *Webster's Collegiate Dictionary,* 5th ed., lists all of these words with ŏ, the "short *o*" of odd. *Webster's New World Dictionary of the American Language* includes the [ʌ] pronunciation for each of these words.

speech of non-native speakers. /ʌ/ is an uncommon sound in other languages and is not too easily distinguished from adjacent phonemes with somewhat similar acoustic values. Such non-native persons should remember that /ʌ/ is normally short and that it is an un-rounded vowel. Listening to the sound and comparing it with other vowels will help establish it in the speech pattern.

2. In a few words, the substitutions of /ɪ/ or /ɛ/ for /ʌ/, as in *just*, *such*, and *brush* are associated with substandard speech. Interestingly enough, these same substitutions (in the same words) are noted as "mispronunciations" in early American spelling books, from the very beginning of the nineteenth century, and they have remained "uncultivated" and "substandard" forms since that time.

THE SYLLABIC /r/ OF *THIRD* AND *MOTHER*: THE CENTRAL VOWELS [ɜ, ɝ, ə, ɚ]

The vowel [ɜ], and its variant [ɝ], are the sounds of stressed syllabic /r/ in English. They are made with the tongue moderately retracted toward the center of the mouth. The front part of the tongue remains relatively flat in the mouth for [ɜ], while an arc is formed with the middle portion of the tongue. (See Figure 29, page 139.) The lips are open and neutral. [ɜ] and [ɝ] are tense, stressed, and usually long vowels. The [ɝ] variant, the more common of the two in American English, results from a retroflexion of the tongue-tip toward the hard palate, a greater retraction of the tongue muscle, or a combination of both. The degree of retroflexion varies from a slight to a considerable turning back of the tongue-tip. [ɜ] is the "*r*-less" vowel sound of *third*, found in Eastern New England, New York City, and the South. It is used instead of the retroflex syllabic /r/, which is heard in most of the country. The retroflex [ɝ] (the symbol actually represents an "*r*-colored" [ɜ]) is the symbol used for stressed syllabic /r/ in the remainder of the country and by some in New York City. Neither of these symbols appear in the IPA chart on page 299 of the Appendix, although they do appear in almost all texts on the phonetics of American English.

[ɚ] is the sound of unstressed syllabic /r/ heard in such words as *father*, *doer*, and *batter*. It is the "*r*-colored" lax, central vowel heard in such syllables throughout the country, except in the "*r*-less" areas of the country: the South, Eastern New England, and, for many, the New York City area. In these areas, [ə] is its normal variant. Thus, unstressed [ə] and [ɚ] vary as do the stressed and higher central vowels [ɜ] and [ɝ].

We recognize that /r/ functions like /l, m, n/ when we compare *battle*, *chasm*, *batten*, and *batter*. In each of these words, /l, m, n, r/ function as syllabic sounds. /r/ is also like the glides /w, j/, as can be seen when comparing the relationship between [u] and [w], [i] and [j], [ɝ] and [r], as was noted in Chapter 6. But in each instance, some special differences make /r/ stand aside. Although /l, m, n/ may function as syllabics, they do so in unstressed syllables only. No words with stressed syllabic /l, m, n/ appear. Yet syllabic /r/ does appear in the speech of most American speakers in both *batter* and *bird*, as an unstressed as well as a stressed syllabic sound. And although the relationships of [i-u-ɝ] to [j-w-r] seem clear, the special circumstance of the [ɜ-ə] of "*r*-less" *murmur*, and their relation to /r/, has no counterpart in the other glides. For these reasons, and those already mentioned in the earlier discussion on /r/, pages 119 to 121, which you should reread, American phoneticians have adopted the four sounds [ɜ, ɝ, ə, ɚ]. The first two allophones of /r/ are used to represent the stressed vowel of *bird*, the last two, the unstressed syllabic of *father*. The [r] symbol is retained for the consonantal form, found before, or between, vowels, as in *red* and *very*.

[ɜ] and [ɝ] are commonly spelled *er* and *ur*, as in *fern* and *burn*. Other spellings are *ear* in *learn*, *ir* in *first*, *or* in *worst*, *our* in *courage*, and *yr* in *myrrh*. The sounds appear initially, medially, and finally in stressed syllables.

[ɚ] and its variant [ə] have almost the same spellings as their stressed counterparts. The common spellings are *er* and *or*, as in *better* and *actor*. Other spellings are *ar*, as in *wizard*, *ir* in *tapir*, *oar* in *cupboard*, *ur* in *murmur*, *ure* in *pressure*, *yr* in *satyr*, and *re* in *sceptre*.

Variations and Modifications of the [ɜ]—[ɝ] Sounds

1. The vowel before intervocalic *r* in *hurry* and *courage* varies between [ʌ] and [ɝ] in American English. Persons who "drop their *r*'s" tend to retain the [ʌ] sound, with the [r] initiating the following syllable: [hʌri], [kʌrɪdʒ]. Those who retain postvowel *r* in their speech pronounce these words with [ɝ] sounds: [hɝi], [kɝɪdʒ], the "*r*-colored" vowel ending the first syllable.

2. When in final position, as in *stir*, *fir*, and *spur*, the sound is either [ɜ] or [ɝ]. In derivative words *(occurrence, stirring, furrier)* some speakers use the variant [ʌ], especially in "*r*-less" areas, by analogy with the sounds in *hurry* and *courage*. Other areas of the country tend to retain the vowel of the stem word. The use of [ʌ] before intervocalic *r* is also found as a variant for [ɝ] in such words as *squirrel*, *stirrup*, and *furrow*. This [ʌ] for [ɜ] substitution is not widespread among educated speakers, although its use seems to be increasing. Authorities differ in their attitudes toward its acceptability.

3. [ɜ] may become [ɜ] plus [r] when the *r* sound is intervocalic, as in *burrow* and *hurry*. The difference is essentially a shift in the syllabification of the word. Those speakers who use [ɝ] split the word as [bɝ-o], the others split the word as [bɜ-ro].

4. [ɜ] becomes [ɜɪ], [ʌɪ], or [ɔɪ] in the speech of some persons. (See Point 2 under *Other Varieties*, below.)

Other Varieties of [ɜ—ɝ]

1. The use of [ʌ] for [ɜ] or [ɝ] as a final vowel, in such words as *her* (stressed), *occur*, *stir*, *sir*, and *blur* is commonly considered a substandard form. This substitution is found sporadically in the speech of cultivated persons but it has not as yet bridged the gap into cultivated usage. Derivative words with the [ʌ] variant, such as *stirring* and *occurrence*, are more widespread (see Point 2 in discussion of variants above).

2. In New York City and the South, the [ɜ] may be diphthongized to become [ɜɪ] or [ʌɪ], and occasionally to [ɒɪ] or [ɔɪ] in such words as

third, *earl*, and *learn*. This diphthongization, often the butt of actors portraying uncultured characters, is widely misunderstood. These forms do appear in the speech of many persons in the South and in New York City. The diphthongs are not limited to the speech of the illiterate, the foreign-born, or the lesser educated, although they are commonly heard in all three instances. Many older native speakers, with fine educational and social backgrounds, use one or more of these diphthongal forms. However, most speakers in both areas use [ɜ] or [ɜə], avoiding the "faulty diphthongs." The common educated forms are [ɜ], [ɝ], or [ɜə]. With a reasonable amount of ear training, it is fairly easy to recognize the subtle differences between the diphthongal forms ending in [ɪ] ([ɜɪ, ʌɪ] or [ɔɪ]) and the [ɜ, ɝ, ɜə] sounds.[2]

THE UNSTRESSED CENTRAL VOWEL /ə/ IN *ALONE* AND *SOFA*

The /ə/ vowel is the lax, central vowel that can occur in any position of a word. It has no such definite position of the articulators as can be noted for any other sound. It is probably best described as a sound made with the articulators in neutral position, with neither spread nor rounded lips, and with the tongue neither forward nor back. Other than for the description of this sound as made in or toward the central part of the mouth, the position of the vowel is indefinite. It is variously called the *schwa* sound, the indeterminate, weak, obscure, or unstressed vowel.

Presently unstressed vowels were somewhat more distinctly pronounced in former times. Although the spelled form of the vowels remained the same, these unstressed vowels gradually became more weak and more indefinite, so that they tended to level into, or to-

[2] A good discussion of the vowels in these words in New York City speech appears in Allan F. Hubbell, *The Pronunciation of English in New York City* (New York, Kings Crown Press, 1950), pp. 67–70. Many of the same points are made in his article on this subject in *American Speech*, Vol. 15 (1940), pp. 372–376. See also John S. Kenyon, *American Pronunciation*, 10th ed. (Ann Arbor, George Wahr Publishing Co., 1951), p. 199; and Charles K. Thomas, *Phonetics of American English*, 2nd ed. (New York, Ronald, 1958), p. 95.

ward, the /ə/ sound. This unstressing is still going on, so that not all unstressed vowels have levelled to /ə/. Thus, the *schwa* sound may be spelled with any vowel, and its formation may approach the position of any other vowel from the central position of the mouth, with the articulators, more or less, in neutral position. The variations of the sound are dependent on the phonetic surroundings of the vowel. It is not an unstressed variety of other vowels, for any stressed vowel may also have an unstressed form. Not necessarily is each unstressed vowel a *schwa*. /ə/ is an entity by itself in our language, and, as such, it is best understood as a separate phoneme.

/ə/ is the vowel commonly found in the monosyllabic definite and indefinite articles, prepositions, conjunctions, pronouns, and helping verbs, as well as many other words not so easily classified: *a, an, the, but, or, for, from, of, her, them, shall, was, can, as* are normally spoken with /ə/, unless stressed. Many other words possess this indeterminate vowel, that cannot be assigned to any other phonemic entity. The italicized vowel of each of the following words is an example of the /ə/ form, as spoken by most, if not by all of us, regardless of regional dialect: remn*a*nt, Portsm*ou*th, circ*u*s, *o*ffend, Tyb*a*lt, purch*a*se, div*i*dend, sep*a*rate, def*i*nite, fright*e*ning, c*o*ndition, c*o*ncise, not*io*n, parl*ia*ment, parc*e*l, par*e*nt, tel*e*vision, hol*o*caust, and des*o*late.

Because of the extensive unstressing of syllables in our language, /ə/ is our most commonly used vowel. It is part of the standard pattern of our language, and its use is not an aspect of "slovenly" or "careless" speech, as so many persons assume. Stressed syllables do not possess this sound, except as the sound may be a nonsyllabic part of a diphthong (see Chapter 10). Unstressed syllables may, of course, possess other short vowels, or the syllabic consonants previously discussed. But /ə/ is the most commonly used vowel sound for completely unstressed syllables of our language.

It is probably not unnecessary to mention that many linguists do not agree with the conclusion that recognizes /ə/ as a separate phoneme. These linguists consider unstressed [ə] merely an allophonic variant of a stressed vowel, no different from the relationship between the stressed and unstressed forms of the same vowels heard in *deem —demonic, speed—speedometer, hiss—historian,* and *spend—Spenserian.* The widely followed Trager-Smith system, described in the Appendix, transcribes the unstressed and stressed vowels of *above* and *under* as [əbˑv/ and /ˈəndər/, and there is strong phonemic justification for this on the basis of complementary distribution (see page 27). However, many other linguists do not agree with this conclusion. They believe that /ə/ may best be conceived of as a separate phonemic category, as an unstressed vowel phoneme, mostly because of the very widely varied nature of the forms that ˎ completely unstressed vowels take, depending on their phonetic surroundings. They see unstressed allophones of /ə/ varying with those of unstressed /ɪ/, /ɨ/, and even /i/, from one dialect to another, and in words of similar surroundings in the same regional dialect. Almost all American phoneticians have found it useful, therefore, to retain the distinction between unstressed [ə] and stressed [ʌ] of *above,* and between the completely unstressed [ə] and the unstressed forms of other vowels which retain greater similarity to their stressed forms than they do to /ə/.

Some linguists, then, prefer using /ə/ as a separate phoneme in American English, recognizing [ə] and [ʌ] as belonging to /ə/. Others, noting the very complex distribution of [ə], believe a separate phonemic category for the unstressed /ə/ is reasonable. The arguments on either side have not culminated in a satisfactory and generally adopted conclusion. We shall follow the widely adopted phonetic tradition and permit /ə/ to exist as a separate, unstressed entity, keeping in mind: that not all unstressed or lesser stressed vowels belong to this phoneme; that the distribution of the unstressed vowels is very complex, and, as yet, hardly detailed for the regional dialects of American speech; that *all* vowels of unstressed syllables are not merely variants of stressed vowels. This last supposition, held too long by many earlier teachers of our language, resulted in a general disregard, if not objection to, the use of [ə] as a normal sound of spoken English. If you are confused by all this, and desire to know a reasonable conclusion, you will have to wait a bit longer. Leastways, whatever conclusions you yourself draw, you will be in good scholarly company.

Modifications and Variations of the /ə/ Vowel

1. In unstressed medial and final syllables, [ə], [ɪ], and [ɨ] are the common forms, with most speakers using [ə] in most words. There is no definite regional pattern, nor for that matter, any evidence that would indicate that one or two of these sounds would be found in certain circumstances to the exclusion of the others. Normally we hear [ɨ] or [ə] before the final labials /p, b, m/, as in *stirrup, scarab,* and *tandem*; [ɪ] or [ɨ] before the final /k/, as in *topic, music,* and *stomach*; [ɪ] or [ə] before final /l/, as in *pencil, metal,* and *funnel.* Some tendency to use [ɪ] or [ɨ] in final syllables when the adjacent consonants are in the alveolar or palatal areas seems prevalent for most of us, as in *parted, scented, fences, roses,* but others of us use only [ə] or [ɨ] in such words. [ɪ] is commonly heard in *horrible* and *animate,* while [ə] is common in *comical, manage, ánimal,* and *hurricane.* In open syllables, [ə] is clearly the more favored vowel, as in *granary, easily, epicure, enemy,* and *tetanus,* although [ɪ] or [ə] are heard in *testify, manicure, Tennyson,* and *codify.* Certainly no "rulelike" conclusion is warranted. If anything, it would seem that the three forms vary freely, as though they belong to a single unstressed phonemic entity. In this regard, however, see pages 149 to 150 and the discussion of /ɨ/ in the next section.

2. The sounds of initial and final lesser stressed and unstressed syllables vary from a shortened, unstressed variant of the vowel, when stressed, to /ɪ, ɨ, or ə/. Note your pronunciation of such words as *event, accept, except, detain, essential, before, command, opinion, Parisian, Afghanistan, affliction, aesthetic, accessory, seasonal, salad,* and *eternal.* Do you need to be reminded that it would be incorrect to assume that a form of the stressed, or spelled, vowel is the preferable form? These weak or unstressed vowels cannot be denied their place in the standard pattern of usage by an attitude that refuses to

recognize them. They are a natural part of our spoken language in all levels of usage.

THE HIGH-CENTRAL /ɨ/ IN *CHILDREN* AND *SWIM*

This high vowel, made with the central part of the tongue high, and with the entire tongue muscle retracted from the position of [i] or [ɪ] toward an "umlauted" or centralized position, is an admittedly "controversial" sound. Known as the "barred *i*," it has come under widespread examination since the publication of the Trager-Smith *Outline of English Structure*.[3] Many students of American pronunciation have tended to relegate pronunciations with [ɨ] to /ɪ/ or /ə/. Writers in the field of descriptive linguistics, however, are beginning to recognize [ɨ] as a separate and distinctive vowel sound. A typical comment is that by H. A. Gleason, Jr.:[4] "The discovery of the phonemic contrast between /ɨ/ and /ə/ has been associated with a complete rethinking of the nature of unstressed vowels."

/ɨ/ has been covered at length on pages 148 to 150, and the details need not be repeated here. It should be remembered that /ɨ/ may not appear in your speech, nor in certain regional dialects of American English, although, as yet, no known data would warrant the latter conclusion. /ɨ/ is a "controversial" sound mostly because we can all avoid using it, usually substituting /ɪ/ or /ə/, without changing the meaning of the word spoken. And, as mentioned in an earlier section, many consider it as an "uncultivated" sound, despite evidence that disputes such a conclusion. Most of us do not hear this sound for the additional reason that it has no special spelled form which can be associated with it.

A fairly clear difference can be heard in the informal or colloquial pronunciation of certain pairs of words. Different sources have presented such pairs and some are repeated here. Not too many stressed forms of /ɨ/ seem to exist in American English. Maybe you can demonstrate others.

[3] *Studies in Linguistics: Occasional Papers, No. 3* (Norman, Okla., Battenberg Press, 1951).

[4] *An Introduction to Descriptive Linguistics* (New York, Holt, 1955), p. 232.

[ɪ]	[ɨ]	[ʌ]
rivet	river	
gist	just (adv., as in "just now")	just (adj.)
Patty	patting	
will he	Willie	
"pretty girl"	"pretty good"	

These stressed forms of [ɨ] are not as common as the use of unstressed [ɨ], where it varies with [ɪ] or [ə] in the unstressed syllables of *children can do, believe, houses, horses, candid.* And you can probably hear, quite easily, the combination of [ɨ] with [u] for *tune, duty,* and *new,* as [tɪun, dɪuti, nɪu], which others might say as [tjun, djuti, nju], or [tuːn, duːti, nuː]. Similarly, words like *shoe, goose,* and *blue* may be heard with this sound too, when not said with a clearly backrounded [uː]: [ʃɪu, gɪus, blɪu].

REVIEW AND PRACTICE SECTION

1. Since the central vowels are sometimes difficult to distinguish from each other, try saying these sets of words, noting the subtle differences in both acoustic effect (including length), and of articulatory position.

[ɑ]	[ʌ]	[ɝ-ɚ]	[ɔ]
bomb	bun	burn	born
cart	cut	curt	cord
stop	stun	stern	storm
hard	hut	hearse	horse
collar	cull	curl	call
upon	pun	pearl	Paul

2. Each of the following words possesses an unstressed, or lesser stressed, initial or final syllable. Which form do you use: [ɪ, ɨ, ə, ɚ] or another lesser stressed vowel?

assort	bigger	duchess	official	anchor	comma
attract	letter	hatchet	orate	languor	music
Apache	Leonard	Abbot	obey	theatre	Barbara
eject	ancestor	barracks	inept	actor	Rose's
uphold	fingered	Elsa	unlearn	record	pencil

3. The medial syllabic unstressed sound in the following words may vary from [ɪ] to [ɨ] to [ə]. Which do you use? Are there certain words here in

which none of these appears, and in which a different, lesser-stressed vowel appears? folio, recollect, percolate, patronize, metaphor, Lillian, Lilliput, seasonal, following, fluidity, comical, penny-wise, ownership, litigate.

4. The subtle distinction in the vowels of the following words is not always heard by non-native speakers. Describe these differences: oil—earl—all; boy—burr—bought; noise—nurse—gnaws.

5. Transcribe the following sentences:

The officers objected to the colonel's threat of a purge.
The surgeon severed the nerve in order to preserve the student's health.
The owner of the theater appeared in the play until the understudy had overcome his nervousness.

CHAPTER 10

The Vowel Clusters: The Diphthongs and Triphthongs of American English

INTRODUCTION

ALMOST ALL the sounds of the language are now known to you. A few sounds still remain to be discussed. These are the vocalic clusters. It is the purpose of this chapter to analyze and detail these clusters of American English, their characteristics, types, and forms. As with the discussion on the consonants and vowels, the common variations of usage are noted, following the introductory discussion of each sound.

The Characteristics of Diphthongs

Diphthongs are best understood when they are compared with vowels. Following are two groups of words and two sentences. Those in the first group are made up of consonants and vowels that have been discussed previously. The second group contains consonants

186

and diphthongs. As you say each word, try to note how the vowels in the first group differ from those of the second group. You must, of course, be sure to listen to the words as you say them, for the spelling alone is not a clue to the presence of a diphthong.

Group 1: fit, get, bat, hot, father, cut

This sentence consists of simple words in which a diphthong does not exist.

Group 2: fight, same, go, toil, sound

Jane tried out Joe's toys.

You can transcribe all of the words and the sentence in Group 1 with the consonants and vowels already discussed. But the words and sentence in Group 2 cannot be transcribed with these sounds. For these, it is necessary to combine certain vowels with certain others to represent the sounds of the words. These vowel-combinations are the diphthongs of the language. They are actually glides, or complex nuclei, consisting of two vowels. Each of these glides begins with a given vowel that *gradually* changes into another vowel. A diphthong, then, is actually a blend of two vowels initiated as one vowel that slowly changes and culminates in the position and acoustic value of a second vowel. Thus, the diphthongs in *pay, my,* and *cow* begin with the [e] or [a] and end with the [ɪ] or [ʊ] sounds. These diphthongs are not two vowels as much as they are glides from one sound to another.

Note also that these diphthongs are one-syllable sounds. Adjacent vowels that are in separate syllables are not diphthongal. The neighboring vowels of *prettier, eon, miscreant,* and *duteous* are separate syllabics ([prɪtɪ-ɚ, i-ən, mɪskrɪ-ənt, djutɪ-əs]), just as are the italicized adjacent vowels in the sentence, "See-*if* H*ugh-i*s going to-*Ann's* part*y-o*n time." The same situation of separate syllabics may be heard in such words as *idiom* [ɪdɪ-əm], *react* [ri-ækt], and *geometry* [dʒi-ɑmətri], where two adjacent vowels exist. Each vowel is the prominent part of its own syllable. But in the words *my, how,* and *joy* [maɪ, haʊ, dʒɔɪ], the two adjacent vowels blend into a diphthong and are part of the same syllable. The prominent part of the diphthong (the first element of these glides) is syllabic, in the same sense that the vowels of *pen* and *pit* are. The second sounds of these diphthongal glides are, therefore, nonsyllabic. They merely close the diphthong, remaining in the same syllable.

It is convenient to recognize the sounds culminating such diphthongs as [aɪ] and [aʊ] as *off-glides*. They are the unstressed parts of these complex nuclei. When the unstressed element initiates the complex nucleus, it is called an *on-glide*, as in [ɪi] or [ʊu]. The peak of sonority of the syllable containing these complex nuclei, or diphthongs, is the point to which, or from which, the on-glide, or off-glide, makes its rapid transition.

Finally, diphthongs are long sounds. Relatively speaking, they are longer than vowels in similar circumstances. Their length varies according to their phonetic surroundings, the stress of the diphthongal word in the sentence, and the nature of the rate and stress pattern of the speaking person. Two generalizations can be noted:

1. The length of a diphthong is dependent on the degree of stress the diphthong-syllable receives in the sentence. The diphthong in *fine* in the sentence, "It's a *fine* tree," is longer than it is in "It's a fine *apple* tree."

2. A stressed diphthong tends to be longer when it appears at the end of a phrase or sentence before a pause than when it appears elsewhere in the phrase or sentence: "Look at that *boy*," *vs.* "Look at that *boy's hat*."

The influence of the phonetic surroundings on a diphthong is not as clear. Most investigations indicate that diphthongs are longer before voiced than before voiceless consonants (compare *house* and *hound*). One study indicates the contrary view, namely that diphthongs are longer before voiceless consonants.[1] Regardless of the resolution of this disagreement, this fact is not as important for our purposes as either of the other two listed.

---

[1] See study by George W. Hibbitt noted in the bibliography. For further comment on this point, see the Parmenter and Treviño, Heffner, and Rositzke sources listed in the bibliography at the end of this chapter.

In summary, the major characteristics of diphthongs may be noted as:

1. A diphthong is a blend of two vowel elements.

2. The vowel blend begins at the position of a certain vowel and glides to that of another vowel, in which position the diphthong ends. There is a continuous change in the vowel quality and acoustic value, from the moment the glide begins until the culminating point.

3. A diphthong is spoken within the confines of a single syllable.

Diphthongs and Shift of Stress

[eɪ]   [aɪ]   [aʊ]   [oʊ]   [ɔɪ]

Take our sample sentence again: "Jane tried out Joe's toys." As you say each of these words now, you are aware that there is a shift in position of the articulators for each diphthongal glide. In addition, each diphthong also manifests a shift in stress from the syllabic or prominent part of the glide to the nonsyllabic or less prominent part of the glide. This shift in stress is characteristic of every vocalic glide. In all of these glides, you can note that the stress recedes or falls from the stressed to the unstressed part of the glide. These glides are, therefore, known as *receding* or *falling* diphthongs. If the stress moves from the unstressed to the stressed part of the glide (as occurs in *see* or *do*, [sɪi, dʊu]) or when we combine the semivowels /w/ or /j/ with a vowel, as in *wet* or *yes* [wɛt, jɛs], the stress moves forward in the word and the result is known as a *rising diphthong*.

The common falling diphthongs are [eɪ, aɪ, ɔɪ, aʊ, oʊ] and all diphthongs ending in [ə] or [ɚ]. The rising diphthongs include the /w/ or /j/ glides plus a vowel, and the two diphthongs [ɪi] and [ʊu] and their variants [ɨi, ɪu, ɨu, ɪu, ɨu]. (See pages 149 and 172.)

Diphthongs and Shift of Position

Although any vowel may theoretically combine with any other vowel to produce a diphthong, there are actually three directions in which our vowel sounds commonly combine. Vowels may go up in the direction of [ɪ] or [i], [ʊ] or [u], toward the high-front or high-back parts of the vowel system, or they may culminate in a vowel made in the central part of the mouth, toward the [ə-ɚ] position. (See Figures 28, 29, 30.) Diphthongs that rise in position, toward [i], are *fronting diphthongs*. Those that rise toward [u] are *retracting diphthongs*, while those culminating in the central [ə-ɚ] are *centering diphthongs*. No dialect of American speech possesses all the combinations with unstressed [ɪ, ʊ, ə-ɚ]. All vowels except [i] may be followed by a high, fronting off-glide: (eɪ, æɪ, aɪ, ɑɪ, ɒɪ, ɔɪ], and the like; all vowels except [u] may be followed by a high, retracting off-glide: [ɪu, iu, ɪu, aʊ, oʊ], and the like; and all vowels except [ə-ɚ] may be followed by the centering [ə-ɚ] off-glide, [ɪə, ɛə, ɑə, ɔə, oə], and the like. Probably all such combinations are heard in the different regions and dialect varieties of American speech.

Fronting diphthongs, culminating in an unstressed off-glide, normally end in the lax vowel [ɪ], while retracting diphthongs usually culminate in the unstressed off-glide [ʊ]. Although front and back diphthongs may end in [i] or [u], the unstressed nature of the off-glide tends to favor a lax [ɪ] or [ʊ] rather than a tense [i] or [u] in these combinations. The stressed nuclei of centering diphthongs are commonly lax, such as [ɪ, ɛ, ɑ, ʊ], or somewhat laxer forms of the normally tense vowels [i, e, ɔ, o]. Diphthongs that rise in stress normally culminate in stressed and tense [i] or [u] as in *see, do, blue*, pronounced as [sɪi], [sɹi], [dʊu], [dɪu], [blʊu], or [blɪu], or in any vowel when preceded by /w/ or /j/.

Incomplete Diphthongs

Diphthongs may be complete or incomplete. The incomplete form commonly occurs in American English with the diphthongs [eɪ] and [oʊ], where the monophthongs [e, o], or these sounds followed by a slight off-glide ([eᴵ, oᵁ]), may appear instead of a full diphthongal form. Our definition of diphthongs should now include the recognition that *they are partial or complete syllabic blends of two vocalic elements that may rise or fall in stress*.

If we consider the possible cluster combinations of vowels that

SOME COMPLEX NUCLEI OF AMERICAN ENGLISH

Vowel	plus [ɪ], [i]	plus [ʊ], [u]	plus [ə], [ɚ]	plus [ɪ] and [ə, ɚ]	plus [ʊ] and [ə, ɚ]
i			[iə]: *we're* [iɚ]: *we're; see her*		[uɪ, ɚu]: *sure, newer*
ɪ	[ij]: *see*	[ɪu]: *new, sue* in Midwest and Mid-Atlantic areas	[ɪə]: *idea* [ɪə, ɪɚ]: *fear, near*		
e	[eɪ]: *bay*			[eɪə, eɪɚ]: *they're coming; fair*	
ɛ	[ɛɪ]: *fail*	[ɛʊ]: *house, out* in Tidewater Va.	[ɛə] as in *yeah;* and as a variant for [æː] or [æə] in *man, bath.* [ɛə, ɛɚ]: *there, care*	[ɛɪ, ɛɪɚ]: *fair*	

Vowel	plus [ɪ], [i]	plus [ʊ], [u]	plus [ə], [ɚ]	plus [ɪ] and [ə, ɚ]	plus [ʊ] and [ə, ɚ]
æ	[æɪ]: heard in the South for *my, high,* etc.	[æʊ]: in *now, cow,* heard as a variant pronunciation for [aʊ] throughout the country	[æə]: *path, bath,* esp. in Atlantic coastal regions; [æə] in *fair, there* in South		[æʊə, aʊɚ] in *flower sour, how* esp. in east coast regions
a	[aɪ]: *buy, bite*	[aʊ]: *now, cow*	[aə]: *park, car* in New England; [aə]: *nice* in South	[aɪə]: *trial, quiet;* [aɪə, aɪɚ]: *fire, higher*	[aʊə]: *fowl, towel;* [aʊɚ]: *flour, tower*
ɑ	[ɑɪ]: *buy, bite*	[ɑʊ]: in *now, how,* esp. in eastern areas; common to stage speech	[ɑə]: *park, car* in New York City and South; [ɑə]: *calm, pa;* [ɑɚ]: *park, car*	[ɑʊə, ɑʊɚ]: *fire, higher*	[ɑʊə, ɑʊɚ]: *towel, flour*
ɒ	[ɒɪ]: *boy*		[ɒə]: variant of [ɔ]; [ɒə] in *law, fall, wash, dog*	[ɒɪə]: *toil;* [ɒɪə-ɒɪə]: *foyer*	
ɔ	[ɔɪ]: *boy*	[ɔʊ]: heard in South for "*you-all*"	[ɔə]: *law, soft;* as variant of [ɔː]. [ɔɚ, ɔɚ]: *course, morning*	[ɔɪə]: *toil* [ɔɪɚ]: *foyer*	

o	[oɪ]: *boy*	[oʊ]: *go, note*	[oə]: *boa; sore, four* in South; [oɚ]: *four, hoarse*	[oʊə, oʊɚ]: *slower, hoarse*
ʊ	[ʊ, uɪ]: *buoy*	[ʊʊ]: *soon, new, food*	[ʊə, uɚ]: *sure, cure, you're*	[uʊə, uʊɚ]: *pure, fewer*
u			[uə, uɚ]: *you're, who're, "two or"* when contracted; rare—more commonly [ʊə, uɚ]	
ɪ	[ɪi]: *see, be* in mid Atlantic areas especially	[ɪu, ɪʊ]: *new, Tuesday* in upper New York State	[ɪə, ɪɚ]: variant of [ɪə, ɪɚ] as in *fear, clear*	[ɪuə, ɪuɚ]: variant of [ɪuə, ɪuɚ] in *sure, newer*
ɜ	[ɜɪ]: *bird, first* in New York and South	[ɜʊ]: *go, hope* in Phila, New York City, and other eastern urban areas	[ɜə]: *third, first*; variant of [ɜː]	
ʌ	[ʌɪ]: New York City, South, for *bird, first; nice:* Ontario	[ʌʊ]: *house, out,* Charleston, eastern Va., and Canada	[ʌə]: *fur, girl* in Atlantic coastal regions	

can produce complex nuclei in our language, we will see that over forty such combinations exist. At least eight simple vowels may combine with [ɪ, ʊ, ə, ɚ]; [ɪ] and [ʊ] may combine with each other and with [ə] and [ɚ]; [ɜ] may combine with [ɪ] and [ʊ] and even with [ə]; the occasionally monophthongal but more normally diphthongal [ɪi, eɪ, oʊ, ʊu] may combine with [ə] and [ɚ] to produce triphthongal clusters; all other diphthongal clusters culminating in [ɪ] and [ʊ] may combine with [ə] and [ɚ] in final *r* words or phrases with following unstressed "are," "or," and the like ("We're going," "Who're you?" "She or I...,"). Some of these clusters are common to all dialects of American speech. Some exist in certain dialects, not in others. No one uses them all. We cannot, of course, detail all these complex nuclei. Both space and knowledge force the limitation to the more commonly heard forms.

Examine the preceding chart of some of these complex nuclei, as heard and reported on in various studies of American speech. At present, there are many gaps in our knowledge of the different combinations of these vowels as they are spoken throughout the country. The speech of the New England farmer, the Texas cattle-hand, the Florida fruit picker, the Dakota rancher, the Michigan factory worker, the New York store clerk, the Alaska fisherman, and the Pennsylvania miner is not completely known to any of us. These gaps will be filled, and maybe completely new clusters inserted, as the evidence of studies now going on indicates.

Representation of Diphthongs

The glide symbols /w, j, r/ are not used for the culminating positions of diphthongs in this text, as in many other texts on the phonetics of American English. A comment explaining the reasons for this appears on pages 112 and 120. These glide symbols are used in phonetic transcription only when they initiate syllables, as in [wɛt] and [jɛs]. Transcription in the Trager-Smith system, previously mentioned, and in other systems adopted by certain phoneticians and linguists, do show these semivowels or glides in culminating positions, so that /w, j (or /y/), r, h/ appear for culminating [ʊ or u], [ɪ or i], [ɚ or ə], respectively. Pronunciations of such words as *now*, *high*, and *far*, transcribed here as [naʊ, haɪ, fɑɚ, fɑə] may appear in these other systems as /naw, haj (or hay), far, fah/. (See Appendix, pages 312–313.)

THE FALLING DIPHTHONGS; THE UPWARD GLIDES: THE /aɪ/ DIPHTHONGAL GLIDE IN *ICE* AND *FLY*

/aɪ/ is found in all positions of words, initially as in *ice*, medially as in *mine*, and finally as in *fly*. It is commonly spelled *i*, although other spellings are used: *ie* as in *lie*, *ai* or *ay* as in *aisle* and *aye*, *ei* or *ey* as in *height* and *geyser*, *uy*, *y*, or *ye* as in *buy*, *fly*, and *lye*.

The initial position of this glide varies between [a] and [ɑ], both [aɪ] and [ɑɪ] being part of the standard, educated pattern. A modified initial element, approaching [ɜ, ʌ, or ə] survives in the eastern sections of the country: in eastern Virginia and eastern Canada (Ontario), where it commonly appears before voiceless consonants, as in *nice* [nəɪs, nʌɪs, or nɜɪs]; in the speech of some older, poorly-educated persons in coastal New England before voiceless or voiced consonants, as in *nice* and *flies* [nɜɪs, flɜɪz].

The substitution of [a] or [ɑ], or these vowels plus the off-glides [ə] or [ɪ], is heard in the South, so that *five* or *time* may be heard as [fa·v, faəv, ta·m, taᶦm, taəm]. This substitution is more common in, if not typical of, the speech of less-educated speakers in the South, although many educated speakers use these forms too. The diphthong is the common educated form, the use of the monophthongal variety increasing as the educational level decreases. The use of [a] or [ɑ] for the diphthong in the contracted forms *I'll* and *I'm* is common to all sections of the country at all levels, so that [ɑːm goʊɪŋ] or [ɑːl si] are not thought of as uneducated forms.

Noticeable retraction of this diphthong to [ɑ˵ɪ], or even [ɔɪ] or [ɒɪ], may be heard in less cultivated speech, as is excessive nasalization of the diphthongal glide as in *fine* or *my*: [fãɪn, mãɪ].

[eɪ] [aɪ] [aʊ] [oʊ] [ɔɪ]
Jane tried out Joe's toys.

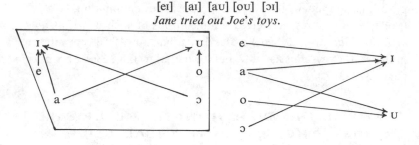

FIG. 32. The common falling diphthongs: stressed to unstressed forms. Upward glides ending in [ɪ] or [ʊ].

THE /ɔɪ/ DIPHTHONGAL GLIDE IN *OIL* AND *JOY*

/ɔɪ/ is found in all positions of words, initially as in *oil*, medially as in *Joyce*, and finally as in *joy*. It is commonly spelled *oi* or *oy*. A less common spelling, *aw*, appears in the word *lawyer*. The initial element of this glide is modified in the speech of many persons to [ɒ]. Both forms, [ɒɪ] and [ɔɪ], are heard in standard American English.

Initial or medial *oi—oy*, as in *oyster* or *boil*, may be heard as [ɜɪ, ɜ̈, or ɝ] in less cultivated speech in the New York City area, so that these words may be heard as [ɜɪstə—ɝstə; bɜɪl—bɝl]. This is not as common a substitution in less cultivated speech as the [ɜɪ] for [ɜ] of *bird* and *third*. Educated speakers in the New York area who may use [ɜɪ] for [ɜ] (see page 178) do not substitute [ɜɪ] for the *oi—oy* words. In their speech, *curl* and *coil*, *oil* and *earl*, *foil* and *furl* are not homonyms. A rare [ɝ] for [ɔɪ] before a consonant may be heard in the South.

In rapid, "careless" speech, /ɔɪ/ before *l* may be shortened to a monophthongal [ɔ·], or [ɔ^ɪ]. "The boiled eggs were spoiled" may sound like [ðə bɔ·ld ɛgz wɚ spɔ^ɪld].

An older /aɪ/ for /ɔɪ/, in such words as *join*, *point*, and *hoist* may be heard in the speech of some older, rural speakers. The former long *i* pronunciation for these words may be seen written as the dialectal "*jine, pint, hist*," [dʒaɪn, paɪnt, haɪst].

A not too uncommon pronunciation of this diphthong in less educated speech results when the initial part of the glide is excessively retracted, with noticeable lip rounding, to [ɔ˞ɪ] or [ɔ'ɪ]. Those speakers who retract the vowel in *ball* and *fall* (see page 167) are more prone to retract the /ɔɪ/ of *joy*. The use of little or no lip rounding, and an attempt to approximate an initial [ɒ], soon removes what most consider a substandard form.

THE /aʊ/ DIPHTHONGAL GLIDE IN *OUT* AND *NOW*

/aʊ/ is found in all positions of words, initially in *out*, medially in *bounce*, and finally in *now*. It is spelled *ou*, *ow*, or *ough*, as in *bounce*, *brow*; and *bough*. Like the other two diphthongs, /aɪ/ and /ɔɪ/, the first element of this glide has two very common forms: [aʊ] and [ɑʊ]. Both are found throughout the country and both are part of the standard speech pattern.

Before voiceless consonants, as in *house* or *about*, a variant [ɜʊ] or [ʌʊ] is found in the speech of all levels in eastern Virginia, Ontario, Canada, and around Charleston, South Carolina, while [æʊ] is heard before voiced consonants, as in *down* and *loud*.

The raising and fronting of the initial element of this glide to [æʊ] is the third major allophone of this diphthong, along with [aʊ] and [ɑʊ]. This fronted glide is common in the South in both educated and less cultivated speech, except of course in the tidewater areas noted in the preceding paragraph. Sometimes Southern speakers are apt to shorten the off-glide to such a point that the diphthong in *how* or *now*, in such phrases as "How are you?" or "Now is the time, "may be heard as [haᵁ (ha:, hæᵁ, hæ:) ɑə ju], [naᵁ (na:, næᵁ, næ:) ɪz ðə taɪm]. [æʊ] for [aʊ] is frequently heard in the Northeast, Midland, and Midwestern sections of the country too, although [aʊ] is the more frequent and favored form.

An excessively lengthened as well as flattened and fronted diphthong, [æ:ʊ], is common in less cultivated speech in the Atlantic coastal regions of the country. This tense, lengthened sound is also commonly nasalized to [æ̃:ũ]. This pronunciation is not common to educated, standard speech.

This diphthong, with its many variant forms, reflects its complex development in America. Our modern diphthong developed from a Middle English long [u:] sound, going through a number of variations of the initial element. Our early spellers in this country first described the sound of *ow* as [ɔu]. Later sources noted it as [ɒu, ɑu, ʌu, and æu], not necessarily in that order. By the nineteenth century, the three sounds [æu], [ɑu], and [ɒu] were common in New England, with a preference for [ɑu] noticed by the 1850's. [æu], or at least a flattened-fronted sound somewhat similar to [æu], was already called a "negligent form," if not a "rustic pronunciation." Earlier, Noah Webster, in his *Dissertations on the English Language* (1789), had called what may have sounded like [æu, ɛu or ᶦæu] a "vulgar singularity of the eastern people...; that of prefixing the sound of *i* short or *e*, before the diphthong *ow*; as *kiow*, *piower*, or *peower*."

As you can see, this diphthong has gone through a number of changes within recent times—from an earlier back [ɔu], through [ɑu] and now to [au, æu]. The direction of the change seems to have been consistently toward the front. [æu] or [aˑu] for [au, ɑu] may not be the favored form today, especially in formal speech, but its use in normal, colloquial speech cannot be "wished away." Many educated speakers use it in their normal pattern of speech. Singers and actors consciously avoid it in favor of the "fuller," more open [au, ɑu].

THE [eɪ] AND [ou] DIPHTHONGAL GLIDES IN MAY AND NO

The diphthongs [eɪ] and [ou] are discussed as nonphonemic variants of /e/ and /o/ on pages 151 and 167–168. These sounds are normally diphthongal, rather than monophthongal [e] and [o], in American English. It will be useful to review those two sections before proceeding to the next section.

THE CENTERING DIPHTHONGAL GLIDES

All front and back vowels may glide into the central vowels [ə] or [ɚ]. Words spelled with *r* following a vowel in the same syllable (such as *fear* or *poor*) are diphthongal forms in our language, inasmuch as the American English /r/ is semivocalic in nature. In the "*r*-less" areas of the country, final /r/ in such words as *fear*, *care*, *for*, and *poor* changes into an off-glide [ə] vowel to form a diphthong with the preceding vowels: [fɪə, kɛə, fɔə, pʊə]. In other areas of the country a nonsyllabic /r/, [ɚ], is heard: [fɪɚ, kɛɚ, fɔɚ, pʊɚ]. In those instances where a final /r/ is dropped, the preceding vowel may be lengthened, compensatorily. *Car* and *scorn* may be heard as [kɑɚ, kɑə, kɑ:] and [skɔɚn, skɔən, skɔ:n].

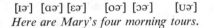

[ɪɚ] [ɑɚ] [ɛɚ]   [oɚ] [ɔɚ]   [ʊɚ]
Here are Mary's four morning tours.

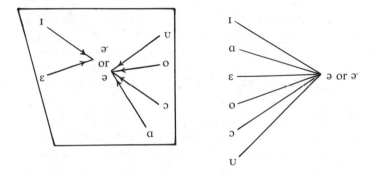

FIG. 33. The common falling diphthongs: stressed to unstressed forms. Centering glides ending in [ə] or [ɚ].

Centering diphthongs, ending in [ə], are heard in certain words where orthographic *r* does not exist. Some, if not most, of the examples listed below probably appear in your own speech. Not all of them are commonly found in every person's speech, nor in each regional dialect of American speech.

1. Vowel plus [ə] before dark [ɫ]: as in *real, really, squeal, veal*—[ɪə] or [iə]; *fail, sail, sailor*—[ɛə] or [eə]; *doll, fall, crawl*—[ɑə, ɒə, ɔə].
2. Normally, syllabic [ə] is absorbed into a glide, reducing the total number of syllables by one, as in *idea* [aɪ-dɪə] instead of [aɪ-di-ə]; *theatre* [θɪə-tɚ] instead of [θi-ə-tɚ]; *theory* [θɪə-ri] instead of [θi-ə-ri]; and *theorem* [θɪə-rəm] instead of [θi-ə-rəm].
3. A normally long vowel diphthongizes, adding an off-glide [ə], as in *Pa* [pɑə]; *log* [lɑəg, lɔəg]; *calm* [kɑəm]; *Omaha* [oməhɑə]; *pajamas* [pədʒɑəməz]; *law* [lɔə]; the informal affirmative *yeah* [jɛə]; *off* [ɔəf]; *Boston* [bɔəstən]; *Spa* [spɑə]; *stand* [stæənd, stæˌənd]; and *bag* [bæəg, bæˌəg].

There is a general tendency to diphthongize all long vowels in English by adding a short, lax vowel to a stressed vowel nucleus. Many of us have no long vowels at all in stressed syllables: [kæn] is always [kæən], [kɔl] is always [kɔəl], and so on. These diphthongal forms are not phonemically different from the simple stressed vowels, but their presence is a factor of considerable phonetic importance. [ɪ] or [ɨ] may be added to front or central vowels, [ʊ] to back or central vowels, and [ə] to all vowels. The Southern tendency to diphthongize most long vowels is probably better known to most of us, for this vowel-breaking tendency seems to be more pronounced in that region than in others. Excessive diphthongization in the South is associated with less cultivated speech: *man* [mæn] > [mæɪn], *head* [hɛd] > [heɪd], *walk* [wɔk] > [wɔᵁk], *gone* [gɔn] > [goᵀᵁn], *fist* [fɪst] > [fɪəst], *apple* [æpl̩] > [æepl̩], *foggy* [fɑgi], [fɒgi] > [fɒəgi].

Diphthongization of English long vowels has a long history, going back in time to before the Modern English period. The tendency to break a long vowel into a vowel plus an off-glide is common to most speakers in all dialects of our language.

Although any vowel may precede [ə] or [ɚ] to produce a centering diphthongal glide, there are five common centering diphthongs. These are [ɪə], [ɛə], [ɑə], [ɔə], [ʊə] and their "*r*-colored" variants [ɪɚ], [ɛɚ], [ɑɚ], [ɔɚ], [ʊɚ] in the words *fear, care, far, for*, and *poor*. The modifications found are those already covered for each stressed vowel of the nucleus, in the chapters on the vowels.

Indicated phonemically, these "*r*-colored" diphthongs may be represented /ɪr, ɛr, ɑr, ɔr, ʊr/. For those regions which possess no postvocalic *r* sounds, the clusters appear as /ɪə, ɛə, ɑə, ɔə, ʊə/. In some regions these clusters vary with each other nondistinctively, that is, both may be heard as variants of the same phonemic entity. Other complex clusters ending in /ə/ or /r/ are used throughout the country. They are noted on the chart on pages 191–193.

TRIPHTHONGAL GLIDES

The upward glides [eɪ, aɪ, ɔɪ, aʊ, oʊ] may culminate in a centering [ə] or [ɚ] in those words where the glides are followed by an orthographic *r*. Triphthongs may be heard in the words *mayor, fire, foyer, hour,* and *blower.* These triphthongs are unstable in our language, however, often breaking into two syllables: [faɪ-ɚ, paʊ-ɚ].

There are no special modifications of the triphthongal forms, except for the insertion of the glides /w/ or /j/ (after [ʊ] or [ɪ]): [meɪjɚ, flaʊwɚ], and so on. Other modifications resulting in such complex vowel clusters are noticed in dialectal Southern speech, when the [æ:] of *last, can't, bad* may become [æɪjə], the [eɪ] of *laid* and *make* may become [eɪjə], and the [ɛ:] of *dress* and *bed* may become [ɛɪjə]. The added /j/ and /w/ in any of these words are common to less cultivated speech, although they do appear sporadically in the speech of some better educated speakers. They are not recognized as part of the standard speech pattern.

Triphthongs may also occur before dark *l*, [ɫ], as in *file, scowl, knoll, pail,* and *foil*: [faɪəl], [skaʊəl], [noʊəl], [peɪəl], and [fɔɪəl]. Although educated speakers are known to use some of these forms, they are found most commonly in less cultivated speech, and are not commonly recognized as part of the educated speech pattern.

THE RISING DIPHTHONGS

/w/ and /j/ plus vowels comprise the other category of diphthongs or triphthongs present in our language. Such words as *we, wear, yes,* and *you* are heard as glide forms, in which the stress moves from the semivowel to the stressed syllabic vowel or diphthong of the word. These rising diphthongs and their variants present no special modifying forms that have not been discussed previously in the preceding chapters. The [ɪi] and [ʊu] rising diphthongal glides are discussed as variants of the /i/ and /u/ sounds in Chapters 7 and 9.

[ʊu]   [ɪi]   [ɪu] or [ju]   [wi]
June's free Tuesdays weekly.

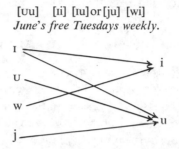

FIG. 34. The common rising diphthongs: unstressed to stressed forms. The nonphonemic diphthongs and /w/ and /j/ initiating diphthongs.

We have now analyzed the sounds of American English—the consonants, vowels, and the sound blends—as they appear in isolation as well as in words and phrases. The common modifications of each are now known to you, and you have had an opportunity to practice your skills of phonetic transcription and sound discrimination. Certain other aspects of our spoken language still need to be discussed for a more thorough understanding of the phonology of American speech. Four of these aspects comprise the final part of this book: pronunciation, sound change, stress, and melody.

REVIEW AND PRACTICE
SECTION—THE DIPHTHONGAL GLIDES

1. Why is it more accurate to call [aɪ] a glide rather than a diphthong (two sounds)? Is the appearance of any vowel following another vowel always a diphthong?
2. Differentiate between rising, falling, incomplete, fronting, centering, and retracting diphthongs.

3. The following list of words contains short, long, and diphthongal syllabic nuclei. Separate them into three columns accordingly, indicating the nucleus for each: *ice, toy, fought, saw, cot, cut, fall, poise, I, kite, dry, first, thirst, foist.*

4. Certain speakers confuse the following pairs. Do you? *pint—point, rile —royal, buy—boy, first—foist, curl—coil, furl—foil.*

5. Describe the differences between the syllabics in each of the following pairs of words: (Example: *mine—Marne.* The diphthongs in both words are falling, the first ending in the off-glide [ɪ], the second in [ə] or [ɚ]. The [aɪ] of *mine* initiates with a low, front vowel, while [aɚ] of *Marne* usually begins with the low, back vowel [ɑ]. The diphthong in *mine* is a fronting diphthong, while that of *Marne* is a centering one.) *toy—turn, tight—tart, cut—kite—cot, got—gout, how—hour, tie—tower —towel, poet—spoke.*

6. The following centering glides are arranged according to the common pronunciations for each group. Have a friend say each word to you. Which does he use?

[ɪə, iə, ɪɚ, iɚ] *fear, sheer, clearly, I see her, Some idea!*
[æɚ, ɛə, ɛɚ]—*there, airy, parent, Hungarian, scarce*
[ɔə, ɔɚ]—*gorge, scorn, morning, horse, border*
[ɔə, oə, ɔɚ, oɚ]—*boarder, hoarse, yore, adore, fourth, store*
[eə, eɪə, ɛə, eɚ, eɪɚ, ɛɚ]—*mail, Bayer, prayer, mayor, player, scale*
[aʊə, aʊɚ]—*flower, devour, scowl, sauerkraut*
[oə, oɚ, oʊə, oʊɚ]—*blower, slower, shoal*

7. Transcribe the following sentences:

Their dinner included clam chowder, sauerkraut, and oysters stewed in brine.

Trying as hard as she could, the child turned the wheel in time to avert the pole.

Each student submitted a critique of the poem studied the night before.

SOURCES FOR FURTHER STUDY

AVERY, Elizabeth, DORSEY, Jane, and SICKELS, Vera, *First Principles of Speech Training* (New York, D. Appleton-Century Co., Inc., 1928), pp. 129–135.

BRONSTEIN, Arthur J., and SHELDON, Esther K., "Derivatives of Middle English O in Eighteenth- and Nineteenth-Century Dictionaries," *American Speech*, Vol. 26 (May, 1951), pp. 81–89.

CAFFEE, Nathaniel M., "The Phonemic Structure of Unstressed Vowels," *American Speech*, Vol. 26 (May, 1951), pp. 103–109.

DE CAMP, L. Sprague, "When Is a Diphthong?" *Le Maître Phonétique*, No. 83 (January–June, 1945), pp. 2–5.

HEFFNER, R–M S., "Notes on the Length of Vowels," *American Speech*, Vol. 12 (April, 1937), pp. 128–134; with W. M. Locke, Vol. 15 (February, 1940), pp. 74–79; with W. P. Lehman, Vol. 15 (December, 1940), pp. 377–380; Vol. 16 (October, 1941), pp. 204–207; Vol. 18 (February, 1942), pp. 42–48; and with W. P. Lehman, Vol. 18 (October, 1943), pp. 208–215.

HIBBITT, George W., *Diphthongs in American Speech* (Privately printed at Morningside Heights, New York, 1948).

HUBBELL, Allan F., "Curl and Coil in New York City," *American Speech*, Vol. 15 (December, 1940), pp. 372–376.

———, "Phonemic Analysis of Unstressed Vowels," *American Speech*, Vol. 25 (May, 1950), pp. 105–111.

HULTZÉN, Lee S., "The Pronunciation of Monosyllabic Form-Words in American English," *Studies in Speech and Drama in Honor of Alexander M. Drummond* (Ithaca, Cornell University Press, 1944), pp. 255–284.

IVES, Sumner, "Pronunciation of 'Can't' in the Eastern States," *American Speech*, Vol. 28 (October, 1953), pp. 149–157.

———, "Vowel Transcription in a Georgia Field Record," *Tulane Studies in English*, Vol. 4 (1954), pp. 147–169.

KENYON, John S., *American Pronunciation*, 10th ed. (Ann Arbor, George Wahr Publishing Co., 1951), pp. 208–234.

MC DAVID, Raven I., Jr., "Derivatives of Middle English [oː] in the South Atlantic Area," *The Quarterly Journal of Speech*, Vol. 35 (December, 1949), pp. 496–504.

PETERSON, Gordon E., and COXE, Malcolm S., "The Vowels [e] and [o] in American Speech," *The Quarterly Journal of Speech*, Vol. 39 (February, 1953), pp. 33–41.

PIKE, Kenneth L., "On the Phonemic Status of English Diphthongs," *Language*, Vol. 23 (April–June, 1947), pp. 151–159.

ROSITZKE, Harry A., "Vowel-Length in General American Speech," *Language*, Vol. 15 (April–June, 1939), pp. 99–109.

THOMAS, Charles K., *Phonetics of American English*, 2nd ed. (New York, Ronald, 1958), pp. 139–146.

———, "Notes on the Pronunciation of *On*," *American Speech*, Vol. 22 (April, 1947), pp. 104–107.

———, "The Dialectal Significance of the Non-Phonemic Low-Back Vowel Variants Before R," *Studies in Speech and Drama in Honor of Alexander M. Drummond* (Ithaca, Cornell University Press, 1944), pp. 244–254.

PART THREE

Sounds and

Context

CHAPTER 11

Sound Changes

INTRODUCTION

IN CHAPTER 1, you became aware of ever-present influences that work against the *status quo* of a language. As a result, the spoken language is never at rest. It is constantly changing, although these changes are never really obvious at any given time. Many of these changes are resisted or delayed, while some are obviated by other strong influences.[1] This chapter analyzes and classifies the more obvious sound changes present in our language. Through a study of the forms of these changes we are able to understand the phonemic relationships between different forms of the same words.

Since these changes are often due to the influence of adjacent sounds, shifts in stress, analogy, or the ease of speech, our discussion must consider the sounds of speech in context with other sounds. Some of these phonetic changes are obvious, others are not. Some are easily explained, while others are seemingly unexplainable. Some changes take place fairly rapidly, while others are slow to take place. Nor is there a point at which we can say that a sound change is about to take place. We can observe change only after it has taken place, or, if enough evidence is available, while it is taking place.

[1] See pages 12–16.

Do not expect to find complete consistency. Sounds surrounded by the same stress and sound patterns will change in certain words, but not in others. The influences that cause phonetic change can be counter-balanced by such other factors as analogy, the psychological barrier of "acceptability," and the spelled form. You will see many such "inconsistencies" in the lists of words demonstrating the different sound changes throughout this chapter.

The matter of "acceptability" deserves special mention here. Certain changed forms have become part of the standard pattern, while others have not. The category of the type of change is not a criterion of acceptability. *Nature* as [neɪtʃʊɚ] and *did you* as [dɪdʒə] reflect the same type of sound change. Your acceptance of one and not the other is only one illustration of the fact that the criterion of acceptability is not dependent on the category of change. It *is* dependent on the extent to which the speech habit is current in educated speech. Widespread use of a changed form will be the sanction it needs for acceptability. If enough students stood and acknowledged a teacher's presence each time he entered the classroom, and if this form of acknowledgement became habitual over a considerable period of time, it would become the *accepted* form of behavior in such situations. Acceptability of the spoken form works very much the same way.

It is also important to keep in mind that sound changes are slow to begin and slow to evolve. Many go on without our being consciously aware of them. And so many have taken place over the period of time during which English has been spoken, that unless we seek them out, we are not aware how different earlier English speaking habits were. No language in use is static. Its grammar, vocabulary, meanings of words, and its phonology are continually being modified. Sound change is probably the most dramatic of these modifications.

Our concern in this chapter does not lead us into a study of the historical changes which have taken place over the history of our language. These are the concern of *historical* or *diachronic linguistics*. Such study accounts for our knowledge of earlier English forms, tracing and explaining such phenomena as the earlier pronunciations of *house* as [hus], of *wife* as [wif], of *point* as [paɪnt], of *father* as [fæðər]. (See "The Background of Our Language" in Appendix A.) And such study in turn leads to the analysis of sounds in related languages, and their comparative development *(comparative linguistics)*, explaining English *day* and German *Tag*; English *three*, Dutch *drie*, and Danish *tre*; French *mère*, Spanish or Italian *madre*, and Portugese *mãe*. The essential concern of this chapter, as it has been throughout this book, is current speech, the study of fairly recent sound changes—those quite recently completed or still going on. Such analysis is a part of *synchronic linguistics* and is separated in intent from the historical approach. Although some diachronic illustrations of sound change may appear, our predominant concern remains synchronic—with the language we use and hear around us.

SOUND CHANGE DUE TO ASSIMILATION

It has long been known that the sounds of a language tend to become similar to, or identical with, a following sound. Latin *ad* and *tenuo* led to the present *attend*, *sit down* may be heard as [sɪd:aʊn], and the two /k/ sounds in *cool* and *key* are influenced by the different positions of the following vowels. These changes result from anticipating the following sound: the *d* of *ad-tenuo* was devoiced in anticipation of the following voiceless /t/; the /k/ sound in *cool* is made farther back in the mouth than the /k/ of *key*, because the tongue anticipates the position of /u/ or /i/ in each word; and the /t/ of *sit* is assimilated into the following /d/ of *down*. These sound changes are the most common in our language. They are known as *anticipatory* or *regressive* changes, because the influence is backwards in the word or phrase, and the speaker anticipates the following sound by changing the preceding one to become more like it. A change in the opposite direction may be noticed in our pronunciation of the word *calls*. The plural form *s* is pronounced as a /z/, while the plural *s* of *cats* remains voiceless. In the former word /s/ > /z/ because of the influence of the voiced *l* before it, while in the latter word, the plural form already follows a voiceless sound. The same kind of a change occurs in *open*, when it is pronounced as [opm̩], where an alveolar /n/ becomes a bilabial /m/ because of the influence of the preceding bilabial /p/. These changes are forward in the word and are known as *forward* or *progressive* assimilations. They are not as common as the anticipatory changes mentioned above.

Any characteristic of a sound may change in the assimilative process. A non-nasal vowel sound may be emitted nasally in *man*: [mæ̃n]. A velar nasal sound, /ŋ/, may be shifted to an interdental position when before a /θ/ sound, as in *length*: [lɛn̪θ]. A voiceless sound may be voiced, as occurs when the /θ/ of *worth* becomes a /ð/ in *worthy*. And a voiced sound may become voiceless, as does the final sound of *walked*.

When one sound is changed *into* a neighboring sound, as in the pronunciation of *horseshoe* as [hɔɚʃu], (s > ʃ), or *cupboard* as [kʌbɚd], (p > b), the assimilation is called a *full* or *complete assimilation*. When a sound is changed *in the direction of* a neighboring sound, as results in the formation of the two /k/ sounds in *key* and *cool*, or when the /n/ of *hand* becomes an /ŋ/ in *handkerchief*, [hæŋkɚtʃɪf], the result is known as a *partial* or *incomplete assimilation*.

An assimilation occurs when a sound becomes more like its neighboring sound. It may become similar to or identical with the sound influencing the change.

Following are a number of assimilations that have already taken place. Some are a normal part of your speech pattern, found in everyday, standard, colloquial usage. Others are not commonly found in educated usage, according to current sources. The failure to use normal assimilated forms may make the speech sound "old-fashioned," "pedantic," or "affected." Widespread use of questionable forms makes the speech sound "careless."

Note each of the following assimilated forms. Those that are considered currently acceptable appear in the first part of each group of words. Those in the second part are either commonly associated with less-educated speech or those for which acceptability is not clearly established.

EXAMPLES OF ANTICIPATORY ASSIMILATIONS

Word or Phrase	Assimilated Forms Found in Colloquial-Educated Speech	Change
comfort	[kʌɱfət	[m > ɱ]
income tax	ɪŋkəm tæks	n > ŋ
pumpkin	pʌŋkɪn	m > n
congress	kɑŋgrəs	n > ŋ
handkerchief	hæŋkətʃɪf	n > ŋ
pancake	pæŋkeɪk	n > ŋ
comptroller	kəntrolɚ	m > n
have to	hæf tu	v > f
used to	justu	z > s
grandpa	græmpɑ	n > m
grandma	græm:ɑ	n > m
on the top	ɑn̪ ðə tɑp	n > n̪
in the box	ɪn̪ ðə bɑks	n > n̪
at the beach	æt̪ ðə bitʃ	t > t̪
newspaper	n(j)uspeɪpɚ	z > s
with time	wɪθ taɪm	ð > θ
horseshoe	hɔɚʃ:u	s > ʃ
don't believe it	dom(p) bəlivɪt]	n > m]

Assimilated Forms
Associated with
Less-Educated Speech

strength	[strɛn̪θ	[ŋ > n
in contact with	ɪŋkɑntækt wɪð	n > ŋ
I can go	aɪ kɪŋgo	n > ŋ
inbred	ɪmbrɛd	n > m
goodbye	gʊbaɪ	d > b
let me	lɛmi]	t > m]

FORWARD OR PROGRESSIVE ASSIMILATIONS

Word or Phrase	Assimilated Forms Found in Colloquial-Educated Speech	Change
open the door	[opm ðə dɔɚ	[n > m
it happens	ɪt hæpm̩z	n > m
wagon train	wægŋ treɪn	n > ŋ
bacon	beɪkŋ̩]	n > ŋ]

	Assimilated Forms Associated with Less-Educated Speech	
ribbon	rɪbm̩	n > m
captain	kæpm̩	tn > m
candidates	kænɪdeɪts	d > n
something	sʌmpm̩	ŋ > m
twenty	twɛni]	t > n]

Reciprocal Assimilations

Reciprocal assimilations occur when both anticipatory and forward assimilations seem to take place simultaneously. Such words as *nature, virtue, picture, mission,* and *vision,* pronounced during the eighteenth century as though spelled "natyure, virtyue, pictyure," and so on, developed palatalized forms with [ʃ] and [ʒ] due to the influence of the /t, s, or z/ and /j/ sounds upon each other. Today, the older forms have disappeared, leaving only the assimilated [neɪtʃɚ, vɚtʃu, pɪktʃɚ, mɪʃən, vɪʒən]. Similar pronunciations, both

assimilated and nonassimilated, were heard for such words as
gradual, graduate, usury, assiduous, and *verdure,* with a favoring of
the assimilated form and a gradual discontinuance of the older,
nonassimilated form. The use of such pronunciations as [neɪtjʊɚ,
grædjʊəl, əprisɪeɪt] in current, educated-colloquial speech is rare
and unexpected. However, *duteous* and *beauteous* are unassimilated,
[bjutɪəs, djutɪəs], while such words as *educate, maturation,* and
nausea are heard both as [ɛdjʊkeɪt, mætjʊreɪʃən, nɔzɪə (nɔsɪə)] and
[ɛdʒʊkeɪt (ɛdʒɚ-), mætʃʊreɪʃən, nɔʒə (nɔʒɪə), nɔʃə (nɔʃɪə)]. The use
of nonassimilated [ɪsju] for *issue* is chiefly British as is the assimilated
[ʃɛjul] for *schedule.*

	Assimilated Forms Associated with	
Word or Phrase	Less-Educated Speech	Change
tune	[tʃun	[tj > tʃ
Indian	ɪndʒən	dj > dʒ
duty	dʒuti	dj > dʒ
he has your coat	hi hæʒjɚ koʊt	zj > ʒ
was your car there	wɑʒɚ kɑɚ ðɛɚ]	zj > ʒ]

VOICING ASSIMILATIONS*

Word or Phrase	Assimilated Forms Found in Colloquial-Educated Speech	Change
letter	lɛtɚ†	t > t̬
butter	bʌtɚ†	t > t̬
thirty	θɝti†	t > t̬
seventy	sɛvn̩ti†	t > t̬
forty	fɔɚti†	t > t̬

* The addition of voice to a voiceless consonant due to the influence of a
neighboring voiced sound.
† The [t] in these words may occur as a weakly aspirated voiceless stop or
as a voiced tap.

Word or Phrase	Assimilated Forms Found in Colloquial-Educated Speech	Change
gosling (from goose)	[gɑzlɪŋ	[s > z
husband (from house)	hʌzbənd	s > z
usurp	juzɝp	s > z
absolve	æbzɑlv	s > z
absurd	æbzɝd	s > z
absorb	æbzɔɚb]	s > z]

	Assimilated Forms Associated with Less-Educated Speech	
got to	[gɑdə	[t > d
notice	noʊdɪs]	t > d]

DEVOICING‡

Word or Phrase	Assimilated Forms Found in Educated Speech	Change
twenty	[twɛnti	[w > ʍ
quiet	kʍaɪət	w > ʍ
quick	kʍɪk	w > ʍ
twice	tʍaɪs	w > ʍ
absorption (absorb)	æbsɔɚpʃən	b > p
resorption (resorb)	rɪsɔɚpʃən	b > p
subscription (subscribe)	səbskrɪpʃən	b > p
prescription (prescribe)	prɪskrɪpʃən]	b > p]

	Assimilated Forms Associated with Less-Educated Speech	
because	[bɪkɔs	[z > s
a good cause	ə gʊd kɔs	z > s
the river flows	ðə rɪvɚ floʊs	z > s
bags	bægs]	z > s]

‡ The removal of voice from a voiced consonant due to the influence of a neighboring voiceless sound or to the pause following the end of the word.

These last four examples are probably more accurately represented by the use of a voiceless z [z̦]: [bɪkɔz̦, kɔz̦, flouz̦, bægz̦]. In normal usage, final z, before a pause, off-glides from the voiced sound to a voiceless sound before the silence: *cause* > [kɔz͡z̦].

DISSIMILATION

An assimilative change, in which one sound is altered to become *more* like its neighbor, is the most common form of sound change. Less common, but equally dramatic, are those changes which occur when one of two recurring sounds is altered to become *less* like its neighbor. In these instances, one of the two repeated sounds is dropped, or it is changed into a different sound. This type of sound-change is known as a *dissimilation*.

You have probably heard the pronunciations [laɪbɛri] for *library*, [gʌvəmənt] for *government*. Dissimilations occur in both instances when the first of the recurring /r/ and /n/ sounds are dropped. A historical dissimilation exists in the word *pilgrim* (derived from the Latin *peregrinum*—note our word *peregrinate*), where an /l/ replaced the first /r/. The word *marble* has an interesting history of dissimilation. The Latin *marmorem* changed in French to *marbre*, the excrescent /b/ acting as a means of separating the two /r/ sounds. Middle English borrowed the French word and showed two forms of it: *marbre* and *marbel*. Our choice today is the dissimilated form [mɑɚbəl]. Some other examples of this type of change are shown below.

Word	Dissimilated Forms Found in Colloquial-Educated Speech	Repeated or Similar Sounds
government	[gʌvəmənt	[n — m
surprise	səpraɪz	ɚ — r
northerner	nɔðənɚ	ɚ — ɚ
library	laɪbɛri	r — r
secretary	sɛkətɛri	r — r
governor	gʌvənɚ	ɚ — ɚ
charivari	ʃɪvəri]	r — r]

		Dissimilated Forms Associated with Less-Educated Speech
chimney	[tʃɪmli	[m — n
environment	ɪnvaɪrəmənt]	n — m]

METATHESIS AND HAPLOLOGY SOUND CHANGES

Two rather peculiar sound changes take place in the pronunciation of certain sounds in context. The first is a reversal of the order of sounds, for example, [æsk] into [æks] for *ask*. This reversal of sounds is known as *metathesis*. The second is the deletion of duplicate elements or syllables, a form of dissimilation known as *haplology*. These sound changes are uncommon. A few of the more common ones are listed below. They are not commonly found in the speech of cultivated speakers.

METATHESIS

relevant	>	[rɛvələnt]
irrelevant	>	[ɪrɛvələnt]
I asked him	>	[aɪ ækst ɪm]
perspire	>	[prəspaɪɚ]
perspiration	>	[prɛspɚreɪʃn]
pronounce	>	[pɚnaʊns]
tragedy	>	[trædədʒi]
elevate	>	[ɛvəleɪt]
rejuvenate	>	[rɪdʒunəveɪt]
hundred	>	[hʌndɚd]

HAPLOLOGY

Mississippi	>	[mɪsɪpi]
Mrs. Smith	>	[mɪs smɪθ]
probably	>	[prɑbli]
particularly	>	[pətɪkjəli]
similarly	>	[sɪməli]

OTHER COMMON SOUND CHANGES

A few other changes of sounds in context occur. These changes have already been covered, in part, in the discussions of the variants of the vowels, diphthongs, and consonants. They are: (1) the nasalization of sounds and (2) the lengthening and shortening of sounds.

Nasalization

Any vowel in the language can be nasalized. The tendency to do so is greatest when there is a nasal sound adjacent to the vowel. Completely assimilated nasality exists for certain vowels in French, where the nasal vowel represents a formerly spelled vowel plus a nasal sound, pronounced as a single nasal vowel at present. If you are a student of French, you know that a nasal consonant, as we know it, does not exist in any of the following words (the nasality has been completely assimilated into the vowel): *faim* [fɛ̃], *Jean* [ʒɑ̃], *bon* [bɔ̃], and *un* [œ̃].[2] In our language, such complete assimilation of the nasal sound does not take place. Some degree of it however, is almost unavoidable when we pronounce such words as *man*, *many*, *candy*, *mean*, and *none*. Such nasalization of the vowels results from the failure of the soft palate to shut off the nasal passage. When nasalization of vowels is excessive, it is considered faulty usage. It results in the kind of speech often labeled as a "nasal twang." Some slight degree of nasality may occur even to *consonants* adjacent to nasal sounds, as in "have more," "He gave Ned . . ." [ṽ]; "with Mary" [ð̃]; "has many" [ž̃]; and so on. Although all speakers are likely to possess some degree of nasality, excessive nasalization is not found in cultivated speech.

The Lengthening and Shortening of Sounds

The lengthening and shortening of sounds is a common occurrence. These concepts too have been discussed previously. They are included here, however, for they are another aspect of sound change.

---

[2] [œ̃] is a rounded [ɛ] sound found in such French words as *chauffeur*, *soeur*, and *coiffeur*.

Lengthening and shortening of vowel sounds are closely associated with the stressing and unstressing of syllables. Stressed syllables normally contain longer vowels, while unstressed syllables possess shorter vowels. Thus the syllable *man* in *dairyman* or *postman* is shortened and weakened to [-mən]. The vowels in the words *have, has,* and *were* are similarly shortened and weakened to [ə] forms when unstressed in such phrases as "I have come," "He has come," and "They were here."

Identical consonants in two syllables are blended into one long consonant in such phrases as *hit Tom, big goose, will Lucy,* and *one night:* [hɪt:ɑm], [bɪg:us], and so on. The three nasals [m], [n], and [ŋ] and the [l] sound are lengthened, normally, when they are in stressed syllables before other voiced consonants, or when final in the phrase. Long vowels tend to break or diphthongize in our language, accounting for the historical change from [hus] to [haʊs], from [wif] to [waɪf], the current pronunciations of *too* and *blue* as [tɪu] and [blɪu], and *candy* and *ask* as [kæ˔əndi] and [æ˔əsk]. The deletion of a post-vowel *r,* in such words as *lark* and *part,* may lead to a compensatory lengthening of the vowel /ɑ/: [lɑːk], [pɑːk].

All these examples of lengthening and shortening of sounds are actually slight variations of the sounds. They are normally disregarded in broad phonetic transcription. They do account, however, for some of the changes of sounds in our language. Further examples of these changes are found below.

The unstressing of a formerly stressed syllable may lead to a change in its phonetic structure. This change is manifested by a change in the vowel toward a shortened form (*man* in *postman* is unstressed and short), the substitution of a syllabic consonant or one vowel for another (*beetle* and *event* become [bitl̩] and [ɪvɛnt]), or the deletion of one or more sounds in the unstressed syllable (*and* may become [n̩d] or [n̩]). The change in a vowel from a stressed form to a lesser stressed or unstressed vowel occurs as a syllable becomes less prominent in the word or phrase. The reverse may occur also—an unstressed vowel may change into a stressed and lengthened form, or into another stressed vowel as the syllable gains prominence. Both of these changes are known as *vowel gradation*. Some examples of each will be found in the lists below.

In certain words the stress-shifts result in the change of a normally unstressed or weaker vowel to a stressed full vowel, as the word assumes a somewhat different form or meaning. The word *the*, in this very sentence, normally contains the unstressed, weak vowel /ə/. When stressed, as in the sentence "This is *the* school," meaning a particular or special school, the phonetic value of the vowel normally changes to /i/. Similar changes of unstressed vowels to other vowels may be heard in the final syllables of each of the following nouns or adjectives as they assume verbal functions: *address, record, separate*; and in the indicated unstressed syllables as the following words assume different forms: *anim̌ate—anim̌ated; vočal—vočalic; Caěsar—Caěsarian.*

LENGTHENED FORMS

Word	Pronunciation with Lengthened Form
card	[kɑ:d
farther	fɑ:ðə
third	θɜ:d
burn	bɜ:n
candy	kæᵊndi
glass	glæᵊs
sings	sɪŋ:z
field	fil:d
take care	teɪk:ɛɚ
set two places	sɛt:u—]

SHORTENED FORMS AS SYLLABLE LOSES PROMINENCE

Word	Shortened Form	Phrase
he	[i or ɪ	Is he here?
her	ə, ɚ, hə, or hɚ	I see her.
she	ʃɪ	Is she coming?
him	ɪm, əm	Give it to him.
them	ðəm, əm	I saw them.
their	ðɚ	It's their own fault.
you	jə	I saw you there.
from	frəm]	Take it from him.

Word	Shortened Form	Phrase
and	[n̩d, n̩	He and John.
could	kəd	I could touch it.
were	wɚ, wə	We were here.
the	ðə	The boy and the girl.
would	wəd	She would see.
was	wəz	He was here yesterday.
there	ðɚ	There aren't any.
shall	ʃəl	We shall come at nine.
can	kən	When can you come?
as	əz	She's as small as he is.
at	ət	He came at once.
does	dəz	What does she do?
had	əd	She had four dresses.
than	ðən	No bigger than a mouse.
what	hwət	I found what I lost.
some	səm	Some other time.
must	məst]	We must go now.

STRESSED FORMS AS SYLLABLE GAINS PROMINENCE
COMPARED WITH UNSTRESSED SOURCE

Source with Unstressed Form	Source with Stressed Form	Sound Change
a	I'll take *a* plum, not two	[ə > eɪ
the	Show her *the* dress	ðə > ði
refer	reference	rɪ > rɛf
associate (adj.)	associate (verb)	ət > eɪt
molecule	molecular	lə > lɛk
spectacle	spectacular	tə > tæk
equal	equality	kwəl > kwɑl
subject (verb)	subject (noun)	səb > sʌb
excellent	excel	sə > sɛl
college	collegiate	lədʒ > li
moment	momentous	mənt > mɛnt
history	historic	tə > tɑr
personal	personality	nəl > næl]

ANALOGY

The change of one sound into another because of the analogy of
a similar word has long been with us. Some of these analogic changes

seem reasonable, others seem strange. We do know that analogic change does not occur easily in commonly-used words. When it does occur, it can often be explained by the lack of such conserving forces as common usage or the spelled form. It is difficult too to explain why analogy will affect one word, but not another just like it.

Our pronunciations of *wife—wives* and *life—lives* should lead us to expect *hoof—hooves* and *roof—rooves*. The pronunciation [huvz] is rare, although our dictionaries do list it. [hufs (or hʊfs)] is the more common form. The plural of *roof* followed the analogy of adding an *s* to the singular form, rather than following the pronunciation with a plural [vz] as in *wives*. The amusing [potɑto] for *potato* results from a mistaken belief that it is pronounced that way by Britishers or New Englanders, by analogy with *tomato* which does possess the [ɑ] in the medial syllable. A popular song appeared out of Hollywood in the thirties, with the words: "You say *tomato* [təmeɪto] and I say *tomato* [təmɑto]; you say *potato* [pəteɪto] and I say *potato* [pətɑto]." Did the lyricist assume that if a Britisher said [təmɑto], he could be sure that he would also say [pətɑto]?

The word *fancy* has an "affected" form. By analogy with such words as *dance, prance, enhance,* and *glance,* which in the Received Pronunciation of British English (or in certain sections of eastern United States) may be heard with [ɑ], *fancy* may appear as [fɑnsi], a created pronunciation of affected speech, since this is not one of the so-called "broad *a*" words. Our pronunciation of *February* as [fɛbjuɛri], possibly explained as an "*r*-dissimilation," can be categorized more readily as a modification of the pronunciation with both "*r*'s," following the analogy of *January* with [-juɛri]. In the earlier discussion of post-vocalic *r* (as in *idea-r* or *law-r-*) you noticed how these "added-*r*" words occurred as a result of analogy with other similar final-*r* words: *fear* was heard as [fɪə], *idea* as [aɪdɪə]; *fear of* as [fɪərəv] led to the analogic *idea-r of* [aɪdɪərəv].

A very interesting use of analogy affecting pronunciation appears in some of our medial "ng" words in English. Have you ever wondered about the confusing use of [ŋ] and [ŋg] in *singer—stronger, youngish—younger*? *Singer* and *youngish* are pronounced with [ŋ], *younger* and *stronger* with [ŋg]. (See pages 106–107.) We know that earlier "ng" was always [ŋg] and that the [g] was dropped when it appeared in the unaccented syllables, as in *walking*, and later whenever final, as in *sing*. The medial "ng" was retained as [ŋg], heard in *finger* and *mingle* and *younger*. But analogy with the [ŋ] of *sing* led to *singer* as [sɪŋɚ], and with *young* to *youngish* as [jʌŋɪʃ], with no velar stops following the [ŋ]. A conflict between analogy and "phonetic law" developed. As a result, we have a confusing use of [ŋg] in *stronger*, but of [ŋ] in *strongly*. *Clangor*, earlier [klæŋgɚ], and still so heard today, has quite recently added the pronunciation [klæŋɚ], by analogy with other "ng" words with suffixed forms. Earlier [hæŋgɑɚ] for *hangar* (the pronunciation during the First World War and thereafter) has given way to [hæŋɚ] so that *hangar* is now a homonym of *hanger*. The pronunciation with the [ŋg] for *hangar* is generally avoided as a "mispronunciation," despite its inclusion in the dictionaries as an educated pronunciation.

Some other minor sound changes occur. Consonants and vowels are modified, in different regional areas and by different speakers in the same regional areas. Such modifications as the fronting, retracting, raising, and lowering of sounds, represented by the symbols [˔, ˕, ˖, ˗], the centralizing of vowels, as in [blü] for *blue*, the vocalizing of certain consonants, as in [mɪʊk] for *milk*, and the restressing of unstressed vowels to new stressed forms, as in [frəm > frəm > frʌm] for *from*, [ɑv > əv > ʌv] for *of*, have been discussed in earlier sections of the text. The addition and deletion of sounds are discussed in the next chapter on "pronunciation."

CONCLUSION

As you can see, sound changes represent one of the most interesting of linguistic phenomena. It was not until fairly recently (the nineteenth century) that the analysis and classification of sound changes were begun. Once uniform phonetic similarities were noticed in the changes taking place, methods for their detection and explanation were presented. Some of these changes seem accidental, failing to fall into a special category. But with the knowledge we now have of the types of change and the phonetic reasons therefore, we are able to appreciate the seeming inconsistencies we sometimes hear around us. With an understanding of sound change, our varying language should make more sense to you than it may have before.

QUESTIONS FOR FURTHER STUDY

1. Define and illustrate the following terms: *assimilation, anticipatory sound change, metathesis.*
2. Can a language ever be static, showing no sound changes over the years?
3. May "careless speech" be defined as that type of speech which permits deletions of sounds? Why?
4. When is a sound change considered part of the standard pattern of usage?
5. Account for the following pronunciations. Indicate whether the change, as noted, is part of standard, educated usage.

was	[wɔz	red top	[rɛt:ɑp
twice	tʌaɪs	going to	gɔnə
envelope	ɛmvəloup	Hogan's here	hougŋz hɪɚ
want to	wɑnə	seventy	sɛvn̩di
had to	hætu	aren't	eɪnt
has she	hæʒʃi	hit you	hɪtʃu
was sure	wɔʒʃuɚ	would you	wudʒə
nice shave	naɪʃʃeɪv	this year	ðɪʃjɪɚ
last show	læʃᵗ ʃou	notice	noṭɪs
call the boy	kɔḷðə bɔɪ	shut up	ʃʌdʌp
pretty	pɚti	children	tʃɪldɚn]
oatmeal	oupmil]		

SOURCES FOR FURTHER STUDY

BLOOMFIELD, Leonard, *Language* (New York, Holt, 1933), "Phonetic Change," Ch. 20, pp. 346–368 and "Types of Phonetic Change," Ch. 21, pp. 369–391. The discussion in this classic text on language details phonetic change with many historical and current examples from English and other languages. A complicated but very valuable discussion.

CARNOY, Albert J., "The Real Nature of Dissimilation," *Transactions* of the American Philological Association, Vol. 49 (1918), pp. 101–113. An older but still excellent account of dissimilation.

FRANCIS, W. Nelson, *The Structure of American English* (New York, Ronald, 1958), pp. 208–220. A short, good review of current (synchronic) sound changes.

HEFFNER, R-M S., *General Phonetics* (Madison, University of Wisconsin Press, 1950), "Speech Sounds in Context," pp. 163–212. A detailed and advanced study of vowel and consonant adaptations, with examples from English and other languages.

KANTNER, Claude E., and WEST, Robert W., *Phonetics* rev. ed. (New York, Harper, 1960), pp. 223–279. Detailing of acoustic and physiologic changes with an especially good discussion on sound incompatibilities on pp. 258–263.

KENT, Roland G., "Assimilation and Dissimilation," *Language*, Vol. 12 (October, 1936), pp. 245–258.

KENYON, John S., *American Pronunciation*, 10th ed. (Ann Arbor, George Wahr Publishing Co., 1951), pp. 76–80. Excellent discussion of assimilation in American English. *r*-dissimilations are illustrated on p. 165; many examples of vowel gradation appear on pp. 96–101.

READ, Allen Walker, "Basis of Correctness in the Pronunciation of Place-Names," *American Speech*, Vol. 8 (February, 1933), pp. 422–426.

SIMONINI, R. C., Jr., "Phonemic Analysis and Analogic Lapses in Radio and Television Speech," *American Speech*, Vol. 31 (December, 1956), pp. 252–263. Analysis of some hilarious contemporary "fluffs" and "bloopers" heard over radio and TV.

STURTEVANT, Edgar H., *An Introduction to Linguistic Science* (New Haven, Yale University Press, 1947), "Assimilation and Dissimilation," Ch. 9, pp. 85–95. Innumerable examples from many languages of these two phenomena.

THOMAS, Charles K., *The Phonetics of American English*, 2nd ed. (New York, Ronald, 1958), pp. 169–190. One of the most readable accounts of the common phonetic changes in American English, with many examples.

WISE, Claude M., *Applied Phonetics* (Englewood Cliffs, N. J., Prentice-Hall, 1957), "Sound Change," Ch. 5, pp. 146–168. A lengthy discussion of sound changes and their causes.

CHAPTER 12

Words

THE DISCUSSION IN THE PRECEDING chapters was concerned, in large part, with an analysis of the sounds of our language. *Pronunciation* is the term used to refer to the result of placing these sounds in context with other sounds, or of combining them to make words and phrases. We commonly refer to the "articulation of a sound," but to the "pronunciation of a word." Our discussion of the pronunciation of words, in this chapter, presupposes an understanding of the nature of these sounds of our language as well as the variant forms they assume.

A study of the pronunciation of words usually implies another concept to most people, the concept of "acceptability." Throughout this text, you have noticed that certain usages are associated with "less-educated speech," while others have been noted as part of "cultivated, or educated-colloquial usage." These pronunciations, not always reflecting your dictionary or even your own impression, have been based on the reported observations of scholars who have studied American pronunciation. These facts of usage, as known and reported, form the basis of acceptability, our own casual impressions or desires, notwithstanding.

Earlier in this text, you were made aware of the phrase "standard speech," and how custom, tradition, authority, sound change, levels and varieties of speech, and regional speech are related to, or associated with, our impressions of "standard." Influences that foster or retard change were presented too. All of these concepts are related to the study of pronunciation, for to a small or large extent, each has an effect upon the pronunciations we use. Three obvious sources affecting pronunciation—spelling, the dictionary, and educated usage—are known to you, for they were discussed, in some detail, in Chapter 1. It will be useful to review a few points about each before we continue our discussion.

For most of us, spelling is our most readily available authority. When time does not permit checking elsewhere, we normally resolve the doubtful pronunciations of words by checking the spelled form. Such dependence on the spelled form is more valuable in a language whose spelling system is closer to a phonemic (phonetic) transcription than ours. Still, this dependence on the spelled form is actually not unwise, *if you are wary of the possibilities that spelling may mislead*, because: spelling does not indicate the variant forms of vowels and consonants; sounds may be pronounced and not spelled; a spelled form may have no spoken counterpart; spelling does not give us any clues to accent or stress. Note what your pronunciation of the following words would be if your only authority in each case was the spelled form: *knee, gnash, knight, one, fete, Esther, sword, whale, anxious, slough, sergeant, deserve, plague, phrase*.

A current, reputable dictionary is a most dependable source for the pronunciation of words, despite the reservations mentioned in Chapter 1. Good dictionaries are readily available to all of us, and the use of a reliable current dictionary is a habit we all must form. It is, of course, essential that we thoroughly understand the sound system (diacritics) of the dictionary we use. And it is necessary to study the key or sample words, the stress-marking system, and the dictionary's comments as to how the sounds should be interpreted. Your check of pronunciation will therefore be accurate only if you interpret the dictionary's sound system accurately.

Many words that you will check in your dictionary will be listed as pronounced in more than one way, indicating that the editors find alternative pronunciations in educated usage. The most usual pronunciation is usually listed first, although one should not interpret from this that the first listing is always preferred. If two alternatives are shown, it is an indication that both are acceptable pronunciations of the word.

No source book is any better than the care and completeness with which it analyzes or represents the speech upon which it is based. A dictionary presents the findings of its editors as they interpret the facts of current usage. The ultimate authority is the language itself, the speech we use to make ourselves understood. Regardless of the biases of its compilers, there is no other accurate source for the editors of dictionaries in making the decisions to include certain pronunciations. Such inclusion is their means of indicating the facts of "acceptable usage." As you already know, a general dictionary does not include *all* the variant pronunciations of its words, even though such variants are known to be "acceptable." The editor selects the most common pronunciations. For other variants, we must refer to pronouncing dictionaries, or texts and manuals particularly concerned with such matters.

We are now ready to look at a few other aspects of the pronunciations of words: the deletion and addition of sounds and syllables in certain words; our pronunciation of "difficult" sound clusters; spelling pronunciations; the pronunciation of foreign terms. The effect of stress, or accent, on the pronunciation of words will be discussed in a separate chapter.

THE DELETION AND ADDITION OF SOUNDS

There are many instances in which sounds are dropped from words as we speak, instances that are not accounted for by assimilative change or dissimilative loss. Many of these deletions are explained by the easing of the speech pattern. Some of them, once considered "careless," are now part of the educated speech pattern. Others have not been able to find their way into educated use.

One special type of sound deletion is already known to you. It is the dropping of a weakened vowel in an unstressed syllable, resulting in a syllabic consonant: *bottle, hidden, chasm* as [bɑtl̩, hɪdn̩, kæzm̩]. The use of syllabic consonants in such words is normal in educated speech. Certain other deletions, not of concern to us now, took place in certain words in former times. Their acceptability today is, of course, unquestioned: *actor + ess > actress; enemy + ity > enmity; cello + ist > cellist.*

/r/, /j/, and /w/ glides are commonly added to certain words in our language. When added within a word or phrase, /j/ and /w/ result from the motion of the articulators from the /i, ɪ/ or /u, ʊ/ vowel positions to the position of the following vowel. In such instances the glides are used as connective sounds. They may be heard in such words or phrases as *higher, flour, high on, he owes, she is, they are, two eyes, now is,* and *you are:* [haɪjɚ, flauwɚ, haɪjɑn, hijouz, ʃijɪz, ðeɪjɑɚ, tuwaɪz, nauwɪz, juwaɚ]. In each instance, the articulators ending the first syllable are close to the initial glide position of the /j/ or /w/ sounds (see pages 113–124). The intruded or added /r/, as in *idea(r) of it and saw(r) it,* has been discussed previously (see pages 121–122).

Sounds are also commonly inserted. Glottal stops may initiate stressed initial vowels, as in "I did," [ʔaɪdɪd] (see page 79). Dark *l* may be preceded by /ə/ as in *feel* [fiəl] and *while* [hwaɪəl]. An /ə/ may appear before the bilabial sounds when preceded by another consonant, as in *dwarf* [dəwɔɚf], *smile* [səmaɪl], and *film* [fɪləm]. The plosive sounds may intrude in *something* [sʌmpθɪŋ], *once* [wʌnts], *bans* [bændz], *farm loss* [fɑɚmblɔs], and *anxiety* [æŋgzaɪəti] (see pages 70, 75, 77).

Some of these deletions or additions of sounds are of such long standing as to have achieved the status of "acceptability." Others still remain the mark of "careless speech." In the lists that follow, currently acceptable forms are separated from those pronunciations for which acceptability is not clearly established.

EXAMPLES OF WORDS WITH DELETED SOUNDS OR SYLLABLES

Word	Pronunciation with Deleted Form, Commonly Found in Educated Speech	Pronunciation with Deleted Form, Commonly Associated with Less-Educated Speech
every	[ɛvri	
chocolate	tʃɑklɪt, tʃɔklɪt	
general	dʒɛnrəl	
interest	ɪntrəst	
considerable	kənsɪdrəbəl	
vegetable	vɛdʒtəbəl	
hygiene	haɪdʒin	
often	ɔfən	
salmon	sæmən	
calm	kɑm	
subtle	sʌtl̩	
almond	ɑmənd, æmənd	
suggest	sədʒɛst	
out of doors	aʊtədɔɚz	
sandwich	sænwɪtʃ]	
geography		[dʒɑgrəfi
poem		poːm
asked		æst
suppose		spoːz
civilization		sɪvləzeɪʃn̩
buffalo		bʌflou
believe		bliv
belong		blɔŋ
liable		laɪbəl
realize		rilaɪz
candidate		kænɪdeɪt
didn't		dɪn̩t
wouldn't		wʊn̩t
crust		krʌs
just wait		dʒʌs weɪt
passed-past		pæs
hold on		houlɑn
recognize		rɛkənaɪz
width		wɪθ
breadth		brɛθ]

	Pronunciation with Deleted Form, Commonly Associated with Less-Educated
Word	*Speech*
acts	[æks
directly	dərɛkli
picture	pɪtʃə
second	sɛkən]

EXAMPLES OF WORDS WITH ADDED SOUNDS OR SYLLABLES

Word	*Pronunciation with Added Form, Commonly Found in Educated Speech*	*Pronunciation with Added Form, Commonly Associated with Less-Educated Speech*
sense	[sɛnts	
once	wʌnts	
prince	prɪnts	
lengthen	lɛŋkθən	
something	sʌmpθɪŋ	
pincer	pɪntsə	
coupon	kjupɑn]	
film		[fɪləm
evening		ivənɪŋ
athlete		æθəlit
grievous		griviəs
school		skuəl
sometimes		sʌmptaɪmz
once		wʌntst
glowing		glouwɪŋ
my own		maɪjoun
highest		haɪjəst
escapade		ɛkskəpeɪd
creator		kriʔeɪtə]

DIFFICULT CONSONANT CLUSTERS

Certain clusters present noticeably difficult problems for the articulators. To promote ease of speaking, certain deletions or substitutions may take place. Some of those commonly associated with less-educated speech may be heard in rapid, or hasty, educated speech, such clusters being difficult to pronounce very quickly. Educated speakers, however, seem to conciously avoid such deletions or substitutions. These substitutions, when made, could well be considered examples of assimilation.

Word	Commonly Found in Educated Speech	Commonly Associated with Less-Educated Speech
clothes (n.)	[klouz]	
sixth		[sɪkst
sixths		sɪksts
depths		dɛpts
hundredths		hʌndrəts
twelfths		twɛlfts
breadths		brɛθs
widths		wɪθs
frosts		frɔs:
expects		ɪkspɛks
insists		ɪnsɪs:]

SPELLING PRONUNCIATIONS

Spelling pronunciation is most noticeable when we come across unfamiliar words. We resort to the spelled form because we are unaware of the normal or traditional pronunciation. Many such spelling pronunciations, when widely enough used, manage to replace traditional pronunciations. The more-commonly used words resist the spelling pronunciations, while less-commonly used words may adopt the spelling pronunciations more easily. In the first group of words listed below, both the spelled and traditional pronunciations appear. In some cases, you will note that the spelled form has become an accepted one, while the traditional form is rare. In the second group of words, the spelling pronunciation is not common in educated speech.

COMMON SPELLING PRONUNCIATIONS IN ACCEPTED USE

Word	Acceptable Spelling Pronunciation	Acceptable Alternative Pronunciation
clothes	[klouðz	[klouz
separate	sɛpəreɪt (v.)	sɛpreɪt (v.)
	sɛpərɪt (n.)	sɛprɪt (n.)
Marlborough	mɑɚlbɚo	mɔlbərə
	mɑlbɚo	mɒlbrə
coxswain	kɑksweɪn	kɑksn̩
Waltham	wɔlθæm – wɔlθəm	wɔltəm
Pall Mall	pɔl mɔl	pɛl mɛl
Mantua	mæntəweɪ	mæntʃʊə – mæntʊə
nephew	nɛfju	nɛvju
every	ɛvɚi – ɛvəri	ɛvri
Thames	θeɪmz	tɛmz—teɪmz
	(for river in U.S.)	(for river in England)
Theobald	θɪəbɔld	tɪbəld
	(American name)	(British name)
vehicle	vihɪkəl	vɪɚkəl
vaudeville	vɔdəvɪl—voudəvɪl	voudvɪl—vɔdvɪl
chocolate	tʃɔkəlɪt—tʃɑkəlɪt	tʃɔklɪt—tʃɑklɪt
government	gʌvɚnmənt	gʌvɚmənt
interested	ɪntərɛstɪd	ɪntrəstɪd
Chatham	tʃæthæm	tʃætəm
forward	fɔɚwɚd	fɔrəd
Wodehouse	wʊdhaʊs	wʊdəs
often	ɔftən	ɔfən
arctic	ɑɚktɪk	ɑɚtɪk
Venetian	vəniʃən]	vəniʃən]

Word	Spelling Pronunciation	Alternative Pronunciation
almond	[ælmənd	[ɑmənd—æmənd
vegetable	vɛdʒətəbəl	vɛdʒtəbəl
extraordinary	ɛkstrəɔɚdənɛri	ɪkstrɔdn̩ɛri
almonry	ælmənri	ɑmənri
constable	kɑnstəbəl	kʌnstəbəl
apothecary	əpɑθəkɛri]	əpɑtɪkɛri (obsolete)]

SPELLING PRONUNCIATIONS NOT COMMON IN EDUCATED SPEECH

chasm	*as* [tʃæzm̩	*for* [kæzm̩
bade	beɪd	bæd
caste	keɪst	kæst
lichen	lɪtʃən–laɪtʃən	laɪkən
schism	skɪzəm	sɪzəm
schismatic	skɪzmætɪk	sɪzmætɪk
sciatic	skaɪætɪk	saɪætɪk
scintillate	skɪntəleɪt	sɪntəleɪt
Scylla	skɪlə	sɪlə
Charon	tʃærən	kærən
sepulcher	sɛpəltʃɚ	sɛpəlkɚ
Charybdis	tʃərɪbdɪs	kərɪbdɪs
Chekov	tʃɛkɔv	tʃɛkɔf
Cimarron	kɪməroʊn, -ɑn	sɪməroʊn, -ɑn
frigate	frɪgeɪt	frɪgɪt
fungicide	fʌŋgəsaɪd	fʌndʒəsaɪd
fungi	fʌngaɪ	fʌndʒaɪ
subtle	sʌbtl̩	sʌtl̩
sword	swɔɚd	sɔɚd
calm	kɑlm	kɑm
annihilate	ənaɪhɪleɪt	ənaɪəleɪt
ptomaine	ptoʊmeɪn	toʊmeɪn
salmon	sælmən	sæmən
alms	ɑlmz]	ɑmz]

THE PRONUNCIATION OF FOREIGN WORDS

No study of pronunciation would be complete without some mention of the pronunciation of foreign words and names. English is a great borrower from other languages. It possesses, in its vocabulary, words from almost every language you have heard. In earlier times, it took many words from Latin and French, and it has since borrowed heavily from many other languages.

The problems involved in the pronunciation of foreign terms are much too complicated to cover in detail here. Pertinent and useful analyses are available in such general sources as *Webster's New*

International Dictionary, W. Cabell Greet, *World Words*, and Claude
M. Wise, *Applied Phonetics*.[1]

There is no fool-proof rule-of-thumb to guide you. The "acceptable" form is best discovered by checking in a current, reliable source.
In general, we tend to retain the native pronunciation of foreign
terms (as much as our phonetic and stress patterns will comfortably
permit) until an Anglicized form becomes established. As these
foreign terms become more and more commonplace, uncommon
phonetic and stress forms become assimilated into our own. Thus
the French-borrowed *valet* is pronounced with a final /t/, *Paris* with
an American /r/ and a final /s/, *garage* with an American /r/ and
an inserted /d/ before the /ʒ/, as an alternate pronunciation to
[gɔrɑʒ]. As to the use of newly arrived foreign names and words,
W. Cabell Greet's words to radio announcers are quoted for your
awareness and caution:[2]

Without seeking to impair any citizen's right to be his own Professor of
English, we look for what is natural, contemporary, and reputable.

... for the most formal occasions and for musical programs, and also in
the case of foreign speakers, the nuance of foreign pronunciations may be
desirable.

The rule, or aspiration, is to adopt the foreign pronunciation insofar as
it can be rendered by customary English sounds in the phrasing and
rhythm of an English sentence.

Following are certain words borrowed from some other languages.
The pronunciations, as listed, are those found in current, educated
American speech. Additional words for practice are found in the
exercise material at the end of the chapter. In the phonetic transcription of each word, a strong or primary stress is indicated by
placing the stress mark *above* and before the syllable, while a medium
or secondary stress will be marked by placing a stress mark *below*
and before the syllable. (A detailed discussion of stress appears in
the next chapter.)

[1] 2nd ed. (Springfield, Mass., Merriam); 2nd ed. (New York, Columbia
University Press, 1948); (Englewood Cliffs, N. J., Prentice-Hall, 1957), Part 4,
pp. 325–532.

[2] *World Words*, 2nd ed. (New York, Columbia University Press, 1948),
pp. xiii, xiv, xv.

THE PRONUNCIATION OF BORROWED WORDS

Source	Word	Current Pronunciation
Latin	alumnus	[əˈlʌmnəs
	de facto	dɪˈfæktoʊ
	habeas corpus	ˈheɪbɪəs ˈkɔɚpəs
	prima facie	ˈpraɪmə ˈfeɪʃɪ
	vox populi	ˈvɑks ˈpɑpjʊˌlaɪ
	per annum	pɚˈænəm
	ecce homo	ˈɛksɪ ˈhomo
	per diem	pɚˈdaɪəm, pɚˈdiəm
French	blasé	blɑˈzeɪ, ˈblɑze
	café	kəˈfeɪ, kæˈfeɪ
	chevron	ˈʃɛvrən
	debutante	ˌdɛbjuˈtɑnt, ˈdɛbjəˌtænt
	attaché	ˌætəˈʃeɪ, əˈtæʃe, əˈtæʃeɪ
	fiancé	ˌfiənˈseɪ, fiˌɑnˈseɪ, fiˈɑnse
	bayou	ˈbaɪu, ˈbaɪju
	divorcé	dəˌvoɚˈseɪ, dəˌvɔɚˈseɪ
	vaudeville	ˈvodəˌvɪl, ˈvodˌvɪl, ˈvɔdəˌvɪl, ˈvɔdˌvɪl
Spanish	pecan	pɪˈkɑn, pɪˈkæn, ˈpikæn
	chocolate	ˈtʃɑklɪt, ˈtʃɔklɪt, ˈtʃɑkəlɪt
	barbecue	ˈbɑɚbɪˌkju
	canyon	ˈkænjən
	patio	ˈpætiˌoʊ, ˈpɑtiˌoʊ
	vigilante	ˌvɪdʒəˈlænti
	mesa	ˈmeɪsɑ, ˈmeɪsə
	matador	ˈmætəˌdɔɚ
	bolero	boˈlɛərou, boˈlerou, bəˈlɛərou
	chihuhua	tʃɪˈwɑwɑ
	caballero	ˌkæbəlˈjɛrou
	rodeo	ˈrodiˌoʊ, roˈdeo
	señorita	ˌsɛnjəˈritə
German	sauerkraut	ˈsauɚˌkraut
	frankfurter	ˈfræŋkfɚtɚ
	schnauzer	ˈʃnauzɚ
	delicatessen	ˌdɛləkəˈtɛsn̩
	meerschaum	ˈmɪɚʃəm, ˈmɪɚʃɔm]

Italian	pizza	[ˈpitsə
	scherzo	ˈskɛərtso
	ravioli	ˌraviˈouli, ˌræviˈouli
	sotto voce	ˈsato ˈvoutʃi
Hebrew	bar mitzvah	ˌbaəˈmɪtsvə
	cabala	kəˈbalə, ˈkæbələ
	kosher	ˈkouʃɚ
	matzoh, matzoth,	ˈmatsə, ˈmatsəθ, ˈmatsəz, ˈmatsəs
	matzohs	
	leviathan	lɪˈvaɪəθən
Chinese	chop suey	ˈtʃapˈsui
	chow mein	ˈtʃauˈmein
Japanese	hara-kiri	ˈharəˈkɪri, ˈhærəˈkɪri
	kimono	kəˈmounə, kəˈmouno
Dutch	cole slaw	ˈkoulˌslɔː
	cruller	ˈkrʌlɚ
	Santa Claus	ˈsæntəˌklɔz, ˈsæntɪˌklɔz
	veldt	vɛlt, fɛlt
American	mocassin	ˈmakəsn̩
Indian	opposum	ˈpasəm, əˈpasəm
	terrapin	ˈtɛrəpɪn
	toboggan	təˈbagən
Russian	bolshevik	ˈbalʃəvɪk, ˈboulʃəvɪk
	intelligentsia	ɪnˌtɛləˈdʒɛntsɪə, —ˈgɛntsɪə
Arabic	mufti	ˈmʌfti
	fakir	fəˈkɪə, ˈfeɪkɚ
Indian	pariah	pəˈraɪə, ˈpæria, ˈparɪə
	dinghy	ˈdɪŋgi]

No complete discussion of the pronunciation of words can be made available in a text. The one source in which you can check the most common pronunciations of many individual words is the dictionary. It is the one authority you can always consult. Nor is there such a thing as *the* dictionary. There are many dictionaries worth consulting, and with which you should have some familiarity. Such dictionaries are noted in the bibliography at the end of this chapter.

QUESTIONS FOR FURTHER STUDY

1. Define and illustrate the following terms: *diacritics, spelling pronunciation, consonant clusters, alternative pronunciation.*
2. In each of the following words, a deleted sound or syllable may occur in colloquial, educated speech. Check the pronunciation of each word, noting the deleted form: *exactly, diamond, generally, interesting, library, government.*
3. A less-cultivated pronunciation (with a deleted sound) is noted for each of the following words. Do you know the "acceptable" form?
   stronger [strɔŋɚ]; *finger* [fɪŋɚ]; *bathes* [beɪz]; *particular* [pətɪkələ]; *five cents* [faɪ sɛns].
4. A less-cultivated pronunciation (with an added form) is noted for each of the following words. Do you know the "acceptable" form?

help [hɛləp]	smell [səmɛl]	across [əkrɔst]
mischievous [mɪstʃivɪəs]	I saw it [aɪ sɔɚrɪt]	see it [sijɪt]
reel [riəl]	the dog's paw	flyer [flaɪjɚ]
escape [əkskeɪp]	[ðə dɔgz pɔɚ]	draw [drɔɚ]
to each [tuʔitʃ]	drowned [draʊndəd]	his own [hɪzʔoʊn]
elm [ɛləm]	blower [bloʊwɚ]	glower [gloʊwɚ]
ringer [rɪŋgɚ]	three in one [θrijɪnwʌn]	two in all [tuwɪnɔl]
clawing [klɔrɪŋ]	iodine [aɪjədin]	raw eggs [rɔɚ ɛgz]
umbrella [ʌmbɚɛlə]	my own [maɪjoʊn]	

5. Check the pronunciation of the following words and names. Indicate the accented syllables.

alumni	brassiere	gigue	Mohave
de jure	crepe	hacienda	dachshund
via	debut	sombrero	prosit
finis	facade	burro	Holstein
gratis	portage	sierra	concerto
data	brioche	junta	adagio
non sequitur	tete-a-tete	cabana	Chianti
Don Juan	Don Quixote	Richard Wagner	Beersheba

6. A number of words possess alternative pronunciations. Some of these alternatives are due to spelling pronunciations, assimilated, or dissimilated forms. Dictionary listings of alternatives signify their occurrence in educated usage. At least two alternative pronunciations exist for each of the following words. Do you know them?

almond	chocolate	generally	Pulitzer
arctic	clapboard	gibberish	pumpkin
absolve	clangor	government	reservoir
absorb	clique	gynecology	room
absurd	clothes	hangar	roof
accolade	combatant	hygienist	route
acoustic	coupon	ideology	status
apparatus	dais	implacable	Singapore
Aryan	data	interesting	sarsaparilla
asepsis	diamond	inveigle	sheathing
baldric	diphthongal	khaki	strata
ballet	diphthongization	lengthen	strength
banquet	digress	length	strengthen
basilica	donkey	Nevada	suggest
beloved	economic	often	tomato
blackguard	ecstatic	pecan	vaudeville
breech	eczema	piano	when
brooch	extraordinary	pianist	where
camphor	forehead	process	
calyx	garage	professional	

SOURCES FOR FURTHER REFERENCE

General Dictionaries

A Dictionary of Americanisms on Historical Principles, 2 vols. (Chicago, University of Chicago Press, 1951). Edited by Mitford M. Mathews. A collection of words and expressions originating in the United States; historical treatment; pronunciation is indicated in the International Phonetic Alphabet.

Funk and Wagnalls New Standard Dictionary of the English Language (New York, Funk and Wagnalls, 1947). Prepared under the supervision of I. K. Funk, Calvin Thomas, and Frank H. Vizitelly. Possesses a section on disputed pronunciations; its special feature is the emphasis upon current information, that is, present-day meanings, spellings, and pronunciations.

The New Century Dictionary of the English Language, 2 vols. (New York, Appleton-Century-Crofts, 1959). Edited by H. G. Emery and K. G. Brewster. A simple diacritic system is used to indicate the pronunciation.

The New Century Cyclopedia of Names, 3 vols. (New York, Appleton-Century-Crofts, 1954). Edited by Clarence L. Barnhart with the assistance of William A. Halsey. The "standard" pronunciation of names from English and other languages, from earlier times to the present day; uses the pronunciation system of *The New Century Dictionary*.

The Oxford English Dictionary, 10 vols. (Oxford, England, The Clarendon Press, 1933). Edited by James H. Murray, Henry Bradley, W. A. Craigie, and C. T. Onions in 10 volumes and a supplement. A monumental work based on the application of the historical method to the life and use of words, showing the history of each word introduced into the language with differences in spelling, meaning, pronunciation over the last 800 years.

Webster's New International Dictionary of the English Language, 2nd ed., unabridged. (Springfield, Mass., Merriam, 1934). Editor in Chief, William A. Neilson, General Editor, Thomas A. Knott, Managing Editor, Paul W. Carhart. Possesses a pronouncing gazetteer, a pronouncing biographical section, and a section on pronunciation written by John S. Kenyon; pronunciation is indicated in the Merriam-Webster diacritic system, following formal, educated speech; the most famous American dictionary.

Desk Dictionaries

The American College Dictionary (New York, Random House), Clarence L. Barnhart, Editor, Jess Stein, Managing Editor.

Thorndike-Barnhart Comprehensive Desk Dictionary, rev. ed. (New York, Doubleday), Clarence L. Barnhart, Editor.

New College Standard Dictionary of the English Language (New York, Funk and Wagnalls), Charles Earle Funk, Editor.

Webster's Biographical Dictionary (Springfield, Mass., Merriam), William Allan Neilson, Editor in Chief, John P. Bethel, General Editor.

Webster's Geographical Dictionary, rev. ed. (Springfield, Mass., Merriam), William Allan Neilson, Editor in Chief, John P. Bethel, General Editor.

Webster's New Collegiate Dictionary (Springfield, Mass., Merriam), William Allan Neilson, Editor in Chief, John P. Bethel, General Editor.

Webster's New World Dictionary of the American Language (Cleveland, Ohio and New York, World), Joseph H. Friend and David B. Guralnik, General Editors.

The Winston Dictionary (Philadelphia, Winston).

Pronouncing and Dialect Dictionaries

GREET, W. Cabell, *World Words*, 2nd ed., revised and enlarged (New York, Columbia University Press, 1948). The pronunciation of some 25,000 personal and place names, and special words; pronunciation is indicated by "a simplified Websterian alphabet" and by a phonetic respelling; especially compiled for radio broadcasters of the Columbia Broadcasting System for which Prof. Greet acts as consultant.

JONES, Daniel, *English Pronouncing Dictionary*, 11th ed. (New York, Dutton, 1956). Pronunciation entries in the International Phonetic Alphabet representing Received Pronunciation of British English.

KENYON, John S., and KNOTT, Thomas A., *A Pronouncing Dictionary of American English*, 2nd ed. (Springfield, Mass., Merriam, 1949). Pronunciation entries in the International Phonetic Alphabet, representing the colloquial speech of cultivated American English with northern eastern, and southern variants.

NBC Handbook of Pronunciation (New York, Crowell, 1943), compiled by James F. Bender for the National Broadcasting Company. Pronunciations are noted in both diacritic and phonetic form, reflecting "General American" usage; prepared for the professional broadcaster.

PALMER, H. E., MARTIN, J. Victor, and BLANDFORD, F. G., *A Dictionary of English Pronunciation with American Variants* (New York, D. Appleton and Co., 1927). Pronunciation entries for Received Pronunciation of British English and containing a column of "American Variants"; in IPA notation; now out of date for many of the American variants shown.

WENTWORTH, Harold, *American Dialect Dictionary* (New York, Crowell, 1944). Deals with dialect in the sense of localisms, regionalisms, and provincialisms; pronunciation is indicated in the International Phonetic Alphabet.

Other Sources

LLOYD, Donald J., and WARFEL, Harry R., *American English in its Cultural Setting* (New York, Knopf, 1956), Ch. 29, "The Dictionary," pp. 458–481.

ROBERTSON, Stuart, *The Development of Modern English*, 2nd ed., revised by Frederic G. Cassidy (New York, Prentice-Hall, 1954), Ch. 11, "The Modern Period-Dictionaries, Spelling," pp. 327–374, and Ch. 12, "The Modern Period-Pronunciation, Variation, and Standards," pp. 375–418.

WEAVER, Carl T., "Don't Look It Up, Listen," *The Speech Teacher*, Vol. 6 (September, 1957), pp. 240–246.

CHAPTER 13

Stress and Pronunciation

INTRODUCTION

THE SOUNDS WE HAVE STUDIED so far are known to students of linguistics as the *segmental phonemes* of our language. As we combine these consonants, vowels, and complex nuclei into words, phrases, and sentences, we add certain other sound-features to these combinations of sounds to make them more noticeable and meaningful. Three conventional sound-features available to us for this purpose are: emphasis or force of utterance, pitch or melodic variations, and pause or the lack of it. These "additives" are known as the *suprasegmental phonemes* of stress, pitch, and juncture. We do not speak without them; our language is always heard with them. We cannot understand the phonology of our language without some analysis of them.

Careful analysis of the distribution of these additional sound-features of our language was begun only recently, and there is not, as yet, real agreement on the details of the conventions of stress, pitch, and juncture. The awareness of these phenomena during the speaking process is not new, however. The arts of the public speaker, reader, and actor have always made special use of these sound-

242

features. Each practitioner of these arts spends much of his time and energy on these features of our language as he prepares his material for performance.

Each of us is aware that normal, conversational speech makes use of such sound-features too. Texts on speech and voice have always dealt with them. The analysis of the distribution of these phenomena of our speech, however, affording us the possibility of isolating some of the special characteristics of each, is a recent contribution to our thinking about the English language. Our function in this section is not to consider stress, pitch, and juncture as they are used by the artistic performer on the platform or stage, but rather as essential aspects of the structure of the language we speak in normal, face-to-face conversation.

STRESS AND THE MORPHEME

The segmental phonemes of our language, when combined in certain conventional ways, provide us with meaningful units of the language. The combination of the phonemes /k/, /æ/, and /t/ may be arranged to produce the English words [kæt], [ækt], and [tæk], while the sounds /i/ and /ð/ may be combined to produce the English utterance [ði]. As meaningful units of the language, these combined phonemes may be spoken with degrees or levels of pitch and stress. Linguists call a minimal, meaningful unit of such phonemes a *morpheme*.

The study of morphemes (morphemics) belongs to the study of grammar and syntax. As such, it is beyond the scope of our study here. The study of morphemes follows the study of phonemes, since morphemes consist of combinations of phonemes. We need not get involved in morphemic study, however, although it will prove useful to understand the concept, since the features of stress, pitch, and juncture are associated with morphemes, or sounds in meaningful context, rather than with isolated phonemes.

The following forms are identified as morphemes: *a, they, the, good, follow*, and *banana*. Note that each consists of one or more phonemes, signifying a minimal, meaningful unit of utterance in our language. The *-ess* of *duchess*, the *-or* of *actor*, and the *-y* of *funny* are morphemes for the same reason, that is, each is a minimal, meaningful unit: the *-ess* ending designates the feminine form of a noun; the *-or* ending denotes "one who does something"; the *-y* ending means "characterized by." The italicized words at the beginning of this paragraph cannot be broken into smaller meaningful forms, or into smaller parts with their own meanings. The *fol* of *follow* is part of the word but it is not separable from the rest of the word as an identifiable form in our language: it has no meaning of its own. It is neither a base or stem of the word, nor an inflected form, such as a prefix or suffix. Similarly the *low* of *follow* cannot be identified as a morpheme, nor can the "oh." Although [loʊ] and [oʊ], in other contexts, are known to us as meaningful units of utterance in English, they are not separable parts of *follow*. We can see, then, that *follow* is one complete, minimal unit, incapable of separation into smaller, meaningful parts. Such units of utterance are known as "free forms" in linguistic study—they can stand alone. *Banana* would be similarly classified, as would *aspirin, gorilla, humid, child, a, they, the*, and *good*.

Princess, singer, and *hairy* are also "words" to us, but we can see that each consists of two identifiable forms: a stem or base, to which the suffixes *-ess, -er*, and *-y* have been added. These latter are known as "bound forms." They are part of larger forms and cannot stand alone.

Morphemes, then, may be bound or free. They may be words, or parts of words. They may combine with other morphemes to create simple words *(speak + ing > speaking; re + ceive + er > receiver)*, compound words *(pen-knife, blackbird)*, and phrases or sentences *(The other day . . . or It is.)*.

The smallest possible morpheme in our language is a monosyllable and, therefore, the smallest unit capable of assuming stress is the syllable. Stress is part of each syllable we speak, and every syllable possesses some degree of it, varying from great, or very strong prominence, to very little or weak prominence. The relationship of pitch and stress is such that a heightening or lowering of one is generally accompanied by a change in the other. Many students of our language do not recognize the existence of stress and pitch as discrete sound features. They designate the different levels of pitch as the concomitants of changes in stress. Still other students of our language have submitted evidence to show that a strong syllabic stress is not necessarily accompanied by a higher or lower pitch, nor by any other *single* acoustic factor. The relationship between stress and pitch still needs to be studied. Our purpose will not be served, however, unless we discuss them separately. Stress is the concern of this chapter, pitch, that of the next.

LIMITATIONS

Our discussion will be limited, at first, to certain aspects of word-stress. We know that the stress attached to a word may change as the word assumes its place in the sentence, depending on the speaker's intent. To begin with, however, we shall not concern ourselves with "sense-stress," the emphasis placed on words in phrases or clauses. We shall not attempt an analysis of the conventional stress patterns found in different declarative or interrogative sentences *(He did go.* vs. *Did he go?)*, nor in enumerative expressions *(She washes bottles, dishes, clothing, and her kitchen floor each day)*. Nor need we concern ourselves here with the different applications of stress which help determine and convey thought, mood, or feeling when reading poetry, acting a part, or making an address.

A final limitation on our discussion of word-stress, is the recognition that many words are stressed differently in different regional areas of the country, and the details of such variation are not fully known. Dialect studies of the sound features of our language do not commonly detail the stress differences heard in the pronunciation of words, as they do other sound features. We know that such variations exist, but we do not know the extent of such variations. Professor Daniel Jones reports that, in educated British English, a change in the stress picture of certain words may be heard from Northern to Southern England. In *The Pronunciation of English*[1] he notes that Northern Britishers pronounce the following words with the stress on the italicized syllable: crit*i*cize, recog*nize*, recon*cile*, inter*view*, *Ju*ly, *mag*azine, *vi*brate, con*cen*trate, and il*lus*trate, while the Southern Britisher normally says *crit*icize, *rec*ognize, *rec*oncile, *in*terview, Ju*ly*, maga*zine*, vi*brate*, *con*centrate, and *il*lustrate. And he further reports that different Received Pronunciation speakers in the South of England pronounce the following words with the different stresses shown below. He points out that the words in the second column demonstrate pronunciations which may be due to northern influence and which are not shown in most dictionaries:

*hos*pitable	hos*pit*able
*ex*quisite	ex*quis*ite
in*ex*plicable	inex*plic*able
*for*midable	for*mid*able
*dir*igible	dir*ig*ible
*con*troversy	con*tro*versy
*in*teresting	inter*est*ing
*in*tricate	in*tric*ate
*jus*tifiable	justi*fi*able

American English possesses similar dialectal stress variations in many words. If you have lived in different parts of our country, you may have heard educated speakers pronounce the following words with seeming regional differences: *ci*gar—cig*ar*, *cig*arette—cigar*ette*, *OK*—O*K*, *al*most—al*most*, *ro*deo—ro*deo*, *pe*can—pe*can*, *in*surance —in*sur*ance, *in*fluence—in*flu*ence, *af*ternoon—after*noon*, *ro*tate— ro*tate*, ad*ver*tisement—adver*tise*ment, *re*late—re*late*, *de*tail—de*tail*. Probably you know many others. Our discussion of word-stress, then, does not preclude the fact that for certain words, the stress pattern may vary due to regional differences. Such instances are not common enough, nor are the variations so different from area to area, that we must alter the conclusions we shall reach.

[1] (Cambridge, Eng., Cambridge University Press, 1950), p. 139.

LEVELS OF STRESS

We recognize syllabic stress as normally resulting from, or accompanying, an increase of loudness, duration, and/or a rising pitch of the voice. Differences of stress are, of course, relative, yet distinctive enough to be noticed by any native speaker of English. Using the symbols /′, ‵, ˇ/ to represent primary (or strong), secondary (or medium), and weak, respectively, the following words may be marked with clearly contrastive stresses: *wĭndў, găráge, sŭ̆fficiĕnt, pérmĭt* (n.), *pĕrmít* (v.) to show strong and weak stresses; *díctiŏnàrў, cóncĕntràte, àntárctĭc,* and *mánĭcùre* to show all three levels of prominence. Some students of American English believe that four distinctive stress levels should be noted, using /′, ^, ‵, ˇ/ for primary (or greatest), secondary (or strong), tertiary (or medium), and weak prominence, respectively. This four level system has been widely adopted by those who believe the three level system overlooks the distinctive contrasts between /^/ and /‵/.[2] They point to such contrasts as the following to prove their contention: *lông íslănd* vs. *Lòng Íslănd, bláckbìrd* vs. *blâck bírd* (the species vs. a dark bird), *bluéfìsh* vs. *blûe físh* (the species vs. a colorful fish), *hîgh cháir* vs. *híghchàir* (a tall chair vs. baby's special chair), *élĕvàtŏr-ôpĕràtŏr* vs. *êlĕvàtŏr òpĕrátiŏn,* and *greèn house* vs. *greénhòuse* (a colored house vs. the plant-house). Those convinced that American English possesses only three clearly distinctive stresses indicate that the /^/ and /‵/ of the four level system may be considered variants of a medium stress, which can be either "full" or "light." They note that the contrasting examples used to demonstrate the four stress system depend on certain special constructions, and that with a recognition of these constructions, three levels of stress are sufficient to point out the relative stress differences.[3]

We are presently concerned with the stresses commonly found in

[2] See, for example, George L. Trager and Henry Lee Smith, Jr., *An Outline of English Structure, Studies in Linguistics, Occasional Papers, No. 3* (Norman, Okla., Battenberg Press, 1951), pp. 35–39.

[3] See, for example, Stanley S. Newman, "On the Stress System of English," *Word,* Vol. 2 (December, 1946), pp. 171–187.

isolated, polysyllabic words, and for such we do not need to identify more than three levels of stress. A clear contrast can be made between syllables with strong prominence and those with less force of utterance by the use of three levels of stress. It is not necessary, for our purposes here, to indicate any "in between" levels.

THE INDICATION OF STRESS

Stress, or accent, marks are conventionally indicated in dictionaries by placing an appropriate mark over and following the stressed syllable: *above¹, re¹gal, lan¹guage, ed¹uca¹tion*. A heavy accent mark is commonly used after primarily-stressed syllables, a lighter mark for secondarily-stressed syllables. Too often dictionaries omit the secondary accent marks, assuming that the reader will recognize that full vowels are normally pronounced with greater prominence than are weaker vowels. Your dictionary will probably show *attenuate* with a stress mark after *-ten-*, but with no secondary mark after *-ate*. A check of the word *demilitarize* will show a primary stress on the second syllable, but no stress mark on the initial *de-* syllable. True, the initial syllable of this word is not shown with the same diacritic symbol of the unstressed *depart*, the long *ē* of *demilitarize* sounding longer and possessing greater stress than the shorter *ĕ* or *ĭ* of *depart*. The difference of stress used in the longer word, however, is not made clear. Dictionary editors have their many problems, and certainly the clear indication of accent marks is not yet resolved by them.

Phonetic transcription has developed its own conventions, placing all stress marks *before* the stressed syllable: stress marks appear above the line for strongly-stressed syllables, and below the line for secondarily-stressed syllables. Weakly-stressed or unstressed syllables are unmarked: [əˈbʌv, ˈbɛndɪŋ, ˈbʊkˌkeɪs, ˈkɑnˌtɛnt]. This system permits the recognition of both stress and sound quality at a glance.

Another system of stress marking has been developed recently and is gaining many adherents. It retains the normal orthographic form of the word (although it can be used for phonetic and phonemic respelling too) and places the appropriate stress mark directly over the syllabic nucleus: an acute accent mark, ('), for strong or heavy stress, a grave accent mark, (`), for medium or secondary stress, and a breve mark, (˘), for weakly-stressed or unstressed syllables—*dĭc-tĭonàrў, ìntĕrrúptĭŏn*. Often the breve marks are omitted as understood. We shall use the last method mentioned for indicating the stress in words spelled in the Latin alphabet—*cóntènt* (n.), *inítiàte* (v.)—as well as the method explained in the previous paragraph when the pronunciations are phonetically transcribed—[ˈkɑnˌtɛnt, ɪˈnɪʃiˌeɪt]—since both are commonly used in phonetic and phonemic discussions.

The term *unstressed syllable* is actually a misnomer. In reality, every spoken syllable is pronounced with some degree of stress, from much to little. An "unstressed syllable" refers to one with minimal stress or prominence, and it should always be so considered. It is not a syllable with no stress at all. "Unstressed syllables" may vary from the lesser-stressed initial syllables of *affect*, *reserve*, and *depart* to hardly any stress or prominence at all, heard in the initial sounds of *among* and *alive*, or in the final syllables of *cover* and *mountain*. (Unstressing as a phenomenon of sound change is discussed under "lengthening and shortening of sounds," and "vowel gradation" in Chapter 11, pages 217–220.)

STRESS IN POLYSYLLABIC WORDS

All words of one syllable possess a strong or primary stress when spoken out of context. Since it is understood that all such words carry stress, the indication of any accent mark is conventionally omitted. Disyllable words possess one primary stress and a lesser-stressed syllable, and most disyllables possess the primary stress on the initial syllable, as in *paper*, *mention*, and *Sunday* [ˈpeɪpɚ, ˈmɛnʃən, ˈsʌndi]. Some two-syllable words, however, are spoken with the stronger stress on the second syllable, as in *allow*, *belong*, and *suggest* [əˈlaʊ, bəˈlɔŋ, səgˈdʒɛst]. The differences between strong and medium stresses may be noticed in the pronunciation of such words as *thìrteén, sénìle, blàsphéme, dígèst* (n.), *cóndùct* (n.), *chíldlìke,* and *núrsemàid.*

In a few polysyllabic words, almost equal strong stresses may be heard, with both stresses spoken as either of almost equal prominence, or one of full medium prominence, the other of strong, primary prominence. Such almost-even stress occurs where each part of a compound word tends to retain most of the original force of its separate identity. In such instances, the two stressed syllables are marked with strong stress marks: *árchbíshŏp, íce-créam, hándmáde, óvĕrféd, sémĭcírcŭlăr,* and *óvĕrpróud.*

Polysyllabic words normally contain one strong, or primary, stress, preceded or followed by weakly-stressed or secondarily-stressed syllables. In *déífy̆, sóciălìze, cóncĕntràte,* and *óctăgòn,* the stress pattern is strong, weak, medium. In *díctĭonàrў* and *sécrĕtàrў,* we use strong, weak, medium, weak stresses; in *ăbómĭnàte* and *pĕrógătìve,* the stresses are weak, strong, weak, medium; in *fèrmĕn-tátĭŏn, pèrsĕcútĭŏn,* and *ùndĕrstándĭng* the pattern of stresses is medium, weak, strong, weak. A check of these and other polysyllabic words will soon convince you that the incidence of syllabic stress is not a simple matter for the uninitiated.

JUNCTURE AND SYLLABIC STRESS

You may have noticed in your pronunciation of those words listed with two strong stresses, that equal primary stress on two parts of the same word does not seem to occur unless the two parts are separated by a break or pause between them. If we pronounce *árchbíshop, íce-créam,* and *hándmáde* as noted, we tend to separate the stressed syllables from each other as we do when we say "good dog," "well done," "not now," and "black bird." This break or pause seems to be heard each time we pronounce two strong stresses next to each other, the break separating the two primary stresses in the three levels of stress system ('-'), or two primaries or a primary and secondary in the system containing four levels of stress ('-^). Before continuing our discussion of stress then, it will be useful to examine this special role played by the break or pause between syllables.

Since the point between two sounds may be called a "juncture," linguistic analysis recognizes two kinds of juncture that may occur between phonemes. They are known as *close* and *open junctures*. The lack of any break between syllables results in a normal transition between sounds. In the words *fry* and *desk*, no break occurs between any of the sounds of each word, [fraɪ] or [dɛsk], nor do we hear a break between the syllables of the words *funny* or *walking*, [fʌni, wɔkɪŋ]. This normal transition between sounds or between syllables may be called a *close juncture*. *Open juncture* is the term used to describe the pause or break that is heard between two syllables of the same word or of adjacent words. There are only a few words containing this open transition between sounds, and as we shall soon see, such open transition seems to be closely associated with stress.

The juncture between sounds may be heard in the contrasting pronunciations of the phrase "not at all," of the name "Plato," or of the phrase "ten tees," when in contrast with the word "tenting"— all with different phonetic modifications. Although we are concerned with juncture and stress, rather than with juncture and phonetic modification, the dividing line between them is not always a clear one. The phonetic modifications that are due to juncture are complicated and are not fully known. Some relationship between any two of the three factors of stress, juncture, and phonetic change may be observed, however, by a simple analysis of the contrasting pronunciations of the words and phrases noted above. The pronunciation of "not at all" with a break, or open transition, before *all* (which we shall indicate with a plus sign, /+/) [ˈnɑtət + ˌɔl] rather than as [ˈnɑtə + ˌtɔl], may change the quality of the /t/ toward the voiced variety. In the second pronunciation, where the juncture and the stress precede the syllable beginning with /t/, the resultant /t/ sound is aspirated. This same kind of /t/ would be heard in the phrase "a tall man," where the juncture and stress precede the word *tall:* [ə + ˌtʰɔl —]. The pronunciation of *Plato* as "plate-oh," with a juncture after the /t/, permits the speaker to use a lesser aspirated /t/

than he would normally use if he said the word as "play-tow." If the speaker pronounced both syllables with a normal transition between them and with no such prominence to the second syllable, [ˈpleɪtoʊ], a voiced /t/, [t̬], would not be uncommon. In "ten tees," an open transition is heard between the two words, and with the stress as indicated here, [ˈtɛn + ˌtiz], an aspirated /t/, [tʰ], would be expected. In *tenting*, pronounced as [ˈtɛntɪŋ], no juncture separates the two syllables, nor does stress appear before the final syllable, and the second /t/ is not as fully aspirated as the first.

One additional instance may serve to point up the relationship of juncture to phonetic modification, and may also serve as a means of identifying the open transition /+/ as a phoneme. The presence of an open juncture in *slyness* [ˈslaɪ+nɪs], not heard in *minus* [ˈmaɪnɪs], results in a relatively longer diphthong in the former word. The length difference is not explained by any other phenomenon.

We may be ready, now, to make some generalizations about juncture:

1. The open juncture between sounds is our means of separating syllables in the stream of speech. Its presence may also be associated with stress. Two strong stresses do not exist next to each other without a pause or break between them. That break may be an open juncture /+/, or a longer one that may occur at the end of a clause or a sentence.

2. The open transition does not normally appear between two syllables when a stressed vowel is followed by an unstressed vowel, as in *seeing*, and *see a man* [ˈsiɪŋ, ˈsi ə ˌmæn]. The open transition may appear between two stressed vowels as in *my own* [ˌmaɪ+ˈoʊn], *aorta* [ˌeɪ+ˈɔ˞tə], or *see ours* [ˌsi+ˈaʊ˞z], when a primary stress appears on the second of the two adjacent vowels.

3. A /+/ may be the only means of establishing sense differences between the same adjacent consonants and vowels, as in *an ice man* vs. *a nice man* [ən+ˈaɪsˌmæn, ə+ˈnaɪsˌmæn], or between the same consonants in separately stressed syllables, as in *nitrate* vs. *night+rate*.

Other details of open juncture still need to be studied before we shall be aware of all its manifestations. We can see, however, that since its presence or absence may result in a minimal contrast between otherwise similar groups of phonemes, it belongs with the other suprasegmental phonemes of English. We do not normally indicate an open transition in phonetic transcription except in words when it is necessary to point out its significance, or when transcribing a phrase as a unit, and the /+/ is needed to indicate the break. At other times, the space between words serves to signify the open juncture between sounds, as do a single bar [|] and double bar [‖] for short and long pauses between phrases and clauses.

RHYTHMIC AND RECESSIVE ACCENT IN POLYSYLLABIC WORDS

A study of large numbers of polysyllabic words will lead us to the conclusion that two tendencies may be noted in the accentuating of these words: one is a rhythmic pattern, the other the tendency to push the accent toward the front of the word. The rhythmic pattern of our speech may be noticed in the tendency for stresses to recur at regular intervals in sentences as well as in words. We quite naturally alternate the syllables of polysyllabic words from strong or medium stress to little stress. Some of the following words show this tendency: *pólkădòt, póckĕtboòk, Hémĭngwày, ăppréciàte, prŏpríĕtòr, ànĭmósĭty̆, cònstĭtútĭon, prŏnùncĭátĭon,* and *dìăléctĭc.*

In contrast with this tendency of an alternating, rhythmic stress pattern is the one which moves the accent forward in the word, as in *próbably, góvernment, véhemence, cháncellor, précipice, génerally, cómparable, áccuracy, présidency, délicately,* and *pérmanently.* The use of this recessive accent is more noticeable in the British pronunciation of certain words, where the strong stress is at the initial syllable and a possible secondary accent deleted: *dictionary* [ˈdɪkʃənrɪ] or [ˈdɪkʃənərɪ], *stationary* [ˈsteɪʃṇərɪ], *oratory* [ˈɒrətrɪ], *territory* [ˈterɪtərɪ] and *dormitory* [ˈdɔːmɪtrɪ]. In certain other words, the British speaker moves the stress toward the front of the word, on the second syllable, losing the secondary accent which we, in America, retain, with a considerable difference in the end result. In each of these words, *laboratory, capillary, obligatory,* and *centenary,* we place the primary accent on the first syllable and a secondary accent on the penultimate syllable (the syllable before the last). Daniel Jones lists the first pronunciation of these words in his most recent edition of *Everyman's English Pronouncing Dictionary* (1956) as [ləˈbɔrətərɪ, kəˈpɪlərɪ, ɒˈblɪgətərɪ, sɛnˈtinərɪ, -ˈtɛn-]. The last pronunciation may also be heard in the United States alongside [ˈsɛntəˌnɛrɪ]. The others remain marks of British pronunciation.

SHIFTING STRESS

A change in the stress picture of certain words ([ˈɪnfluəns—ɪnˈfluəns, ˈkænˌnɑt—ˌkænˈnɑt, ˌjɛsˈsɝ—ˈjɛsˌsɝ]) may be attributed to dialectal or individual preference. A change in the stress pattern of a word may be the result of a desire to indicate a contrast between two similar words, as when a speaker desires to point out the difference between *biologic* and *geologic, offense* and *defense, fourteen* and *fifteen,* when the differences in similar words receive the primary stress which permits the desired contrast. Either of the stress shifts mentioned causes no change in the meaning of the word. In other instances, however, a change in the stress pattern of a given word is noted as the result of the change in the function of the word or in the syntactic circumstances in which the word is found.

Where words may function both as nouns (or adjectives) and verbs, the difference in the stress is our clue to meaning: *dischàrge* (n.) vs. *dischárge* (v.), *dèsèrt* (n.) vs. *dèsért* (v.), *úpsèt* (n.) vs. *ùpsét* (v.), *fréquĕnt* (adj.) vs. *frĕquént* (v.). The use of primary stresses and an open juncture /+/ between both of the following syllables indicates we have said two words rather than a compound word with a different meaning: *híghchàir* vs. *hígh+cháir,* the species *blúefìsh* vs. the colorful *blúe+físh,* the gardener's *gréenhòuse* vs. the painted *gréen+hóuse,* Mr. *Gréenhùt* vs. a *gréen+hút,* and the species *bláckbìrd* vs. a *bláck+bírd.* A similar meaningful change results from a stress

change in the following phrases: *the Frènch teácher* (from France) vs.
the Frénch tèacher (in the language department), *the òrange treés*
(painted by the child) and the *órange trèes* in the grove, [ˈbɛ˞skɪn]
(bearskin) and [ˌbɛ˞ ˈskɪn] (bare skin), *wálking stìck* (carried by an
older person) and the impossible, *wàlking stíck*. In each of these
instances, the primary stress on the adjective results in a compound
noun, while the use of a primary stress on the noun permits
the continued functioning of the preceding word as a descriptive
word.

In certain words a stress change occurs because a stressed syllable
is placed before another one and the alternating rhythmic pattern of
the language ˙asserts itself. Words of this type possess variable
accents, depending on their place in the sentence. Note how you
pronounce the indicated word in each of the following sentences:

ideal: This place is ìdéal. This is an ídéal pláce.
nineteen: He is just nínèteen. He is nìnèteen yéars old.
upstairs: Take the package úp + stáirs. Put it in the úpstàirs róom.
tight-lipped: She is very tíght + lípped. She is a tíght-lìpped pérson.
almost: The child is a genius, àlmóst. He is álmòst a genius.
red-hot: The stove is réd + hót. It's a réd-hòt stóve.

Some of the above generalizations do not always hold true, however. There are certain disyllabic words which retain a primary stress
on the second syllable for both nouns and verbs. The words *pérmit*,
áddress, and *rédress* (relief) are nouns; their verbal forms shift the
primary accent to the second syllable. But *permít*, *addréss*, and
redréss are heard as nouns too. The nouns *detail* and *defect* are heard
with the primary accent on either syllable: *détail* and *défect* or *detáil*
and *deféct*. Nor is it always true that all "adjective-noun" constructions (like *orange trees* or *French teacher*) retain the primary stress
on the nouns when the intent is "adjective-noun" and on the descriptive word when it is a "compound noun." There are other factors
which may influence the stress pattern: for example, *girl scouts* is
normally heard with (´ `) when we desire to contrast them with the
expression "boy scouts." "A big house" will be spoken with a different stress pattern when we compare the house with other houses

or when we contrast it with cottages or mansions. And certain forms may be "institutionalized." Do you change the stress pattern when you talk about *Sitting Bull* (the man) from the one you might use in "a sitting bull"? Don't you keep the primary stress on *bull* (or *Bull*) both times?

In a provocative article called "Stress and Information,"[4] Dwight L. Bolinger makes the point that the only way we can predict the stresses used would be to know the "dynamics of the utterance." However we may ultimately analyze the stresses of English, it is difficult to avoid the conclusion that a complete study of the phenomena of stress will have to lead us into the study of syntax, speaker-impressions, and communicating-desires—the areas of grammar and interpretation. Both are beyond the scope of the phonological treatment here.

In general, then, (1) stress shifts may result from the desire to intensify the contrast in similar words; (2) in most disyllabic words which may function as nouns, or adjectives, and verbs the stress shifts from the first syllable of the adjective or noun to the second syllable in the verb: *cóntract, éxtract, dígest, ínsult, cónvict, próject, cóncert, súrvey,* and *íncrease* are nouns, while *contráct, extráct, digést, insúlt, convíct, projéct, concért, survéy,* and *increáse* are verbs; (3) in other pollysyllabic words, we tend to omit the secondary accent for the nouns or adjectives, retaining them for the verbs: *éstimate, cómpliment, órnament, delíberate* are nouns or adjectives, while *éstimàte, cómplimènt, órnamènt,* and *delíberàte* are verbs (note well that some American speakers make no distinction between the noun and verb forms of *compliment* and *ornament*); (4) stress shifts in certain words may be an indication of individual or regional preference; (5) stress shifts may result from the presence or absence of stress in neighboring words; (6) stresses appear differently in special grammatical constructions, or as the impressions or desires of the speaker necessitate his making such changes.

⁴ *American Speech*, Vol. 33 (February, 1958), pp. 5–20. See also Lee S. Hultzén, "The Poet Burns' Again," *American Speech*, Vol. 31 (October, 1956), pp. 195–201.

CONCLUSION

Our discussion of stress cannot be disassociated from the meaning intended, for although it is possible to confine our discussion to the incidence of accent or stress in words, it soon becomes evident that the utterances may change as the intensity desired for the word in the sentence changes. Although each word is stressed when uttered alone, each such word would not carry a strong stress in a sentence. Each of the words *the—boy—is—good* will carry a strong stress when said alone. In the sentence "The boy is good," only two strong stresses normally appear. Should the speaker decide that any one word is more important than another, the stress given that word will be of greater intensity than would be used in other situations.

A first-grade child may read the words of a sentence as though each word is of equal import, giving to each word equal stress. Such reading, sounding as if it were a series of items on a grocery list, does not convey the information expected from a normally spoken sentence. With the child's ability to read will come his use of the varied stress patterns we associate with literate, intelligible reading and speaking. Actually when we think of a word, we think of it as it is spoken in the context of a phrase or sentence, for except in a list of words, any given word is merely a transition from one utterance to another in the verbalized train of thought. Words, as we know them, are not isolated combinations of a few phonemes which are separable from other such utterances in the sentence. We do not think of the pronunciation of words isolated from the pronunciation of the rest of the sentence. Therefore, the stresses with which we hear words spoken are the stresses they receive as part of larger contexts. There can be no question about the fact that stress cannot be disassociated from meanings intended.

The phonetic changes resulting from the changes in syllabic stress were mentioned in Chapter 11, pages 217–220. These changes need not be discussed again except to remind us that a change in stress is inseparable from some phonetic modification of the sounds in the syllable. Changes may be heard in the length of the sounds affected, as in [hit ɪt ˈʌp] vs. [gɛt səmˈhiː t]; in a change of the syllabic nucleus, as in [ˈgɛt mi ˌsʌm] vs. [ˌgɛt səˈmː it]; in the loss of certain sounds as the syllable unstresses, as when *and* becomes [n̩] in [nɛd n̩ læri]. As already mentioned, phonetic changes may also result from the addition of a juncture to a group of sounds. The open transition heard in *Plato* as "play + tow" rather than as "plate + oh" or "playto" permits our hearing not only the break between the sounds as indicated, but also an aspirated variety of /t/ rather than an unaspirated, or even voiced, variety. Since /t/ assumes a different phonetic form when before a stressed vowel from the form used when before an unstressed vowel or when it completes a syllable, [ˈpleɪ+ˌtʰoʊ], [ˈpleɪt+ˌoʊ], and [ˈpleɪt̮oʊ] may be heard not only with different transitions, but with different phonetic forms of /t/.

Recent investigations of the structure of American English have led to the recognition of the phonemic interpretation of stress. We already know that a change in the use of a primary stress will change the noun *cóntènt* to an adjective *cŏntént*, or that the addition of stress to the last syllable of *estimate* will change it from a noun to a verb. (The pronunciation of *estimate* with stress on the last syllable will change it from [ˈɛstəmɪt] to [ˈɛstəˌmeɪt]. [ˈɛstəˌmɪt] is not a normal form.)

Similar stress changes are used as we intend a sense change in various sentences. Using the system of four stress phonemes in connected speech (/ ′ ^ ` ˇ/ for primary, secondary, tertiary, and weak stress, respectively), the meaning of the following sentence undergoes a radical change as we change the stress pattern. The sentence "She likes Mary's dress," with the following pattern, Shê likes Máry̆'s drèss, means she prefers Mary's, not Jane's dress. Should the stress pattern change to Shé likes Màry's drêss, the implication now is, "She may like it, but I don't." The meaning of a speaker is made clear by the different phonemic stresses used. Although there are allophonic variations of stress, just as there are allophones of consonants or vowels (and even if there is, as yet, no real agreement on the actual number of stress phonemes found in the dialects of American English), there is no doubt that without an understanding of the phonemic concept of stress, we are unable to complete our discussion of the phonology of our language.

We have discussed stress with barely a mention of how pitch or melody are affected by stress, or how stress may be affected by pitch. As noted earlier, changes in the levels of stress are normally accompanied by changes in pitch levels. Just what these pitch levels are, and how they function, are the concern of the next chapter.

QUESTIONS FOR FURTHER STUDY

1. Demonstrate how a stress may change because of meaning or the influence of adjacent stresses in a phrase.
2. Why can stress be considered a phoneme in our language?
3. What happens to the stress pattern in the following words and phrases?

> *left-handed*   vs. *left-handed pitcher*
> *ice-cream*   vs. *ice-cream soda*
> *big-boned*   vs. *big-boned man*
> *heart-broken* vs. *heart-broken girl*

4. Transcribe the following words with primary and secondary stress markings: *apple pie, contract* (n.), *straightedge, milkman.*
5. How would you indicate the differences between: *known eater—no neater*; *Jensen—Jen sent*; *sincere—sin-seared*; *gray skies—Grace Kize.*
6. Arrange the following words by placing all with primary accents on the initial syllables in one column and those with primary accents on the second syllables in another column: *general, athletic, kindergarten, vehement, genesis, evasion, battalion, gunwhale, socialize, curator, pregnant, prejudice, pneumatic, chronoscope, garage, America, government, tyranny, marathon.*
7. Transcribe the following words with primary and secondary stress marks: *ammonia, chameleon, withdraw, familiar*; *inquisition, ostentation, predication, animosity, marijuana, genealogy*; *appreciation, portfolio, abominate, proprietary*; *octogenarian, dialectician, diagrammatic, osteopathic*; *psychoanalytic, counterrevolution*; the nouns: *refuse, increase, produce, combine, convert*; the verbs: *refuse, increase, produce, combine, convert.*
8. How might a stress and juncture shift change the meaning of:

She swims like a weakfish, not a weak fish.
He bought six tea-towels, not sixty towels.

9. Each of the following words possesses an alternative pronunciation which is due to a shift in the stress of the word. Do you know two pronunciations of each?

abdomen	harass	applicable
detail	defect	decadence
exquisite	primarily	alloy
acclimate	decorous	precedence
adult	despicable	aerial
advertisement	adverse	allies
exchequer	perfume	chauffeur
illustrate	conversant	resource
gladiola	hospitable	quintuplets

CHAPTER 14

Pitch and Melody in

American English

IF YOU WERE TO WALK into a room full of talkative people, you could tell whether they were speaking English or some other language, even if you couldn't hear the words they were saying. Our language is spoken in certain patterned melodies, and there are instances where the melody we use carries almost as much meaning as the words themselves. You know that a skilled violinist can make his instrument "speak." He can play a melody which we recognize as a question, the doubtful acceptance of an opinion, or the strong affirmation of a belief. If skilled enough, the violinist can make the violin sound like a speaker from another country by playing those melodic patterns associated with another language. We can appreciate his skill because we know, even without careful analysis, that there is a structure to the language melodies we use, and that the different pitches and the connectives between them are not random and haphazard, but quite definite and distinctive from other melodic forms. These variations, or contours, of melody are combinations of different phonemic pitches and terminal inflections. As such, they are morphemes of our language, just as are other meaningful combinations of phonemes. In order to complete the study of our language, the student of American-English pronunciation must understand what these pitch phonemes are and how he can record them.

Stress, juncture, and pitch are the three recognized suprasegmental phonemes mentioned in the preceding chapter. All are interdependent in English. Although there is no actual correlation between stress and any one acoustic phenomenon, stressed utterances are normally spoken at higher pitch levels than are lesser-stressed or unstressed syllables, so that a change of stress in the sentence normally affects the pattern of pitches used. Stressed utterances do not *necessarily* possess higher or lower frequencies, longer durations, greater intensities, nor special vocal qualities. (Some recent studies indicate that stress can probably be analyzed more accurately by a study of bodily (muscular) motion than in terms of any single acoustic phenomenon.)[1] Similarly, the different pauses we use in the stream of speech are related to the pitch patterns preceding them. Recognizing this relationship does not prevent us from analyzing the distinctive features of each separately, as was done with stress and juncture in Chapter 13, and which will be done with pitch here.

Intonation is defined as a contour of melody consisting of different pitches and a terminal inflection. To understand intonation we must identify the different pitch levels we use, the shifts of pitch between or on syllables, and the melodic characteristic of the terminal points of an utterance. Intonation cannot be disassociated from the meaningful content of speech. It is also one of the means through which the speaker may express the emotional coloration he adds to the spoken words. The study of intonation is complicated because it is so variable, being influenced by so many factors. A speaker's mood may be angry, petulant, cordial, declarative, or matter-of-fact. Each mood may affect certain parts of the melodic contours he normally uses. In addition, the situation in which the speaker appears affects the melodic line. The actor and reader on the stage, the

[1] See, for example, Peter Ladefoged, M. H. Draper, and D. Whitteridge, "Syllable and Stress," *Miscellanea Phonetica III* (London, International Phonetic Association, 1958), pp. 1–14.

speaker on the campaign platform, over the radio, or TV, and the conversationalist in the living or dining room, make varying use of the normal intonation contours and the pitch levels which are part of them. Our concern in this chapter is to isolate and describe some of the essential features of American-English intonation, as well as to indicate their methods of representation. How the professional actor, public speaker, or reader applies pitch and melody is not analyzed here. Such belongs to the special art of the theater and the public platform. Our concern is the analysis of the melodies we all use in normal, conversational situations. The artist-performer's is the artistic use of them.

Since 1775, when Joshua Steele first studied the pitch changes as they occur on syllables, leading him to a system of pitch notation for speech, many students of speech and voice have made significant contributions to the study of English speech melody. Many more studies will be made before we know as much about the melody of speech as we know about the sound structure of our language or the function of the parts of the mechanism which produce speech and voice.[2]

[2] Joshua Steele's study was called *Prosodia Rationalis*. His contribution is analyzed in John B. Newman, "The Phonetic Aspect of Joshua Steele's System of Prosody," *Speech Monographs*, Vol. 18 (November, 1951), pp. 279–287; and in the same author's "The Role of Joshua Steele in the Development of Speech Education in America," *Speech Monographs*, Vol. 20 (March, 1953), pp. 65–73. Soon after Steele's work, John Walker published his *Elements* of *Elocution* (1783), in which he attempted an exhaustive analysis of melodic inflection and grammatical structure. Among other contributions worth noting are those of James Rush, who, in 1827, published a detailed system for noting vocal pitch; Daniel Jones, who recognized the constant movement of pitch during a spoken line (1909); Harold Palmer, who established the melodic parts of a sentence (1922); Walter Ripman, who indicated three different levels of pitch (1922); Lilias Armstrong and Ida C. Ward, who developed a system of dots and curves between two lines to represent the height of the voice on each spoken syllable, and explained the meaningful significance of rising and falling melodic patterns (1926). More recently, Hans Kurath has worked on the relationship between meaning, the speaker's attitude, and intonation, while Bernard Bloch, George L. Trager, Henry Lee Smith, Jr., Lee S. Hultzén, Dwight L. Bolinger, Rulon Wells, and Kenneth Pike, among others, have been interested in the analyses of pitch levels, and contours, and the relation between stress and pitch. These studies are listed at the end of this chapter.

Let us begin by noting that the melodic pattern of one language differs from that of another, and that, by itself, it is an important characteristic of that language. The melody, or intonation, is an indication of a particular dialect of a language too. The dialects spoken in Boston, Massachusetts, Atlanta, Georgia, and Glasgow, Scotland differ not only in the vowels and consonants the people use; they possess slight or great differences in melody too. Russian, Italian, English, and Hebrew possess distinctive melodic patterns. These melodic patterns, known as the "tunes" or "intonations" of a language, are a part of what we call "accent" or "brogue." When you appeared in your first foreign-language class, you heard your professor speak that language with a stress and melody pattern peculiar to that tongue. When you read aloud your first German, French, or Italian sentence in class, you undoubtedly sounded like an American-English speaker of that language, that is, you were speaking German (or French or Italian) with an "American-English accent." Your speech possessed this "accent" in the foreign language, not only because you were using some American phonemes instead of German, French, or Italian ones, but also because you were using the melodies and stresses peculiar to our language, patterns not commonly found in the speech of the natives of Berlin, Hamburg, Marseilles, Paris, Naples, or Rome.

The following questions will need answering: What are the common melodies we use in American English? Do they signify different meanings, or are they merely insignificant variations used by different speakers? Are these melodies based on specific pitch levels? If so, how many such levels are used in American English?

PITCH LEVELS AND CLAUSE TERMINALS

Four relative, significant pitch levels exist in our language, going from the lowest (1), to the highest (4). The normal pitch level for each of us is the mid level (2). Pitch level (3) is high, normally used for the stressed points of the utterance. Pitch level (4) is usually reserved for very special emphasis, and pitch level (1) is commonly used for the unstressed and lesser stressed syllables toward the end of the utterance. To some students of American English, the highest pitch level (4) does not seem distinctive enough to warrant a desig-nation separate from pitch level (3). For such (and for almost all normal speaking situations) three levels of pitch suffice, the fourth level, when used, being considered a nondistinctive variant of level (3).

None of these pitch levels is meaningful by itself. Each is part of the contour of melody we use when speaking, and thus, each serves as a beginning, mid, or end point of each clause we speak. The pitch levels serve as those points which establish the characteristic contour used. The pitch of each syllable between pitch levels need not be noted. They will vary somewhere between the levels preceding and following. We may indicate these pitch levels graphically, or by numbering the levels used:

"He's coming to morrow." (231);   "I found my paper." (231)

"I thought it was green er." (241).

You must not gain the impression that the melodic pattern shown for each of these three sentences is the only possible way of saying them. As the speaker changes the stress on any word, in order to change the intended meaning, the contour may have the pitch level (3) or (4) come earlier. A stress on *coming, my,* or *it* will move the (3) or (4) toward the front of each sentence. The contour pattern will remain the same, however: (231, 231, 241). The contour will change also if the speaker does not make a statement but desires to ask a question instead. The statement "He's coming tomorrow." becomes the question "He's coming tomorrow?" as we change the contour to (23). (See page 273.)

Since we speak in phrases, terminating each with a pause, it is also essential that we indicate the nature of this pause by some appropriate symbol. Three significant pause-types can be noted in our language, one appearing at the end of every phrase. These pauses act as either terminal points in an utterance, or as a transition to a following phrase. Imagine the following conversation between two friends:

1. Hello, John.
2. Hi, Jim.
3. Did you finish the report?
4. No.
5. Will you be able to?
6. Well—I'm not sure.
7. You'd better.
8. Why!
9. Mr Jones, and the rest of the staff, are depending on it.
10. They are?
11. Yes.

Let us concern ourselves with the pauses between sentences. It is here that the speaker's voice may take one of two forms: it may fade into silence along with a gradual decrease in pitch and volume (↓) as after sentences 1 and 2, or it may rise in pitch with a comparatively abrupt decrease in volume (↑) heard after "well" in sentence 6, as well as after sentences 3, 5, 8, and 10. A shorter pause may be heard in sentence 9, before and after "and the rest of the staff," with a sustaining of the pitch level, and a prolongation of the syllable before the pause (→). It is convenient to add these arrowheads to the graphic system, and to use the juncture signs (|, ||, #) to represent (→, ↑, ↓), respectively, with the numbered pitch levels. The melodic pattern following the transcription of some of the above sample sentences might then appear as: [hɛlou dʒɑn]—(231#); [haɪ dʒɪm]—(31#); [wɛl | aɪm nɑt ʃuɚ]—(23||231#); [mɪstɚ dʒounz | ənd ðə rɛst əv ðə stæf | ɑɚ dɪpɛndɪŋ ɑn ɪt]—(232|232|231#).

When we add the melodic contours to demonstrate the pitch levels used, the transcription will appear as below. Pitch shifts between words or syllables are connected with upright lines, while a pitch glide on a syllable is written with a slant line through the syllable. Pitch (2) appears directly beneath the word, pitch (3) directly above, pitch (4) a space above (3), and pitch (1) a space beneath (2).

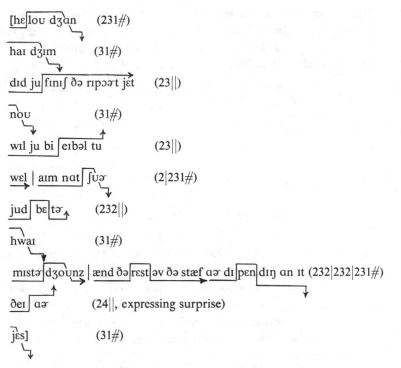

The close relationship between stress and the melody contour may be clearly seen in the above lines, as can the pitch phonemes to each other. The first stressed syllable receives a different pitch from those syllables preceding it. Those syllables preceding the first stressed syllable are commonly spoken on pitch level 2. When the stress appears on the last syllable of the phrase, the pitch glides from one level to another through the syllable. The phrase itself is indicated by the presence of two features: stress and pause. Each phrase contains at least one stressed syllable, one or more pitch phonemes, and a pause (or clause) terminal.

Some students of phonetics find the level and contour system just described somewhat restrictive and prefer to use a more phonetic method of indicating intonation. In one such widely-used system, heavy and light dots are used to represent stressed and unstressed syllables respectively, and melodic changes on a syllable are shown by adding appropriate lines to the dot. In this system, the relative place of the dot on the line indicates its pitch relationship to other adjacent syllables. Here are some examples of this system:[3]

He left an hour ago.	. . · ᳒ ..
Her dog has fleas. Mine doesn't.	᳒ .. ᳒ ᳒..
How good of you.	. ⌐᳒ ..
Did he break it?	.. ᷜ ·
Did you walk, run, or ride?	.. ᷜ ᷜ · ᳒

The advantages of this system are obvious, but we must not forget that this system is phonetic rather than phonemic. The dot system permits the relative insignificant contrasts between pitches to be shown, and it is a notably simple system to use. The pitch-level system is not concerned with pitch differences unless they are in contrast. It would show the first sentence above as

He left an⌐hour⌐ago.

In the dot system as shown above, the first four words of the same sentence use ascending pitches to the highest syllable—the fourth. The phonetician might be interested in showing such relative pitch changes. The phonemicist need not.

MELODY AND MEANING

In the following conversation:

Did you see him?
No.
No?
I didn't.

[3] Other examples of this marking system may be seen in the sections on intonation in Daniel Jones, *Outline of English Phonetics*, 8th ed. (New York, Dutton, 1956).

the word *no* appears twice and its meaning is largely dependent on the pitch shifts the speaker uses. The first *no* is a simple negative answer, conveying the common lexical or dictionary meaning. The questioned *no* ("No?") would be spoken with a changed meaning, such as "You mean you really didn't see him?" The meaning of this second *no* is conveyed through the rising melodic contour used on the word, while that of the first *no* would be spoken with a 31# contour. The melody we use is not an inherent part of the word.

The meaning of a word or phrase may be, and often is, changed by the use of the special melodic features that indicate the attitude of the speaker at the moment, and the particular situation in which he finds himself. Sometimes the pitch shifts merely enhance the lexical meaning of the word. At other times, thay may convey an emphatic, questioning, or even the opposite concept of the word or phrase. Daniel Jones notes six different meanings for the word *yes* in an intonation exercise that demonstrates this very point.[4] He uses the dot and line system, the dot showing the relative level of the pitch, the line indicating the melodic rise or fall on the syllable:

meaning "that is so."

meaning "most certainly."

meaning, "Yes, I understand what you have said. Please continue."

meaning "It may be so."

meaning "Of course it is so."

meaning "Is it really so?"

[4] *The Pronunciation of English* (Cambridge, Eng., Cambridge University Press, 1950), p. 146.

Melodic variations may be added to phrases and sentences with similar effects, so that a speaker, using the same words, may convey many different ideas. Here are some possible meanings of the sentence "I like Biology." Try to say each sentence with the special meaning listed, and see how your use of certain melodic contours provides the clue to your intended meaning. Indicate the contour next to each line and test your reading with a friend as listener. Does he interpret your melody with your intended meaning?

"I like Biology." *to mean*

_____ 1. "Yes, I find it a pleasant course.

_____ 2. "I *love* Biology."

_____ 3. "If anything, I dislike Biology."

_____ 4. "Someone else may like Biology, but I find it very distasteful."

_____ 5. "Chemistry isn't for me, but Biology is just right."

_____ 6. "Now that you ask, I think I do."

All the shades of meaning noted above can be conveyed by the speaker by some change in the stress and pitch pattern of the sentence. Like the notes of a musical selection, the words are there to be interpreted by the performer, and the music and words may convey different impressions when performers or speakers approach them with different attitudes. Words, even more so than musical notes, are capable of so many nuances of expression. You may recall the famous words of Lady Macbeth, "We fail?" when replying to her husband's hesitancies about doing away with the king.

> MACBETH: If we should fail?
> LADY MACBETH: We fail?
> But screw your courage to the sticking-place,
> And we'll not fail.

With these two words, the actress can convey quite a few possible meanings. Does she imply "But don't think about it," or "We

probably shall fail," or "It's inconceivable that we shall or can,"
or "Your attitude disgusts me," or "We shall fail only if *you* fail,"
or "We cannot fail," or "Our failure would be catastrophic. We
must not fail," or "You fool!" or "Be brave and we shall succeed,"
or "You weakling! If it were my task rather than yours, the thought
would never occur."?

Each of these meanings is conveyed by a stress and melody change.
The actor or actress soon learns that the lines to be spoken are
quite barren, unless the melodic pattern enhances the lexical meaning
of the words. Through gestures, motion, pause, and most importantly,
melody, the actor *interprets* his lines so that the audience clearly
understands the author's intent. As speakers, we do the same thing.
Note such expressions as "Did he mean what he said?" "She said
it with a smile," "He was certainly angry when he said it," "You
knew that he meant every word of it," "She said it with a sneer,"
and "He speaks very earnestly." All these attitudes may be conveyed
from speaker to listener through changes in voice quality, tempo,
stress, and pitch as they are added to the thoughts we express.

Let us look now at the common melody contours of our language.
We shall use the graphic form of representing the melody, with
pitch shifts between syllables shown as upright lines, pitch glides on
syllables as slant lines through the nucleus of the syllable. It will be
good to recall that the pitch levels shown are phonemic, that the
pitch of any given speaker may not rise or fall at *exactly* the point
so marked, that the pitch change from one part of a phrase to
another is usually gradual in conversational speech, being made over
the different syllables present in the one pitch level, before the next
pitch level is sounded.

THE RISE-FALL INTONATION (231#)

The rise-fall contour, ending in pitch level (1) and a falling
terminal, is the pattern we commonly use when we make a simple
statement of fact, issue a command, or ask special questions which

require specific information in the answer. These special questions
begin with an interrogative word, such as *How, When, Where*, and
Why, and, of course, can not be answered by a "yes" or "no."
In all these intonations, there is at least one syllable with a primary
stress which will commonly have a higher pitch (usually (3); (4)
when special emphasis is desired) than all the preceding unstressed
or lesser stressed syllables, which will normally be spoken on level
(2). The terminal in all these clauses is low and falling (↓).

Come ⌐here.   (231#)

What's ⌐wrong?   (231#)

How did you ⌐come?   (231#)

The library closes at ⌐nine.   (231#)

Don't drive so ⌐fast.   (231#)

Should the stress shift in any of these sentences, the general
pattern remains the same, the high pitch (3) coming wherever the
stressed syllable appears. The meaning of each sentence below
changes as the speaker indicates the changed stress and pitch pattern:

Don't drive so ⌐fast.

Don't ⌐drive so fast.

Don't ⌐drive so fast.

In each instance the falling pitch shift occurs on, or immediately
after, the stressed or emphasized word. If more than one concept
is emphasized by the speaker, two falling pitches are heard; and
after each of the first pauses, a sustaining juncture is heard, while
after the terminating part of the sentence, (↓) is heard:

Don't drive so ⌐fặst, it's ⌐dangerous.   (232|231#)

Nọ, what's wrong with the ⌐other time?   (32|231#)

All of the contours above are of the rise-fall pattern, ending in pitch level (1). The general impression of these statements is one of completeness or finality. The falling pitch is heard on the last stressed syllable of the phrase, and the terminal part of the sentence, following the last stressed syllable, fades into silence. The same pattern is followed even if the attitude of the speaker indicates a special emotional state, such as surprise or anger, calling for greater emphasis (pitch level (4)) on a given syllable. Following the higher pitch normally used for special emphasis, the pitch level again drops to pitch level (1).

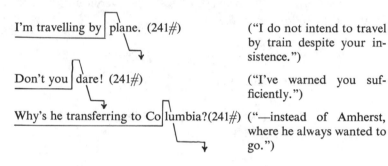

I'm travelling by ⌐plane. (241#)   ("I do not intend to travel by train despite your insistence.")

Don't you ⌐dare! (241#)   ("I've warned you sufficiently.")

Why's he transferring to Co⌐lumbia?(241#)   ("—instead of Amherst, where he always wanted to go.")

THE RISING INTONATION (23‖)

The rising intonation is normally used whenever we ask a question that may take a "yes" or "no" answer. We do this when the sentence reads as a question, as in "Will you call me tomorrow?" or if it reads as a statement of fact, but spoken with the questioning tone: "You'll call me tomorrow?" In such questions, the speaker's voice rises to pitch level (3) on the last stressed syllable and trails off with a short terminal pitch rise at the end of the sentence (↑). The contour is marked (23‖). It may be graphed as follows:

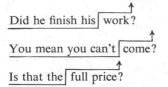

In each sentence the listener is expected to provide the falling ending which will indicate a sense of completion, for the rising intonation implies that something more needs to be said to make the thought complete.

The same melodic contour (23) and a sustaining or rising terminal (→, ↑) may be heard whenever we mention a series of items connected by *and* or a series of alternatives connected with *or*. The (23) contour occurs on all items except the last in the series, unless it is part of a question that normally takes the (23) contour, as may be heard in the following sentences:

He bought to � matoes, � oranges, � apples, and � plums.

Does she speak � Russian, Italian, and � French?

These contours are part of incomplete thoughts and are covered separately in the next section.

THE INCOMPLETE INTONATION PATTERN
(23 ‖, or 232 │)

Parts of sentences followed by a slight pause do not end by dropping to pitch level (1) and fading off into silence. Instead we tend to sustain the previous pitch level spoken, or end with a rising intonation on pitch level (3). This intonation pattern occurs on the stressed words of a series (except the last), or on the terminal part of a phrase, which is separated from the remainder of the sentence by a slight pause, usually represented by a comma. These phrases are terminated on levels (2) or (3). They are finally resolved when either of the other two contours, discussed earlier, terminate the thought expressed.

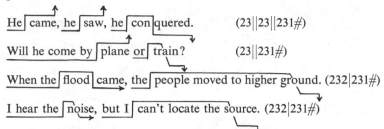

These are the simple, normal, melodic patterns used by all of us. Variation from these patterns do occur as a result of many factors, but the general contour patterns sound like one of the three mentioned. As previously noted, pitch level (4) is rarely used in normal conversational speech, except as the speaker desires to exaggerate or emphasize a given word or syllable for special effect:

Give me my ⌐pen! (241#) ("I've asked you twice and I want it now.")

Is that⌐your book? (24‖) (A surprised reaction by the speaker who would have used 23‖ if he had meant to ask a simple question.)

Two other variations from the norm might be mentioned: Question words may begin sentences and the melody may not follow the expected (231 #) contour. For example, in the sentence, "Where are we going tomorrow?" a speaker might use the melody (32‖) rather than (231 #). The sentence said the first way might be the question asked of a parent by a child who has heard something about the family going someplace tomorrow and who hasn't been informed

of the plans yet: "Where are we going tomorrow?" The (231 #) contour would be heard in the following conversation with the same child:

Did you enjoy the movie today?

Yes I did. Where are we going to⌐morrow?

Let's wait until morning before we decide.

Similarly, certain statements may be spoken with slightly changed pitch contours, with resultant changes in meaning:

You like⌐ fish. (13‖)   ("That's strange. Never expected you to.")

You⌐ like fish. (32|)   (—the hostess says, rather hopefully, as she serves the platter to her guest. Her expression indicates that she is looking for a nod or smile, rather than recoil on her guest's part.)

A more complete detailing of the melody patterns is not necessary for our purpose, which is to indicate how melody may be noted in transcription, and the common forms we use in American English. Many contour varieties are detailed in one of the most complete studies of this subject presently available.[5]

CONCLUSION

Melodic contours result as we use different pitch levels to indicate the information we desire to convey. And, at times, melody can convey more than information. Through it, the speaker can indicate his mood or attitude. The singsong or monotonous (tone of) voice of one speaker is as indicative as the loudness or softness of tone, the rapid or slow tempo, the steady or broken rhythm of speech, the special qualities of voice of another speaker. All of these characteristics of voice and speech may be added to the normal phonemes of our language. These additives, still in need of careful, objective analysis, help make for the variety of speech we all hear.

The subtle details of melodic patterns as they differ from dialect to dialect have not been studied. There is little question that melody plays its part in dialect differences, although present knowledge seems to indicate that the melodic contours outlined above are used by most American speakers. Some slight variations undoubtedly occur, but with the recognition of the relative differences, the student of phonetics can mark his transcription with sufficient accuracy to record them all.

[5] Kenneth L. Pike, *The Intonation of American English* (Ann Arbor, University of Michigan Press, 1946).

QUESTIONS FOR FURTHER STUDY

1. Transcribe and indicate the melody contours of the following sentences, being sure to say them aloud with the meaning listed:

   It's a fine day for swimming. (simple statement of fact)
   It's a fine day for swimming? (Is it?)
   It's a fine day for swimming! (It certainly is not.)
   I like your dress. (It's nice.)
   I like your dress. (Don't you like mine?)
   I like your dress. (I wonder if you shouldn't have bought the other.)
   I like your dress. (It doesn't compliment you one bit.)
   I like your dress? (How could I like it? The store sold me the very same one!)
   How do you do it? (a simple, polite question)
   How do you do it? (Show me *how* to do it.)
   How do you do it? (*I* do it differently.)
   How do you do it? (I understand what you mean but I still don't know *how* to *do* it.)
   Is that so? (simple question)
   Is that so! (I'm quite annoyed about it.)
   Is that so! (Don't threaten me!)
   Is that so? (Did it really happen? I'm very surprised.)
   Is that so! (Boy, am I glad to hear that!)

2. Say each of the following words with the indicated terminal shift. A possible meaning is noted to assist you.

   John ↓   (Stay away from there.)
   John ↑   (Is that you?)
   Say ↓   (I like that!)
   Funny ↑   (Do you think it was?)
   Mary ↓   (You're very sweet)
   Eileen ↑   (Is that you, Eileen?)
   Hold still →   (While I tie your shoelace)
   Why ↓   (Why did you do it?)
   Why ↑   (Are you asking me 'why'?)

3. Say each of the following with the (231) contour, changing the position of the (3), or stressed syllable, at least once. Try saying each sentence with a (241) contour.

   Physics is a difficult course.
   He plays the violin beautifully.
   Why should we go today?

4. What melodic pattern would you use for each of the following:

I won't do it. (simple statement)
I won't do it. (anger)
He isn't the same boy? (surprise)
I don't like snakes, mice, or worms.
Is the house surrounded by trees? (simple question)
Is the house surrounded by trees? (consternation)
I'll pay you thirty cents a pound. (and that's final)
I'll pay thirty cents a pound. (but I'd rather pay 25 cents)
I'll pay thirty cents a pound (as agreed)

5. Using the dot and line system, note the melody for each of the following sentences.

The jury system is ǀfair.
The jury system ǀis fair.
The ǀsystem is fair; it's the ǀpeople who ǀserve on it that give him pause.
Learning a ǀforeign ǀlanguage is ǀeasier than you think.
Learning ǀGerman is easy.
Learning ǀGerman is ǀvery easy.
Knowing German and ǀusing it are ǀtwo ǀvery ǀdifferent things.

SOURCES FOR FURTHER STUDY

ARMSTRONG, Lilias E., and WARD, Ida C., *Handbook of English Intonation* (Leipzig and Berlin, B.G. Teubner, 1926).
BOLINGER, Dwight L., "Intonation: Levels vs. Configurations," *Word*, Vol. 7 (1951), pp. 199–210.
——, "Stress and Information," *American Speech*, Vol. 33 (February, 1958), pp. 5–20.
HOUSEHOLDER, Fred W., Jr., "Accent, Juncture, Intonation, and My Grandfather's Reader," *Word*, Vol. 13 (August, 1957), pp. 234–245.
HULTZEN, Lee S., "The Useful Study of Phonetics," *The Quarterly Journal of Speech*, Vol. 41 (April, 1955), pp. 105–109.
——, "Stress and Intonation," *General Linguistics*, Vol. 1 (Spring, 1955), pp. 35–42.
JONES, Daniel, *The Pronunciation of English* (Cambridge, Eng., Cambridge University Press, 1950), esp. pp. 144–158.
LEE, W. R., "Fall-Rise Intonations in English," *English Studies*, Vol. 37 (April, 1956), pp. 62–72.
LEHISTE, Ilse, "Phonetic Study of Internal Open Juncture," *Phonetica*, Supplement to Vol. 5 (1960), 49 pp.

MORGAN, Bayard Q., "Question Melodies in American English," *American Speech*, Vol. 28 (October, 1953), pp. 181–191.

NEWMAN, Stanley S., "On the Stress System of English," *Word*, Vol. 2 (1946), pp. 171–187.

PALMER, Harold E., *English Intonation* (Cambridge, Eng., W. Heffer and Sons, 1922).

PIKE, Kenneth L., *The Intonation of American English* (Ann Arbor, University of Michigan Press, 1946).

SLEDD, James, "Review of *An Outline of English Structure* by George L. Trager and Henry Lee Smith, Jr.," *Language*, Vol. 31 (April–June, 1955), pp. 326–329.

SMITH, Henry Lee, Jr., *Linguistic Science and the Teaching of English* (Cambridge, Mass., Harvard University Press, 1956), pp. 47–61.

———, "The Teacher and the World of Language," *College English*, Vol. 20 (January, 1959), pp. 172–178.

TRAGER, George L., and SMITH, Henry Lee, Jr., *An Outline of English Structure, Studies in Linguistics: Occasional Papers*, No. 3 (Norman, Oklahoma, Battenberg Press, 1951), pp. 41–52.

TWADDELL, W. Freeman, "Stetson's Model and the Suprasegmental Phonemes," *Language*, Vol. 29 (October–December, 1953), pp. 415–453.

WELLS, Rulon, "The Pitch Phonemes of English," *Language*, Vol. 21 (January–March, 1945), pp. 27–39.

APPENDIX A

The Background of Our Language

THE ENGLISH LANGUAGE today, although seemingly unchanging, is certainly a very different language from that used by earlier English-speaking people. The members of the court of King Alfred the Great, who spoke Old English, would not be able to understand us. Chaucer and his contemporaries spoke a form of English much more similar to our own, yet different enough to warrant a different label. We recognize three major periods in the development of English: Old English, the language of the fifth to approximately the twelfth century; Middle English, approximately from the twelfth through the fifteenth century; and Modern English, from the sixteenth century to the present.

The time boundaries of these three periods are, of course, vague. They are merely approximations, for no exact time-lines can be drawn in the developmental history of a language. It is undoubtedly true that many spoke what we call Middle English before the invasion by the Normans in the eleventh century. And later versions of Middle English were still being spoken in the early part of the Modern English period. These divisions are matters of convenience, arbitrarily chosen from a continuing development of a language now in use for fifteen centuries.

Like any social phenomenon, the English language has a history—a parentage of sounds, structure, and usage. It is our purpose here to glance at part of this background.

The earliest language we can trace to the British Isles was spoken by the Celts, an ancient people who first came to the islands sometime before 500 B.C. It appears they came from the mainland in two large and separate invading groups, known as the Gaelic and Brittanic invasions. No trace of the speech of those absorbed or routed by the Celts remains. The conquerors' languages have come down to modern times, however. Scotch-Gaelic, Irish, and Manx (the now almost extinct language of the Isle of Man) are the modern languages of the Gaelic group, while the descendants of the Brittanic group are Welsh, Breton, and the now extinct Cornish.

The Celts experienced no threat to their control of the islands until they also saw two invasions of their homeland, first by the Roman army of Julius Caesar, in 55 B.C., and later by Emperor Claudius' legions in 43 A.D. Caesar's campaign was of little import. The natives successfully resisted his making any headway during the first landing from Gaul, and he soon returned to the continent. On his second attempt, a year later, his landing was somewhat more successful, his soldiers managing to penetrate some of the island. The expedition lasted only a short while and the Roman army returned to Gaul.

Emperor Claudius' expedition was, however, more than a military campaign. It was a thorough conquest of most of the land of the Celts. The Romans established a military government, built roads, developed communities, built villas and public baths, evidence of which may still be seen. The Latin language of the conquerors may have been adopted by the more wealthy and by the urban dwellers, but it was not widely enough used to displace the Celtic tongues, which continued to be spoken by the native people. The Romans remained until 410 A.D., when Rome, beset by internal dissensions and barbaric invasions of its own territories, called its soldiers home. The Britons were now left to govern themselves and to protect themselves. Our English language and literature had their beginnings as a result of the Britons' inability to successfully accomplish the latter of these two tasks.

OLD ENGLISH

Soon after the withdrawal of the Romans, certain Teutonic tribes, known as the Angles, Saxons, and Jutes, began to invade and settle the British Isles. They came in migratory waves that continued for more than a hundred years, and they came in such force that they assumed control of the entire island. Their continental homelands (and the actual dates of their migratory invasions) are matters of dispute, but it is generally believed that they came from the Danish peninsula and from regions in

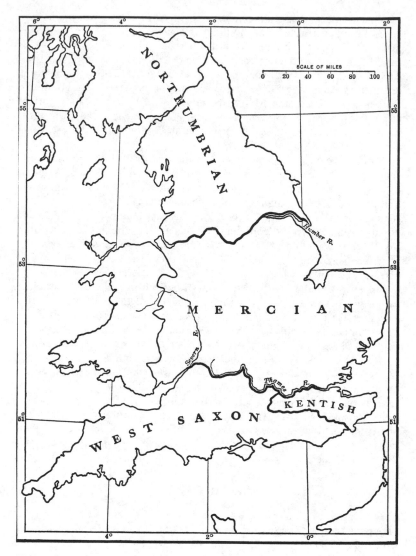

FIG. 35. The principal dialects of Old English. (From Albert C. Baugh, *A History of the English Language*, 2nd ed. (New York, Appleton-Century-Crofts, Inc., 1957), p. 61, with permission.)

northern Germany. Accounts of these invasions, and of other smaller ones (especially from the Scandinavian countries) that occurred toward the end of the Old English period, are reported by Bede in his *Ecclesiastical History of the English People*, completed in 731, and in the *Anglo-Saxon Chronicle*, the name of the annals of England begun during King Alfred's reign during the ninth century and continued until the year 1154.

The language of this period (from approximately the fifth to the twelfth centuries), known to us as Anglo-Saxon, or more commonly Old English, was the result of the mixture of the related dialects spoken by these invading tribes. It is the language of *Beowulf*, the earliest known Old English epic, and the language of Caedmon, Cynewulf, Alfred the Great, and Ælfric.

The language of Old English times differed from region to region. Four major dialects existed: Northumbrian, Mercian, West Saxon, and Kentish. The first two were the dialects used by the Angles. Kentish was the dialect spoken by the Jute settlers. West Saxon was the dialect of the West Saxon kingdom, the dialect in which nearly all Old English literature is preserved and about which we know most. West Saxon is thus the basis of the study of Old English.

What we know about its pronunciation has been learned from the spellings found in the documents of the time, and from our knowledge of related or cognate languages. In addition, the Latin alphabet has been a help. The letters of this alphabet were introduced with the Latin language at the time of the Christianizing of Britain. In time, English writers discontinued using runic inscriptions, which may still be seen on the Ruthwell and Bewcastle crosses in Dumfries, Scotland and Cumberland, England. Instead, writers employed the letters of the Roman alphabet to represent English sounds which corresponded closely to the value of the sounds they had in Latin. Scholars have been able to arrive at certain conclusions about Old English by comparing the sounds with the known values of the Latin letters of the seventh century.

The language of Old English times was considerably different from the English we speak today—in pronunciation, vocabulary, and grammar. Here are a few samples of Old English, with a translation of each and a respelling of the last sample into a phonetic system representing one probable pronunciation.

Fæder ūre, þū þe eart on heofonum, sī þīn nama gehālgod.
Our father, who art in heaven, hallowed be thy name.

Da wæs æfter manigum dagum þæt sē cyning cōm tō þǣm eālande.
Then it was after many days, that the king came to the island.

Ic ðāra frætwa Frēan ealles ðanc,
For these treasures, Lord, all thanks
Wuldur-cyninge, wordum secge
to the King of Glory, let me words say
ēcum Dryhtne, þē ic hēr on starie
to the Eternal Lord, for what I here behold
þæs ic mōste mīnum lēodum
That I must for my people
ǣr swylt-dæge swylc gestrȳnan.
Before the day of my death, gain such a gift.

A more poetic and meaningful translation of this extract from *Beowulf*, lines 2794–2798, was made by William Ellery Leonard.[1] It reads:

For this splendor-booty   be thanks unto the Lord,
Unto the King-of-Glory,   for what I here behold,
To God, the everlasting,   in that 'tis mine to give
Such gifts unto my people,   while an hour I live.

The pronunciation is based on Henry Cecil Wyld's reading for Lingua-phone Institute, New York,[2] with some slight modifications. The symbols used to indicate the pronunciation are explained on pages 28–30.[3]

[ɪtʃ θɑːrɑ frætwɑ fræːɑn æːlːɛs θaŋk
wuldur kynɪŋgɛ wɔrdum sɛdʒɛ
eːtʃum dryçtnɛ θeː ɪtʃ heːr ɔn stɑrɪɛ
θæs ɪtʃ moːstɛ miːnum leːodum
æːr swylt dæjɛ swylk jɛstryːnɑn]

[1] *Beowulf*, trans. by William Ellery Leonard (New York, Appleton-Century-Crofts, Inc., 1923). By permission.

[2] "Pronunciation of Anglo-Saxon," *English Pronunciation Through the Centuries*. By Permission.

[3] The pronunciations represented by the [y] and [ç] in [kynɪŋgɛ] and [dryçtnɛ] do not exist in Modern English. [y] is the vowel sound in the German words *über* and *Mütter* or French *tu* and *lune*. [ç] is the symbol used for the *ch* in German *ich* and *mich*, or the Japanese *h* before *i*, as in *hito*. The [j] of *dæge* and *gestrȳnan* was a voiced, spirant consonant, made in the area of present-day [j] but sounding more like a fronted, fricative [g] sound. The ȳ of *gestrȳnan* is represented by some scholars as a complex sound, beginning with [y] and culminating in the direction of [ɪ]. For further analyses of Old English phono-logy, see the references by Hockett, Moore, and Stockwell at the end of this chapter.

MIDDLE ENGLISH

Middle English is the label given to the English language during the period from approximately the twelfth to the sixteenth century. It was during this time that the language changed from one that is almost a foreign language to us at the beginning, to a more familiar Early Modern English by the end. The language of this period shows many changes from its parent, Old English. Grammatical forms are much simpler now, most readily noticed in the loss of inflectional endings. For example, by the end of the Middle English period *good* replaces earlier different forms of the word that appeared as *gōda* (masculine) and *gōde* (neuter and feminine) for the singular-nominative forms, and *gōdan* (masculine and feminine), *gōde* (neuter), for the singular-accusative forms. Similarly, the plural ending *-s* (or *-es*) appears for almost all indications of plurals now, while the exceptional *-en* of *oxen*, *brethren*, and *children* remain to remind us of a former declension, now forgotten.

An event of great importance to England took place during the eleventh century. In 1066, William the Conqueror, Duke of Normandy, invaded and conquered England. William was the noble leader of the Normans, an essentially French people. With the Normans and their victory and settlement came their language. Although the conquered English continued to use their native tongue, Norman French became the language of the upper social classes. It was used in the Court and in the conduct of the business of the land and retained its hold for over two hundred years. By the fourteenth century, English had regained its place as the language of the country, relegating French to the position of a foreign tongue. However, many French words made their way into the vocabulary of English, such as *crown*, *prince*, *petticoat*, *peasant*, *beauty*, and *vision*. And by this time, some Old English words, such as *belīfan* (remain) and *wlitig* (beauty), had dropped out, and of course some meanings of words had changed too. (*Stench* now referred to an unpleasant smell, rather than to any kind of odor or scent, as it once did.)

French declined for many reasons, not the least of which was the growth of a nationalistic feeling which associated French with an alien people. By this time, the socio-economic position of the English-speaking middle class had improved and there was a strong feeling that English was the proper language for Englishmen. Authors were now aware that their writings would be read by English speakers, and the business of the land used English as its means of communication. Although French left its imprint on the language, it was no longer the native tongue of any of the social classes. English had resumed its place as the language of the country.

The evidence is fairly clear that the continuity, or growth and change,

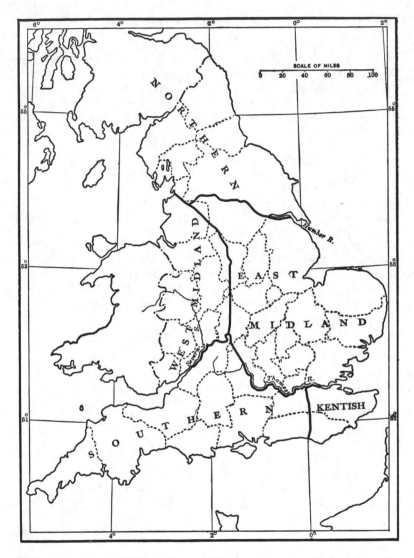

FIG. 36. The principal dialects of Middle English. (From Albert C. Baugh, *A History of the English Language*, 2nd ed. (New York, Appleton-Century-Crofts, Inc., 1957), p. 230, with permission.)

of the English language was neither broken nor noticeably delayed by the Norman conquest. Nor do authorities consider the actual pronunciation changes noticed during this period as caused by the invasion of the Norman people. As far as we can judge, the Middle English changes from Old English were a result of the forces already at work in the language during the Old English period.

Dialectal differences of the Middle English period are separated into four principal areas, as noted in Figure 36. East Midland emerges as the predominant dialect of the period, spoken in the capital city of London and at the seats of higher learning, Oxford and Cambridge Universities.

The Middle English period was one of great literary achievement. It saw the development of the literary romances, of which the Arthurian romance is the outstanding example. In addition, it fathered Layamon's *Brut*, Malory's *Morte d'Arthur*, the development of the miracle, mystery, and morality plays, and the works of John Wycliff, William Caxton, and of its most notable figure, Geoffrey Chaucer.

Following is a short sample of Middle English with a phonetic transcription indicating the pronunciation. A translation follows the selection. Note that the spelling and word order are quite close to the modern forms, and that the sample pronunciation listed doesn't sound quite as foreign to our ears as the earlier Old English sample does. It should be kept in mind that the pronunciation indicated (like that of the earlier Old English sample) is only one sample of many dialects and forms that must have existed at the time. Much variation of pronunciation was present and no real consistency obtained. This selection is taken from the "Prologue" to Chaucer's *Canterbury Tales*, East Midland dialect, at the end of the fourteenth century.

1. Whan that Aprille with his shoures sote
   [hwɑn θɑt ɑpril: wɪθ (h)ɪs ʃurəs sotə

2. The droghte of Marche hath perced to the rote,
   θə druxt ɔf mɑrtʃ hɑθ persəd to θə rotə

3. And bathed every veyne in swich licour,
   ɑnd bɑðəd ɛvrɪ væin ɪn swɪtʃ lɪkur

4. Of which vertue engendred is the flour;
   ɔf hwɪtʃ vɛrty ɛndʒɛndrəd ɪs θə flur

5. Whan Zephirus eek with his swete breeth
   hwɑn zɛfɪrus e:k wɪθ (h)ɪs swetə bræθ

6. Inspired hath in every holt and heeth
   ɪnspirəd hɑθ ɪn ɛvrɪ hɔlt ɑnd hæθ

7. The tendre croppes, and the yonge sonne
   ðə tɛndər krɔp:əz ɑnd θə juŋgə sunə

8. Hath in the Ram his halfe cours y-ronne,
   haθ ɪn θə ram hɪz halvə kurs ɪ rʊn:ə
9. And smale fowles maken melodye
   and smalə fuləs makən mɛlɔdiə
10. That slepen al the night with open yë
    θat slepən al θə nɪçt wɪð ɔpən ijə
11. So priketh hem nature in hir corages.
    sɔ prɪkəθ həm natyr ɪn hɪr kuradʒəs.]

When April with his showers hath pierced the drought
Of March with sweetness to the very root,
And flooded every vein with liquid power
That of its strength engendereth the flower;
When Zephyr also with his fragrant breath
Hath urged to life in every holt and heath
New tender shoots of green, and the young sun
His full course within the Ram hath run,
And little birds are making melody
That sleep the whole night through with open eye,
For in their hearts doth Nature stir them so.[4]

THE MODERN ENGLISH PERIOD

The linguistic forces already at work during the Middle English period culminated in a number of changes closely approximating the sounds of the present day. From the available evidence, scholars of the English language have concluded that by the end of the fifteenth century the typical Middle English pronunciations had disappeared and a great number of characteristically modern-sounding pronunciations had already developed. Middle English short *a*, [a], was now a fronted sound, [æ], as in current *man*, *cat*, and *hand*; long *i*, [i], had become a diphthong (the first of a series of diphthongal changes), culminating in our current [aɪ] as in *blind*, *wife*, and *write*; long *u*, [u], had diphthongized too, ultimately

---

[4] The phonetic transcription is based on the reading done by Professor Henry Cecil Wyld for *English Pronunciation Through the Centuries*, Linguaphone Institute, New York, with some slight modifications. The translation is by Frank Ernest Hill, Longmans Green and Co., 1935, reprinted with the publisher's permission. The symbols used to indicate the pronunciation are explained on pages 28–30. The pronunciation represented by the [x] symbol, as in [druxt], does not exist in Modern English. [x] is the phonetic symbol used for the *ch* sound in German *ach* or *Loch* or for the Spanish *j* in *jota* or the *g* in *gente*. A note on the [y] symbol appears on page 284.

culminating in our current pronunciation [aʊ], as in *house, mouth,* and *plow.* These and other vowel changes, commonly called the "Great Vowel Shift," act as a boundary marker between Middle English and Early Modern English. The actual values of the vowels were not those of the twentieth century, as the two samples below will demonstrate. But the language was now in a new period. At least, it could no longer be called Middle English.

Following are two samples of earlier Modern English pronunciation. The first represents Elizabethan English of the late sixteenth or early seventeenth century, as spoken in the south of England. The pronunciation is based on the recording done by Daniel Jones for the Linguaphone Institute, cited earlier, and the phonetic transcription noted for the same selection by Helge Kökeritz.[5] They are in substantial agreement. Where they are not, the pronunciation suggested by Kökeritz appears. Elizabethan pronunciation has been carefully studied by other scholars, and in most instances all are in agreement.

The second selection represents the speech of approximately one hundred years later, that of early eighteenth-century London English. It is based on the recording made by Henry Cecil Wyld for the Linguaphone Institute, cited above.

1. All the world's a stage,
   [ɔːl ðə wɜːrldz ə stɛːdʒ|

2. And all the men and women merely players:
   ən(d) ɔːl ðə mɛn ən wɪmɪn miːrlɪ plɛːərz|

3. They have their exits and their entrances,
   ðɛː (h)ɛːv ðər ɛksɪts ən ðər ɛntrɔnsɪz|

4. And one man in his time plays many parts,
   ən(d) oːn mæn ɪn ɪz təɪm plɛːz mɛnɪ paːrts|

5. His acts being seven ages. At first the infant,
   (h)ɪz æk(t)s biːn sɛvn̩ ɛːdʒɪz|| ət fɜːrst ðɪ ɪnfənt|

6. Mewling and puking in the nurse's arms.
   mjuːlɪn ən pjuːkn̩ ɪn ðə nɜːrsɪz armz||

7. Then the whining schoolboy, with his satchel
   ðɛn ðə hwəɪnɪn skuːlbɒɪ wɪð (h)ɪz sætʃəl

8. And shining morning face, creeping like snail
   ən ʃəɪnɪn mɔrnɪn fɛːs| kriːpn̩ ləɪk snɛːl

9. Unwillingly to school. And then the lover,
   ʌnwɪlɪnlɪ tə skuːl|| ən ðɛn ðə lʌvər|

10. Sighing like furnace, with a woeful ballad
    səɪən ləɪk fɜːrnəs| wɪð ə woːfʊl bæləd

[5] *Shakespeare's Pronunciation* (New Haven, Yale University Press, 1953), pp. 356–357.

11. Made to his mistress' eyebrow. Then a soldier,
    mɛːd tu (h)ɪz mɪstrɪs əɪbrəʊ‖ ðən ə soː(l)dʒər
12. Full of strange oaths, and bearded like the pard,
    fʊl əv strɛːn(d)ʒ oːðz| ən bɛːrdɪd ləɪk ðə paːrd
13. Jealous in honour, sudden, and quick in quarrel,
    dʒɛləs ɪn ɒnər| sʌdn̩ ən kwɪk ɪn kwɑrəl|
14. Seeking the bubble reputation
    siːkn̩ ðə bʌbl̩ rɛpətɛːʃɪən
15. Even in the cannon's mouth.
    iːn ɪn ðə kænənz məʊθ‖]

Act II, Scene vii, As You Like It

1. Such were the notes thy once-loved poet sung
   [sʌtʃ wə(r) ðə noːts ðʌɪ wʌns lʌvd poɪt sʌŋ
2. Till Death untimely stopped his tuneful tongue.
   tɪl dɛθ ʌntʌɪmlɪ stɒpt hɪz tjunfl̩ tʌŋ‖
3. Oh just beheld and lost! admired and mourned!
   o dʒʌst bɪhɛld ənd lɒst| ədmʌɪə(r)d ənd moː(r)nd|
4. With softest manners, gentlest arts adorned!
   wɪð sɒftɪst mænə(r)z dʒɛntlɪst æː(r)ts ədoː(r)nd|
5. Blest in each science, blest in every strain!
   blɛst ɪn etʃ sʌɪəns| blɛst ɪn ɛvrɪ stren‖
6. Dear to the Muse! to Harley dear – in vain!
   diə(r) tə ðə mjuz| tə hæː(r)lɪ diə(r) ɪn ven][6]

Alexander Pope, Epistle to Robert Harley

ATTITUDES TOWARD PRONUNCIATION IN THE SIXTEENTH-EIGHTEENTH CENTURIES

The concept of a "standard" or "preferred" pattern of speech, begun during the Middle English period, did not continue a steady development during the early part of the Modern period. The sixteenth century demonstrated no serious effort to define or detail a standard, or acceptable, form of English. This Elizabethan period was an era of linguistic permissiveness, and prescriptions of "right," "wrong," or "preferred" are not commonly found. Although the seventeenth century did indicate a knowledge of the existence of a concept of standard speech, by sporadic attempts to dictate "correct" forms, these attempts were not lasting.

[6] The *r* sound is placed in parentheses to signify that it was either very weakly pronounced or lost.

The eighteenth century, however, marks the growth of a strong interest in the usage of the English language, especially in pronunciation. This was a dictionary-conscious age, reflecting a desire for conformity, so contrary to the permissiveness of the Elizabethan period. The eighteenth century saw the dictionaries of Bailey, Johnson, Sheridan, Walker, and others, as well as many technical dictionaries and glossaries. Pronunciation was recognized as an important aspect of the language. In 1730, Nathan Bailey published his *Dictionarium Britanicum*, the first dictionary to show an indication of accent by placing a stress mark over the stressed vowel *(chèwing, chìcken)*. And in 1755, when Joseph Scott published the Scott-Bailey *A New Universal Etymological English Dictionary*, he considered it necessary to call the attention of prospective buyers to the value of including accent marks, by writing about it on his title page.

LANGUAGE AND THE CLASSICAL TRADITION

The purifying attitude of the eighteenth century stemmed partly from the strongly followed classical tradition of the times. This tradition revered the systematic representation of thoughts, especially as they could be expressed in Latin and Greek, which seemed to offer logical and reasonable sets of constructions. There appeared to be little guesswork in these languages as to meaning, less as to method of sentence construction, and still less as to the pronunciation of the sounds of each language. Latin and Greek were, therefore, "reasonable" languages; they were "logical" and "exact." Students could learn them from sets of rules, tried and proved. Thus, the more like Latin English could be, the better. Adherence to rules, it was felt, would stop the "degeneration" of the language and return it to the pristine state it so rightly deserved.

Finding themselves armed with a philosophy and a critical system already tried and found serviceable, the "men of rules" dominated the eighteenth century. The prevailing attitude was that language must conform to a "standard of reason." The eighteenth century has been called an "Age of Classicism and Formal Rules," an age in which the laxity of the Elizabethans was frowned upon in favor of formality and regularization of language.

The Seeds of Usage as a Criterion.

A few writers did manage to introduce an opposing concept. They believed that a modern language often develops in a rather haphazard fashion, allowing considerable variation in usage even among the educated and cultivated speakers and authors. But this new concept made no serious

A NEW

UNIVERSAL ETYMÓLOGICAL

ENGLISH DICTIONARY:

Containing not only

EXPLANATIONS of the WORDS

IN THE

ENGLISH LANGUAGE;

And the Different SENSES in which they are ufed;

WITH

AUTHORITIES from the BEST WRITERS, to fupport thofe which appear Doubtful;

BUT ALSO THEIR

ETYMOLOGIES

FROM THE

ANCIENT and MODERN LANGUAGES:

AND

ACCENTS directing to their Proper PRONUNCIATION;

Shewing both the

ORTHOGRAPHY and ORTHOEPIA of the *ENGLISH* TONGUE.

ALSO,

Full and Accurate EXPLANATIONS of the Various TERMS made ufe of in the feveral
ARTS, SCIENCES, MANUFACTURES, and TRADES.

Illuftrated with COPPER-PLATES.

Originally compiled by *N. BAILEY.*

Affifted in the Mathematical Part by *G. GORDON*; in the Botanical by *P. MILLER*; and in the
Etymological, &c. by *T. LEDIARD,* Gent, Profeffor of the Modern Languages in *Lower Germany.*

And now Re-publifhed with many CORRECTIONS, ADDITIONS, and LITERATE IMPROVEMENTS,
by Different HANDS.

The Etymology of all TERMS mentioned as derived from the *Greek, Hebrew, Arabic,* and other *Afiatic* LANGUAGES,
being Revifed and Corrected

By *JOSEPH NICOL SCOTT,* M. D.

LONDON:

Printed for T. OSBORNE and J. SHIPTON; J. HODGES; R. BALDWIN;
W. JOHNSTON, and J. WARD.

MDCCLV.

FIG. 37. Title page of the Scott-Bailey dictionary, 1755.

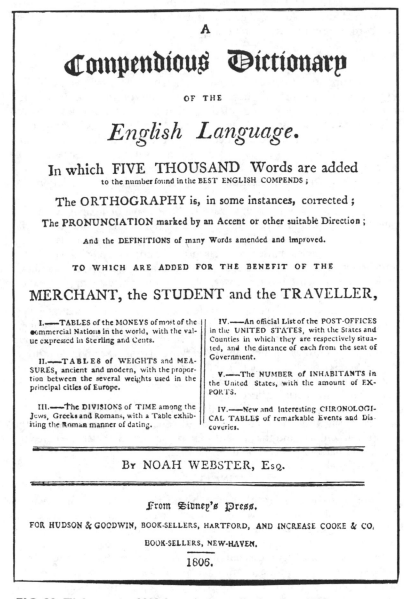

A

Compendious Dictionary

OF THE

English Language.

In which FIVE THOUSAND Words are added
to the number found in the BEST ENGLISH COMPENDS ;

The ORTHOGRAPHY is, in some instances, corrected ;

The PRONUNCIATION marked by an Accent or other suitable Direction ;

And the DEFINITIONS of many Words amended and improved.

TO WHICH ARE ADDED FOR THE BENEFIT OF THE

MERCHANT, the STUDENT and the TRAVELLER,

I.——TABLES of the MONEYS of most of the commercial Nations in the world, with the value expressed in Sterling and Cents.

II.——TABLES of WEIGHTS and MEASURES, ancient and modern, with the proportion between the several weights used in the principal cities of Europe.

III.——The DIVISIONS of TIME among the Jews, Greeks and Romans, with a Table exhibiting the Roman manner of dating.

IV.——An official List of the POST-OFFICES in the UNITED STATES, with the States and Counties in which they are respectively situated, and the distance of each from the seat of Government.

V.——The NUMBER of INHABITANTS in the United States, with the amount of EXPORTS.

IV.——New and interesting CHRONOLOGICAL TABLES of remarkable Events and Discoveries.

By NOAH WEBSTER, Esq.

From Sidney's Press.

FOR HUDSON & GOODWIN, BOOK-SELLERS, HARTFORD, AND INCREASE COOKE & CO.

BOOK-SELLERS, NEW-HAVEN.

1806.

FIG. 38. Title page of Webster's first dictionary, 1806. By now, the pronunciation of all entries was considered an essential part of a dictionary. (Courtesy of G. & C. Merriam Company, publishers of the Merriam-Webster Dictionaries.)

inroads into the bulk of the writings of the period. If anything, it was considered distasteful to a consciousness that demanded a strict social standard of pronunciation and usage.

THE NINETEENTH CENTURY

Some support for current usage ("the language as it is") as a criterion of language acceptability began to take hold during the nineteenth century. At least the writings of the period demonstrate a desire to recognize the actual custom of the language. Authors were beginning to be aware that speech possessed definite dialect variations, even among educated speakers, as well as class dialects and substandard or less reputable forms of speech. These variations were considered "provincialisms" by some, and "mispronunciations" or "peculiarities of pronunciation" by others.

Thomas Sheridan and John Walker, the two major lexicographers of late eighteenth-century England, exerted a tremendous influence on the writers of American dictionaries and pronunciation manuals. Many authors in America patterned their pronunciation keys and *Guides to Pronunciation* after them. Departures from accepted British standard, especially as noted by Walker, were often accompanied by apologies and explanations.

Despite this strong dependence, a study of the period demonstrates that American authors were beginning to realize that they could not overlook the usage of competent speakers in this country. Noah Webster was one of the first to protest against an arbitrary regulation of language (known as the "prescriptive approach") and to recognize the concept of current usage as a criterion (the "descriptive approach" to language study). At least the groundwork had been laid.

Thus, the nineteenth century reflects these two divergent concepts of standard usage: the more widely-followed "doctrine of correctness" of the eighteenth century, and the attitude that attempts to consider the language as it is, rather than as it should be.

CONCLUSION

None of us is unaware that even before we entered the first year of formal schooling, most of us were already speaking understandable and "acceptable" English. None of us has escaped being corrected in the ways we have used the English language from the very beginnings of our struggles with it. Suggestions continue to come as we seek a more careful style, a more appropriate form, or a more clearly understandable pronunciation. The question of "usage" or "acceptability" cannot be disregarded. But we have progressed beyond the eighteenth-century approach that dictated "right" or "wrong" based on an unchanging rule or a whole set of rules. We know that if there are any rules in a language, they come from the actual, common usages found therein, and that both rules and particular usages may change. Nothing can really be labeled "acceptable" until the evidence permits and sanctions.

The question of "right" and "wrong" was the subject of the first chapter, and, in many ways, of this entire text. You know now that it is not easy to arrive at the conclusion of which usage is right and which usage is wrong. Actually, such conclusions have not been our immediate concern. Instead, we have sought the evidence of the linguistic behavior of native speakers of American English. Our intent has been to understand and analyze what we say, who says it, how, when, and where it is said. This text should have helped you collect some of the evidence. If pronouncements must be made, let them come when, after the study of our linguistic behavior, we are more capable of not only having an opinion, but of defending it.

QUESTIONS FOR FURTHER STUDY

1. How does a language reflect the attitudes current in the social and cultural scene?
2. Should language be guided by the proved rules of use, as geometry is by the axioms?
3. Earlier dictionaries did not recognize the pronunciations of *nature* and *picture* as "natshure and "pictshure." Your dictionary does not indicate "didja" for *did you*, although you may have heard it. What does this seeming discrepancy indicate?
4. Can you think of any pronunciations or grammatical usages that you use today but which your parents or grandparents did not consider acceptable in their youth?
5. Can you define the following terms?
   a. usage
   b. linguistic prescription
   c. the "doctrine of correctness"
   d. lexicography

SOURCES FOR FURTHER STUDY

BAUGH, Albert C., *A History of the English Language*, 2nd ed. (New York, Appleton-Century-Crofts, Inc., 1957).

BRONSTEIN, Arthur J., "Nineteenth-Century Attitudes Towards Pronunciation," *Quarterly Journal of Speech*, Vol. 40 (December, 1954), pp. 417–421.

DOBSON, Eric J., *English Pronunciation 1500–1700*, 2 vols. (London, Oxford, The Clarendon Press, 1957).

HOCKETT, Charles F., *A Course in Modern Linguistics* (New York, The Macmillan Company, 1958), Ch. 43, "Old and Middle English," pp. 372–379.

KÖKERITZ, Helge, *Shakespeare's Pronunciation* (New Haven, Yale University Press, 1953).

LEONARD, Sterling A., *The Doctrine of Correctness in English Usage, 1700–1800* (Madison, University of Wisconsin Studies in Language and Literature No. 25, 1929).

MARCKWARDT, Albert H., *Introduction to the English Language* (New York, Oxford University Press, 1942).

McKNIGHT, George H., *Modern English in the Making* (New York, D. Appleton and Co., 1928), esp. Ch. 15, "Eighteenth-Century Grammarians," pp. 377–397, and Ch. 18, "Fixing the Pronunciation," pp. 428–459.

MOORE, Samuel, *Historical Outlines of English Sounds and Inflections*, rev. by Albert H. Marckwardt (Ann Arbor, Michigan, 1951).

ROBERTSON, Stuart, *The Development of Modern English*, 2nd ed., rev. by Frederick G. Cassidy (Englewood Cliffs, New Jersey, Prentice-Hall, Inc., 1954), esp. Ch. 5, "The History of English Sounds," pp. 87–108.

SHELDON, Esther K., "Walker's Influence on the Pronunciation of English," *Publications of the Modern Language Association*, Vol. 62 (March, 1947), pp. 130–146.

SHERIDAN, Thomas, *A Complete Dictionary of the English Language, Both with Regard to Sound and Meaning*, 2nd ed. (London, C. Dilly, 1789).

STOCKWELL, Robert P., "The Phonology of Old English: A Structural Sketch," *Studies in Linguistics*, Vol. 13, Nos. 1–2 (Spring, 1958), pp. 13–24.

VIËTOR, Wilhelm, *Shakespeare's Pronunciation* (Marburg, N. G. Elwert, New York, Lemcke and Buechner, 1906).

WALKER, John, *A Critical Pronouncing Dictionary* and *Expositor of the English Language* (London, G. G. J. and J. Robinson, 1791).

WEBSTER, Noah, *Dissertations on the English Language* (Boston, Isaiah Thomas and Co., 1789). Reprinted by Scholars' Facsimiles and Reprints (Gainesville, Fla., 1951).

WYLD, Henry C., *A Short History of English*, 3rd ed., rev. and enl. (London, John Murray, Ltd., 1927).

——, *Studies in English Rhymes from Surrey to Pope* (London, John Murray, Ltd., 1923).

ZACHRISSON, Robert E., *Pronunciation of English Vowels, 1400–1700* (Göteborg, Zachrisson, 1913).

APPENDIX B

Charts, Maps, Samples of
Phonetic Transcription

	Bi-labial	Labio-dental	Dental and Alveolar	Retroflex	Palato-alveolar	Alveolo-palatal	Palatal	Velar	Uvular	Pharyngal	Glottal
CONSONANTS											
Plosive	p b		t d	ʈ ɖ			c ɟ	k g	q ɢ		ʔ
Nasal	m	ɱ	n	ɳ			ɲ	ŋ	N		
Lateral Fricative			ɬ ɮ								
Lateral Non-fricative			l	ɭ			ʎ				
Rolled			r						ʀ		
Flapped			ɾ	ɽ					ʀ		
Fricative	ɸ β	f v	θ ð, s z, ɹ	ʂ ʐ	ʃ ʒ	ɕ ʑ	ç ʝ	x ɣ	χ ʁ	ħ ʕ	h ɦ
Frictionless Continuants and Semi-vowels	w ɥ	ʋ	ɹ				j (ɥ)	(w)	ʁ		
VOWELS											
Close	(y ʉ u)						Front i y · ɨ ʉ · Back ɯ u				
Half-close	(ø o)						e ø · ɘ · ɤ o				
Half-open	(œ ɔ)						ɛ œ · ɜ · ʌ ɔ				
Open	(ɒ)						a · ɑ ɒ				

(Secondary articulations are shown by symbols in brackets.)

OTHER SOUNDS.—Palatalized consonants: ţ, ḑ, etc.; palatalized ʃ, ʒ : ʆ, ʓ. Velarized or pharyngalized consonants: ɫ, đ, ẕ, etc. Ejective consonants (with simultaneous glottal stop): p', t', etc. Implosive voiced consonants: ɓ, ɗ, etc. ɼ fricative trill. σ, ℧ (labialized θ, ð, or s, z). ƫ, ʓ (labialized ʃ, ʒ). ɹ, ʗ, ʖ (clicks, Zulu c, q, x). ɩ (a sound between r and l). ŋ Japanese syllabic nasal. ƕ (combination of x and ʃ). ʍ (voiceless w). ɩ, ʏ, ɵ (lowered varieties of i, y, u). ɜ (a variety of ə). ɵ (a vowel between ø and o).

Affricates are normally represented by groups of two consonants (ts, tʃ, dʒ, etc.), but when necessary, ligatures are used (ʦ, ʧ, ʤ, etc.), or the marks ‿ or ⁀ (ts or t͡s, etc.). ⁀ also denote synchronic articulation (m͡ŋ = simultaneous m and ŋ). c, ɟ may occasionally be used in place of tʃ, dʒ, and ʒ, ʑ for ts, dz. Aspirated plosives: ph, th, etc. r-coloured vowels: ɛɹ, aɹ, ɔɹ, etc., or eʴ, aʴ, ɔʴ, etc., or ɵ, aᶤ, ɒᶤ, etc.; r-coloured ə : əɹ or əʴ or ɹ or ᶕ, or ᶕ.

LENGTH, STRESS, PITCH.— ː (full length). · (half length). ˈ (stress, placed at beginning of the stressed syllable). ˌ (secondary stress). ˉ (high level pitch); ˍ (low level); ꜛ (high rising); ꜜ (low rising); ˋ (high falling); ˎ (low falling); ˆ (rise-fall); ˇ (fall-rise).

MODIFIERS.— ˜ nasality. ̫ breath (l̫ = breathed l). ̬ voice (s̬ = z). ˙ slight aspiration following p, t, etc. ͜ labialization (n̮ = labialized n). ̩ dental articulation (t̩ = dental t). ˙ palatalization (ż = ʑ). ˌ specially close vowel (ẹ = a very close e). ˌ specially open vowel (ę = a rather open e). ⊣ tongue raised (e⊣ or ẹ = ẹ). ⊢ tongue lowered (e⊢ or ę = ę). ⊦ tongue advanced (u⊦ or ų = an advanced u, t̟ = t̟). ⊢ or ╺ tongue retracted (i̱ or ɨ = ɨ̱, ṯ = alveolar t). ˙ lips more rounded. ˗ lips more spread. Central vowels: ɪ̈ (= ɨ), ü (= ʉ), ë (= ɵ), ö (= ɵ), ë, ö. ˌ (e.g. n̩) syllabic consonant. ˴ consonantal vowel. ʃˆ variety of ʃ resembling s, etc.

FIG. 39. The International Phonetic Alphabet (revised to 1951). (Reproduced by permission of the International Phonetic Association.)

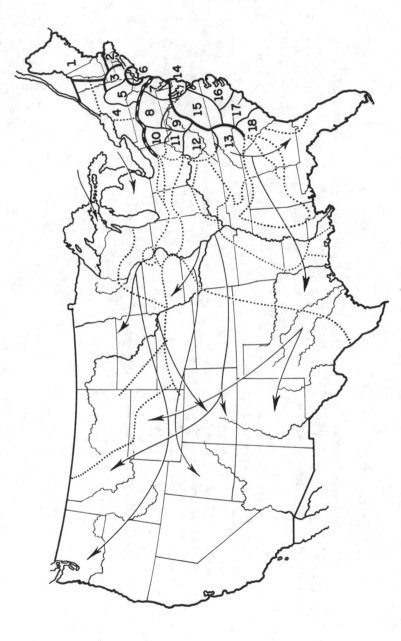

FIG. 40. Dialect areas of the United States. (From Hans Kurath, *A Word Geography of the Eastern United States*, Fig. 3. Copyright by the University of Michigan, Ann Arbor, 1949. Kurath indicates only the Atlantic Seaboard areas. The tentative dialect boundaries of the remainder of the country and the arrows indicating the directions of migrations are from W. Nelson Francis, *The Structure of American English*, Map. 2, p. 580. Copyright, 1958, by the Ronald Press Company) contributed by Virginia McDavid.

The North

1. Northeastern New England
2. Southeastern New England
3. Southwestern New England
4. Upstate New York and western Vermont
5. The Hudson Valley
6. Metropolitan New York

The Midland

7. The Delaware Valley (Philadelphia Area)
8. The Susquehanna Valley
9. The Upper Potomac and Shenandoah Valleys
10. The Upper Ohio Valley (Pittsburgh Area)
11. Northern West Virginia
12. Southern West Virginia
13. Western North and South Carolina

The South

14. Delmarva (Eastern Shore of Maryland and Virginia and southern Delaware)
15. The Virginia Piedmont
16. Northeastern North Carolina (Albemarle Sound and Neuse Valley)
17. The Cape Fear and Peedee Valleys
18. South Carolina Low Country (Charleston)

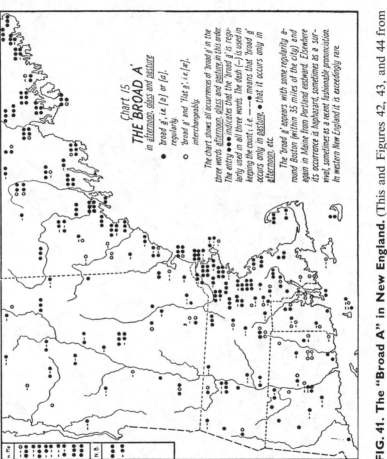

FIG. 41. The "Broad A" in New England. (This and Figures 42, 43, and 44 from the *Handbook of the Linguistic Geography of New England* by Hans Kurath, with the collaboration of Marcus L. Hansen, Julia Bloch, and Bernard Bloch (Washington, D.C., American Council of Learned Societies, 1939), p. 34, with permission.)

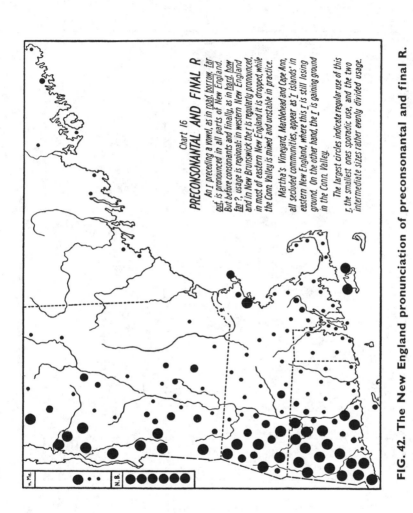

FIG. 42. The New England pronunciation of preconsonantal and final R.

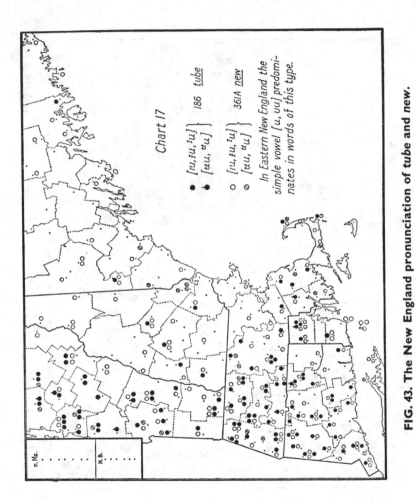

FIG. 43. The New England pronunciation of tube and new.

THE BOSTON AREA

EASTERN WORDS AND PRONUNCIATIONS

x   in general use
/   fairly common
·   rare

	FOCAL AREA							MARGIN			WEST	
	Maine	Eastern New Hampshire	Essex County	Merrimack Valley	Boston Area	Plymouth Area	Rhode Island	Worcester Area	Upper Connecti-cut Valley	Eastern Connecticut	Lower Connecti-cut Valley	Western Vermont
101 [r] lost in *barn*	x	x	/	x	x	/	x	x	x	x	/	·
59 [3] in *thirty*	x	x	/	x	x	/	/	/	/	/	·	
192 [a] in *calf*	x	x	/	x	x	x	/	x	x	·	·	
311 [a] in *glass*	x	/	x	·	x	·	/	·	·	·	·	·
45 [ɒ] in *rod*	x	x	x	x	x	x	x	x	/	x	·	
550 [ɒ] in *law*	x	x	x	x	x	x	x	·	/	/	/	·
142 [ɪ] in *towel*	x	x	x	x	x	x	x	/	x	x	/	·
558 [u] in *butcher*	x	x	x	x	·	x	x	·	·	/	·	

FIG. 44. The pronunciation of certain words in the Boston area.

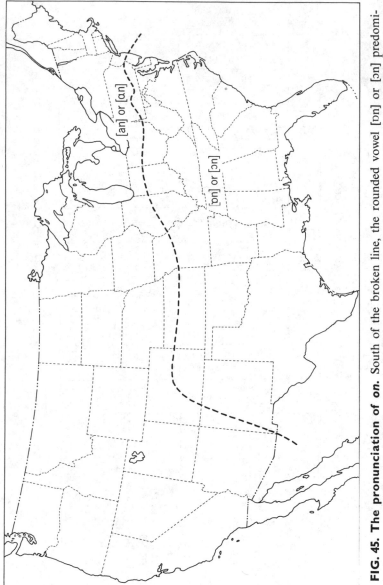

FIG. 45. The pronunciation of on. South of the broken line, the rounded vowel [ɒn] or [ɔn] predominates; north of the line, the unrounded vowel [an] or [ɑn] predominates. (After C. K. Thomas, "The Linguistic Mason and Dixon Line," in Donald C. Bryant, ed., *The Rhetorical Idiom*, p. 254. Copyright, 1958, by the Cornell University Press.

SAMPLE PHONETIC TRANSCRIPTIONS

The following transcriptions appeared in four earlier issues of *American Speech* at a time when that journal included some sample transcriptions of American speech in each issue. The first transcription appeared in the December, 1939 issue, pages 288–289. It was made from a radio recording of part of an address given by President Emeritus James Rowland Angell of Yale University at the University of Rochester in November, 1935. The speaker was born in Vermont. The second transcription was made from a recording of a broadcast made on July 18, 1940, at which time Franklin D. Roosevelt accepted his party's nomination for the Presidency. It appeared in the October, 1940 issue, page 301. Transcription III was made from a recording of a radio broadcast made by then President Isaiah Bowman of Johns Hopkins University on February 24, 1941. Dr. Bowman was born in Waterloo, Ontario, Canada. This transcription appeared in the April, 1941 issue, page 121. Transcription IV was made from a recording made by William Jennings Bryan of his "Cross of Gold" speech (Gennett Record, No. 400000A). Mr. Bryan was born in Salem, Illinois, in 1860. This transcription appeared in the February, 1942 issue, page 49.

These four transcriptions are reproduced with the permission of the Editors of *American Speech* and the Columbia University Press. Many other samples of American speech appear in a volume edited by Jane Dorsey Zimmerman, *Phonetic Transcriptions from "American Speech,"* Revised Edition (New York, Columbia University Press, 1939). Single and double bars, [|, ||], represent short and long pauses, respectively.

I

... ɪf junɪ'vɝsɪtɪ 'mɛn ɑɚ tə 'kleɪm| 'fridəm ʌv 'tɪtʃɪŋ| æn 'fridəm ˀʌv 'θɔt| ænd 'spitʃ| ðeɪ 'mʌst ɪn 'tɝn| 'dʒʌstɪfaɪ ðə 'kleɪm|| naṭ 'oʊnlɪ baɪ eɪ 'dɪsənt rɪ'spɛkt| fɔ ðɪ ə'pɪnjən əv ˌmæn'kaɪnd| bʌṭ 'ɔlso baɪ soʊ'braɪətɪ əv Pʌtrəns| ɒn æ'kjutlɪ kɑ̃tɚ'vɝsɪəl Pɪʃjuz| ðeɪ mʌst bi 'sɛnsɪtɪv| tu ðə 'dɪkˌteɪts əv 'gʊd 'sɛnˈts| æn 'gʊd 'teɪst| æz ðə 'greɪt 'mæs əv ðəm Pɔlwɪz Pɑ|| Paftər 'ɔl| ðɪ junɪ'vɝsɪtɪ Pɪz| ˀeɪ 'krɪtʃɚ ˀʌv ðə sə'saɪətɪ ʌɪtʃ sə'pɔɚts ɪt| ænd ɪz 'sɛt tə 'sɝv ðə 'dɪpɪst æn 'moʊst ɛn'duəɪŋ 'ɪntɚəs: ɒv 'ðæt sə'saɪətɪ|| ɪt 'ðɛɚ'fɔɚ 'kænnɑt 'waɪzlɪ| bi ɪn'dɪfɚənt tu 'fɔɚsɪz| haʊPɛvɚ ɪ'ræʃənəl| ðæt ɑ 'moʊmən'tɛrəlɪ 'muvɪŋ ðə 'θɔt æn 'filɪŋ| ˀʌv 'ɑnəst foʊk|| ænd ʌaɪl ɪt mʌst 'faɪt· tu ðɪ 'ɛnd| fɔ ðə 'fridəm əv ðə 'skɒlɚ| tu 'sɝtʃ fɔɚ 'truθ| æn pə'naʊns 'fɪɚləslɪ| ə'pʌn hɪz 'faɪndɪŋz| ɪn ðə 'fild 'fɔ ʌɪtʃ hi hæz bɪn 'spɛʃəlɪ 'treɪnd| ɪt meɪ 'wɛl 'ɝdʒ ɪts 'mɛmbɚz tu ˌkɑn'sɪdɚ ðə 'trædʒɪk 'pɛnəltɪz| ʌɪtʃ meɪ ə'raɪz| frəm eɪ 'kɛɚləs mɪs'jus| ʌv ðɪs 'mætʃləs 'prɪvəlɪdʒ| ðæt 'mɛmbɚʃɪp ɪn eɪ 'greɪt junɪ'vɝsɪtɪ ˌkɑn'fɝz| ə'pɒn ɪts poʊ'zɛsɔɚ|| ...

II

... djʊrɪŋ ðə ˈpast ˈfju ˈmʌnts| wɪð ˈdju kənˈgrɛʃnəl əˈpruvəl| ðə juˈnaɪtəd ˈsteɪts hæz bɪn ˈteɪkɪŋ ˈstɛps tʊ ˈɪmpləmɛnt ðə ˈtoʊtl dəˈfɛns əv əˈmɛrɪkə|| aɪ kænat fəˈgɛt ðət ɪn ˈkɛrɪŋ ?aʊt ˈðɪs ˈproʊgræm| aɪ hæv ˈdraftəd ɪntʊ ðə ˈsɝvɪs əv ðə ˈneɪʃn ˈmɛnɪ ˈmɛn ænd ˈwɪmɪn| ˈteɪkɪŋ ðɛm əˈweɪ frəm ɪmˈpɔtnt ˈpraɪvət əˈfɛɾəz| ˈkɔlɪŋ ðɛm ˈsʌdnlɪ frəm ðɛə ˈhoʊmz ænd ðɛə ˈbɪznəsɪz|| aɪ hæv ˈaskt ðɛm tə ˈlɪv| ˈðɛə Iˀoʊn ˈwœk| æn tə kənˈtrɪbjut ˈðɛə ˈskɪl æn ɪkˈspɪrɪəns| tə ðə ˈkɔz əv ˈðɛə ˈneɪʃn|| ˈaɪ| æz ðə ˈhɛd əv ˈðɛə ˈgʌvənmənt| hæv Iˀaskt ðɛm tə ˈdu ˈðɪs|| rəˈgadləs əv ˈpaʈɪ rəˈgadləs əv ˈpœsnəl kənˈvɪnjəns| ˈðeɪ ˈkeɪm|| ˈðeɪ Iˀansəd ðə ˈkɔl||. ...

təˈdeɪ ˈɔl ˈpraɪvət ˈplænz| ˈɔl ˈpraɪvət ˈlaɪvz| həv ˈbɪn ɪn ə ˈsɛns rəˈpɪld baɪ ən Iˀoʊvəˈraɪdɪŋ| ˈpʌblɪk ˈdeɪndʒə|| ɪn ðə ˈfeɪs əv ˈðæt ˈpʌblɪk ˈdeɪndʒə ˈɔl ˈðoʊz hu kən bi əv ˈsɝvɪs tə ðə rəˈpʌblɪk| hæv ˈnoʊ ˈtʃɔɪs bət tʊ Iˀɔfə ðəmˈsɛlvz fə ˈsɝvɪs| ɪn ˈðoʊz kəˈpæsətɪz fə ʍɪtʃ ˈðeɪ ˈmeɪ bi ˈfɪtɪd|| ˈðoʊz ˈmaɪ ˈfrɛndz ɑ ðə ˈrɪznz ʍaɪ aɪ hæv hæd tʊ ədˈmɪt tʊ maɪˈsɛlf| ænd ˈnaʊ tə ˈsteɪt tə ˈju| ðət ˈmaɪ ˈkʌnʃəns| wɪl nɒt ˈlɛt mi ˈtœn maɪ ˈbæk| əˈpɒn ə ˈkɔl tə ˈsɝvɪs||

ðə ˈraɪt tə ˈmeɪk ˈðæt ˈkɔl| ˈrɛsts wɪð ðə ˈpipl| ˈθru ðɪ əˈmɛrɪkən ˈmɛθəd əv eɪ ˈfri əˈlɛkʃn| Iˀoʊnlɪ ðə ˈpipl ðəmˈsɛlvz| kæn ˈdraft eɪ ˈprɛzədənt|| ɪf ˈsʌtʃ ə ˈdraft ˈʃʊd bi ˈmeɪd əˈpɒn mi| aɪ ˈseɪ tu ju ɪn ðɪ Iˀʌtmoʊst sɪmˈplɪsətɪ| aɪ wɪl wɪð ˈgɒdz ˈhɛlp| kənˈtɪnju tə ˈsɝv| wɪð ðə ˈbɛst əv ˈmaɪ əˈbɪlətɪ| ænd wɪð ðə ˈfulnəs əv ˈmaɪ ˈstrɛŋkθ||

tu ˈju ðə ˈdɛlɪgeɪts əv ˈðɪs kənˈvɛntʃn| aɪ ɪkˈsprɛs ˈmaɪ ˈgrætɪtjud| fə ðə səˈlɛkʃn əv ˈhɛnrɪ ˈwaləs fə ðə ˈhaɪ ˈɔfəs əv ˈprɛzədənt [sic] əv ðɪ juˈnaɪtəd ˈsteɪts|| hɪz ˈfɝst ˈhænd ˈnalɪdʒ əv ðə ˈprabləmz əv ˈgʌvənmənt| ɪn ˈɛvrɪ ˈsfɪər əv ˈlaɪf| ænd ɪn ˈɛvrɪ ˈsɪŋgl ˈpat əv ðə ˈneɪʃn| ænd ɪnˈdid əv ðə ˈhöl ˈwœld| ˈkwɒləfaɪz hɪm wɪˈðaʊt ˌrɛzəˈveɪʃn|| hɪz ˈpræktɪkl aɪˈdiəlɪzm| wɪl bi əv ˈgreɪt ˈsɝvɪs tʊ mi ˌɪndɪˈvɪdʒʊəlɪ| æn tu ðə ˈneɪʃn æz ə ˈhöl||

ænd| tu ðə ˈtʃɛəmən| ʌv ðə ˈnæʃnəl kəˈmɪtɪ| ðə ˈpoʊst ˈmastə ˈdʒɛnrəl əv ðɪ juˈnaɪtəd ˈsteɪts| ɔ əz aɪ ˈlaɪk ˈbɛtə tə ˈkɔl ɪm| ˈmaɪ Iˀoʊldˈfrɛnd| ˈdʒɪm ˈfalɪ|| aɪ ˈsɛnd| əz aɪ hæv Iˀɔftn bəˈfɔə| ænd wɪl ˈmɛnɪ ˈtaɪmz əˈgeɪn| ˈmaɪ ˈmoʊst əˈfɛkʃnət ˈgritɪŋz|| ˈɔl əv əs ə ˈʃʊə| ðət hi wɪl kənˈtɪnju tə ˈgɪv| Iˀɔl ðə ˈlidəʃɪp ən səˈpɔət ðət hi ˈpɒsəblɪ ˈkæn| tə ðə ˈkɔz əv əˈmɛrəkən dəˈmakrəsɪ||. ...

III

ˈðɪs ˈneɪʃn hæz ɪmˈfætɪkəlɪ ɪkˈsprɛst ɪts dɪˌtɝməˈneɪʃn| tʊ ˈseɪfˈgaɚd ɪts ˈoʊn dəˈmakrəsɪ| æn tʊ ˈhɛlp Iˀʌðɚ dəˈmakrəsɪz| ˈðæt ˈɪz| Iˀʌðɚ ˈkaɪndz æn diˈgriz əv dɪˈmakrəsɪ|| ˈðɪs ɪnˈvalvz ˈkanflɪkt| ɪnˈtɛns ?æn proˈlɒŋd ˈkãⁿflɪkt|| ˈʍɛðɚ ɔɚ ˈnat wi ɚ ət ˈwɔɚ||

wi rəˈdʒɛkt ðə ˈnju ˈɔɚdɚ əv ˈnatsɪ ˈdʒɝmənɪ| ˈnaʊ ðə dɪˈkleɚd Iˀɛnəmɪ

ˈʌv dɪˈmakrəsɪz| bɪˈkɔz |ˈdʒɝmən ˈlidəz ɪnˈtɝprət ˈðɛə ˈnju ˈɔɔdə| ˈounlɪ
ɪn ˈtɝmz əv ˈdɛθ tʊ ˈɔ ˈʌðə ˈɔədəz||

ˈhu ɪz rɪˈspansəbl fɔə ə ˈpis| ˈðæt wɪl pəˈmɪt eɪ ˈrɪznəbl ˈnju ˈɔədə tə bi
ˈfɔədʒd|| ɪz ɪt ˈnat ðə ˈvɪktə|| ɪf ðə ˈvɪktə ɪz rɪˈspansəbl fə ðə ˈkansᵊkwɛnsəz
əv hɪz ˈvɪktɔɪ| ˈwi ðə ˈpipl əv ðɪ juˈnaɪtəd ˈsteɪts ɝ ˈnau ˈfeɪst wɪð ˈtu
ˈtɛɔəblɪ ˈɝdʒənt ˈkwɛstʃnz|| ˈhau ʃəl wi ˈhɛlp ˈˈwɪn ˈvɪktɔɪ| æn ʍat ʃəl wi
ˈˈdu wɪð ˈvɪktɔɪ ʍɛn wi həv ˈwʌn ɪt||

ðə ˈpiplz əv ðə ˈwɝld ˈθɪŋk ðət ˈvɪktɔɪ wɪl ˈbrɪŋ ˈpis|| ˈðeɪ ˈlʊk ˈfɔɔwəd
tə ðə ˈbɝθ əv prasˈpɛɔətɪ| ðə ˈtʃaɪld əv ˈpis|| ʍatˈɛvə ˈɛls ðə ˈfjutʃə meɪ
rɪˈvil| ˈðɛə ɪz ə ˈdeɪndʒə ˈsɪgnəl əˈhɛd fɔə ⁱᵖɛvrɪ ⁱᵖɪntrɪst ʍɪtʃ ðə ˈskʊlz əv
əˈmɛɔəkə ⁱᵖædvəkeɪt æn dɪˈfɛnd||

æz ˈfɑɝ æz ˈspid æn ˈkɔsts ə kənˈsɝnd| wi ɑɝ ˈgouɪŋ əˈbaut ˈauɝ
dɪˈfɛnsɪv ˈmɪlətɛɔɪ ˌprɛpəˈleɪʃnz| æn ˈmʌst ˈgou əˈbaut ðɛm| æz ɪf wi wɝ
ɔlˈrɛdɪ ət ˈwo:ɝ|| ˈnau ˈðɛɝ ɪz bət ˈwʌn ˈweɪ əv ˈʌltəmətlɪ ˈmitɪŋ ˈðouz
ˈkɔsts| ʌv ˈpeɪɪŋ fɔə ˈwo:ɝ| ɔɝ ˌprɛpəˈleɪʃnz fɔə ˈwo:ɝ| ɪt ɪz baɪ ˈlouɝɪŋ
ðə ˈstændəd əv ˈlɪvɪŋ|| ˈðɪs ɪz ðə ˌjuniˈvɝsl ˈsɪnjɝɪdʒ ʍɪtʃ ˈmɑɹəz ɪkˈstrækts
frəm ɑɝ ˈsouʃl ˈkɔɪnɪdʒ|| ɪt ɪz ˈtʃɪzld ˈaut əv ˈskʊlz mjuˈziəmz| ⁱᵖaɝt
ˈgælɝɪz| ˈkwalətɪ ænd əˈmaunt əv ˈfud| ˈkloumdɪŋ| ˈhaus ˈfɝnɪʃɪŋz| ˈsɔɪl
ˌprɛzɝˈveɪʃn| ˈkɛɝ əv ðə ˈblaɪnd ænd ðɪ ɪnˈseɪn| ˈpraɪvət ən ˈpʌblɪk
ˌhɒspɪtlaɪˈzeɪʃn| ˈroud rɪˈpɛɝ| ænd ˈauɝz əv ˈliʒɝ| fɔə ˌrɛkrɪˈeɪʃn| ɪnˈkludəd
ɪn ðə ˈlɪst ɪz ˈpʌblɪk ˈmɔɔˈæl| ʍɪtʃ ˈsʌmz ʌp ðə ˈnæʃənəl ˈkæɹɔɪktə əˈfɛkt
əv ˈɔl ðɪ ˈʌðəz|| ⁱᵖivn ðə ˈvɪktə| kən kənˈtraɪv no ˈweɪ əv əˈskeɪp frəm ðə
ˈdʒɛnrəl əˈfɛkt| fɔə ðə ˈwɝld ɪz ˈbaund təˈgɛðɝ ɪn ˈwɛlˈfɛɝ| æz ɪn ˈtreɪd||
ˈvɪktə æn ˈvæŋkwɪʃt ˈʃɛːɝ| ði ˌɪnɪsˈkeɪpəbl ˈkɔsts əv ˈwo:ɝ| ɪn ˈgreɪtɝ ɔɝ
ˈlɛsɝ dɪˈgri|| ðə ˈhoul ˈwɝld ˈpeɪz| æn ˈpeɪmənt ˈkʌmz ˈaut əv ən əˈkaunt
ˈkɔld ˈstændɝd əv ˈlɪvɪŋ||. . . .

<h2 style="text-align:center">IV</h2>

ˈmɪstə ˈtʃɝmən| ⁱᵖæn ˈdʒɛntlmən əv ðə kənˈvɛntʃən|| ⁱᵖaɪ wʊd bi prə-
ˈzʌmptʃuəs ɪnˈdid| tʊ pɝˈzɛnt ˈmaɪˈsɛɝf| əˈgɛnst ðə dɪsˈtɪŋgwɪʃt ˈdʒɛntlmən
tʊ ˈhum ju hæv ˈlɪsənd| ɪf ˈðɪs wɝ eɪ ˈmɪɝ ˈmɛʒɝɪŋ| ⁱᵖʌv əˈbɪlətɪz| bʌt
ˈðɪs ɪz ˈnɒt ə ˈkɒntɛs| bəˈtwin ˈpɝsənz|| ðɪ ˈhʌmblɪst ˈsɪtəsən ɪn ˈɔl ðə
ˈlændz| ʍɛn ˈklæd ɪn ðɪ ˈaɔmɝ əv ə ˈraɪtʃəs ˈkɔz| ɪz ˈstrɔŋgɝ ðən ˈɔl ðɪ
ˈhousts əv ˈɛɔrɝ|| aɪ ˈkʌm tʊ ˈspik tə ˈju ɪn ðɪ dɪˈfɛns əv ə ˈkɔːːz| ⁱᵖæz
ˈhoulɪ əz ðə ˈkɔːːz əv ˈlɪbɝtɪ|| ðə ˈkɔːːz ⁱᵖʌv hjuˈmænətɪ||

ʍɛn ˈðɪs dɪˈbeɪt ɪz kənˈkludəd| eɪ ˈmouʃn wəl bi ˈmeɪd tʊ ˈleɪ əpən ðə
ˈteɪbl| ðə ˌrɛzəˈluʃən ˈɔfɝd ɪn ˌkɒmənˈdeɪʃən əv ðɪ ædˌmɪnɪsˈtreɪʃən| ənd
ˈɔlso ðə ˌrɛzəˈluʃən ˈɔfɝd ɪn ˌkɒndɛmˈneɪʃən| ⁱᵖɒv ðɪ ədˈmɪnɪsˈtreɪʃən||
wi əbˈdʒɛkt tʊ ˈbrɪŋɪŋ ðɪs ˈkwɛstʃən ˈdaun tʊ ðə ˈlɛvl əv ˈpɝsnz|| ðɪ
ˌɪndɪˈvɪdʒuəl ɪz ˈbʌt ən ˈætəm| hi ɪz ˈbɔɝn| hi ˈæks| hi ˈdaɪz|| bʌt ˈprɪnsəplz
ⁱᵖɔɝ iˈtɝnəl| ənd ˈðɪs hæz bɪn eɪ ˈkɑntɛst| ˈouvɝ eɪ ˈprɪnsəpl||

ˈnɛvɚ bəˈfoɚ ɪn ðə ˈhɪstrɪ əv ˈðɪs ˈkʌntrɪ| hæz ðɚ bɪn ˈwɪtnəst ˈsʌtʃ eɪ
ˈkɑntɛst| æz ˈðæt θru ˈmɪtʃ wi həv ˈdʒʌst ˈpæst|| ˈnɛvɚ bəˈfoɚ ɪn ðə ˈhɪstrɪ
əv əˈmɛrɪkən ˈpɒlɪtɪks| hæz ə ˈgreɪt ˈɪʃu| bɪn ˈfɔt ˈaut æz ˈðɪs ˈɪʃu hæz ˈbɪn|
baɪ ðə ˈvoutɚz| əv ə ˈgreɪt ˈpɑrtɪ|| ɒn ðə ˈfoɚθ əv ˈmɑɚtʃ| ˈeɪˈtin ən ˈnaɪntɪ
ˈfaɪv| eɪ ˈfju ˈdɛməkræts| ˈmoust əv ðəm ˈmɛmbɚz əv ˈkɒŋgrəs| ˈɪʃud ən
əˈdrɛs tu ðə ˈdɛməkræts| əv ðə ˈneɪʃən| æˈlsɚtɪŋ ðət ðə ˈmʌnɪ ˈkwɛsˈʃən
wəz ðə ˈpærəmaunt ˈɪʃu əv ðɪ ˈauɚ|| dɪˈklɛrɪŋ ðæt ə məˈdʒɑɚɪtɪ əv ðə
ˈdɛmokrætɪk ˈpɑɚtɪ| hæd ðə ˈraɪt tu kənˈtroul ðɪ ˈækʃən əv. ðə ˈpɑɚtɪ|
ɒn ˈðɪs ˈpɛɚɾəmaunt ˈɪʃu| æn kənˈkludɪŋ wɪð ðə rəˈkwɛst| ðæt ðə bɪˈliːvɚz
ɪn ðə ˈfri ˈkɔɪnɪdʒ əv ˈsɪlvɚ| ɪn ðə ˈdɛmoˈkrætɪk ˈpɑɚtɪ| ˈɔɚgənaɪz| ˈteɪk
ˈtʃɑɚdʒ ˈʌv| æn kənˈtroul ðə ˈpɒlɪsɪ ɒv| ðə ˈdɛmokrætɪk ˈpɑɚtɪ|| ˈθri
ˈmʌnθs ˈleɪtɚ æt ˈmɛmfəs| æn ˌɔɚgənəˈzeɪʃən wəz pɚˈfɛktəd ʔæn ðə ˈsɪlvɚ
ˈdɛməkræts ˈwɛnt ˈfoɚθ ˈoupənlɪ| æn kɚˈreɪdʒəslɪ proˈkleɪmɪŋ ðɛɚ bəˈlif|
æn dɪˈklɛɚɪŋ ðæt ɪf səkˈsɛsfʊl| ðeɪ wud ˈkrɪstəlaɪz ɪntu ə ˈplætfɔɚm| ðə
ˌdɛkləˈreɪʃn| ˌmɪtʃ ˈðeɪ hæd ˈmeɪd|| ˈðɛn bɪˈgæn ðə ˈkɒnflɪkt|| wɪð ə ˈzɪl
əˈproutʃɪŋ ðə ˈzɪl| ˌmɪtʃ ɪnˈspaɪɚd ðə kruˈseɪdɚz| hu ˈfɒloud ˈpitɚ ðə
ˈhɚmɪt| ʔauɚ ˈsɪlvɚ ˈdɛməkræts ˈwɛnt ˈfoɚθ frəm ˈvɪktɔɪ ʌntu ˈvɪktɔɪ|
ʌnˈtɪl ðeɪ ɚ ˈnau əˈsɛmbld| ˈnɑt tu dɪsˈkʌs| ˈnɑt tu dɪˈbeɪt| bʌt tu ˈɛntɚ
ˈʌp ðə ˈdʒʌdʒmənt ɔlˈrɛdɪ ˈrɛndɚd baɪ ðə ˈpleɪn ˈpipl| əv ˈðɪs ˈkʌntrɪ||
ɪn ˈðɪs ˈkɑntɛst ˈbrʌðɚ hæz bɪn əˈreɪd əˈgɛnst ˈbrʌðɚ| ˈfɑðɚ əˈgɛnst ˈsʌn||
ðə ˈwɔɚməst ˈtaɪz əv ˈlʌv| ʌˈkweɪntəns| ænd əˌsousɪˈeɪʃən| hæv bɪn ˌdɪsrɪ-
ˈgɑɚdəd|| ˈould ˈlidɚz hæv bɪn ˈkæst əˈsaɪd| ˌmən ðeɪ rɪˈfjuzd tu ˈgɪv
ɪkˈsprɛʃən| tu ðə ˈsɛntəmənt əv ˈðouz hum ˈðeɪ wud ˈlid| æn ˈnju ˈlidɚz|
hæv ˈsprʌŋ ˈʌp tu gɪv dɪˈrɛkʃən tu ˈðɪs ˈkɔz əv ˈtruθ|| ˈðʌs həz ðə ˈkɑntɛst
bɪn ˈweɪdʒd| ənd wi hæv əˈsɛmbld ˈhɪɚ| ˈʌndɚ əz ˈbaɪndɪŋ nd ˈsɒləm
ɪnˈstrʌkʃn| əz wəz ˈɛvɚ ɪmˈpouzd əpɒn ðə ˌrɛprəˈzɛntətɪvz ʌv ðə pipl||

V *

aɪ ˈnou ˈɔl əˈbaut ðə ˈtrʌblz ju kn ˈhæv wɪð ə ˈhaus n ˈgɑdn, ənd aɪ
ˈsɪmpəθaɪz wɪð ju, bət aɪ m ˈʃɔ ju ˌwʊdnt bɪ ˈhæpɪ ɪn ə ˈflæt. ˈaɪ ˌlɪvd ɪn
wʌn wɛn aɪ ˈfɜs ˌgɒt ˈmærɪd, əm wɪ ˌhæd ə ˈkʌpl u ˈkwɒrld ˈɔl ˈdeɪ ən
ˈnaɪt bɪˈlou əs, ˈænd ə trɒmˈboun ˌpleɪər əˈbʌv əs. ɪt bɪˌkeɪm ˈsou ˈbæd,
ðət aɪ ˈjus tə ˌlʊk ˈfəwəd tə ˈgɛtɪŋ tə ðɪ ˈɒfɪs, fər ə ˈbɪt əv ˈpis n ˈkwaɪət.
ɪn ðɪ ˈɛnd, maɪ ˈwaɪf wəz ɒn ðə ˈvɜdʒ əv ə ˈnɜvəs ˈbreɪkdaun, sou aɪ
dɪˈsaɪdɪd tə ˈdʒɔɪn ðə ˈmɪljənz ɪn ðə ˈsʌbɜbz. əv ˈkɔs, aɪ ˈhæd tu əˈreɪndʒ
ə ˈmɔgɪdʒ tə ˈpeɪ fə ðə ˈhaus, bət ɪts ˈplɛznt tə ˌkʌm ˈhoum ˈhɪər ɪn ðɪ
ˈɪvnɪŋ, əˈweɪ frəm ðə ˈnɔɪz n ˈdʌst əv ˈlʌndən. ðə ˈtrʌbl ˈɪz maɪ ˈwaɪfs
ˈnau kəmˈpleɪnɪŋ ðət ɪts ˈtu ˈkwaɪət n ˈlounlɪ.

* The following transcription was made by Mr. A. C. Gimson, Department
of Phonetics, University College, London. It is included here as a sample of
Southern British speech and is reproduced with Mr. Gimson's permission. Mr.
Gimson uses commas and periods to express short and long pauses.

PHONEMIC TRANSCRIPTION SYSTEMS

Probably the most widely followed phonemic analysis of the sounds of American English is that presented by George L. Trager and Henry Lee Smith, Jr. in their *An Outline of English Structure*.[1] Their ninety-two page pamphlet contains forty-two pages on the phonology of American English and their comments are based on a wide acquaintance with different dialects of American speech. Their conclusions are admittedly tentative and they note in their Preface the desire for "the widest possible comment and criticism by linguistic scientists." The publication of this pamphlet induced widespread comment, ranging from severe disagreement to very sympathetic, if not enthusiastic, acceptance. Most of the scholarly reviews of the *Outline* are too complicated for student reading. You may, however, get a taste of scholarly "battles" and probing by glancing at some of the following reviews. The chances are you will understand neither the *Outline* nor the reviews unless you can afford to give them much time and careful study. See, for example, those by Raven I. McDavid, Jr., in the *Journal of English and Germanic Philology*, Vol. 52 (1953), pages 387–391; Harold Whitehall in the *Kenyon Review*, Vol. 13 (1951), pages 710–714; James Sledd in *Language*, Vol. 31 (April–June, 1955), pages 312–335; and Hans Kurath, "The Binary Interpretation of English Vowels," *Language*, Vol. 33 (April–June, 1957), pages 111–122.

The Trager-Smith symbolization uses the same forms for the consonants as used in this text, except for /c, j, š, ž, y/ which are represented in this text by the IPA symbols /tʃ, dʒ, ʃ, ʒ, j/. Nine simple or basic vowels are symmetrically arranged as follows:

	Front	*Central*	*Back*
High	i	ɨ	u
Mid	e	ə	o
Low	æ	a	ɔ

	as in	
pit	"jist"	put
pet	putt	obey, *or*
		whole (ENE)
pat	pot	pot (ENE), *or*
		aural

[1] *Studies in Linguistics: Occasional Papers, No. 3* (Norman, Okla., Battenberg Press, 1951).

To each of these simple vowels may be added one of three semivowels /y, w, h/, making a total of thirty-six possible simple and complex nuclei. Not all of the thirty-six nuclei appear in any one dialect of American speech nor in any one person's speech.

The diphthongs, or complex nuclei, mentioned above, consist of two phonemes, a simple vowel plus one of the three glides. Those that end with /y/ glide from one of the simple vowels to a higher and fronter tongue position: /ay/ or /ey/ as in *my* and *day*, phonetically [aɪ] or [eɪ]. Nuclei ending in /w/ glide from a simple vowel to a higher, back, and more rounded tongue position: /aw/ or /ow/ as in *bout* and *boat*, phonetically [aʊ] and [oʊ]. Nuclei ending in /h/ glide from a simple vowel to a more central tongue position or to a lengthened version of the same vowel: /ih/ or /ah/ as in *idea*, or ENE *fear*, and *calm*, or ENE *farm*, phonetically [ɪə], [ɑə] or [ɑ:], [aə] or [a:].

This phonemic symbolization, despite its tentativeness and certain strong objections, has been widely followed in much linguistic writing and it will be to your advantage to become acquainted with it. A glance at page 316 of this Appendix will soon show that not all linguists who are strongly in favor of this phonemic arrangement agree with the identical system of representation. This is especially noticed with the transcription of the second element of the complex nuclei.

Other students of our language have found it useful to work with other systems of transcribing the phonemes of American English. Kenyon *(American Pronunciation)* and Thomas *(Phonetics of American English)*, both of which sources have been cited many times in this text, follow the International Phonetic Alphabet, although they do not make use of differentiating slants and brackets. Although both Kenyon and Thomas have written "phonetic texts," their books are essentially attempts to treat the phonemes of English and their allophonic variants. Clifford H. Prator, Jr., in his *Manual of American English Pronunciation*, uses the IPA symbolization with slight modifications. In his Introduction, he notes: "The system of phonetic transcription adopted is almost entirely phonemic, and the norms presented are phonemically defined . . ."[2] He presents eleven simple vowels and eight diphthongs for the users of his text who are learning English as a second language. Charles C. Fries, in his *Teaching and Learning English as a Foreign Language*, and Kenneth L. Pike, in his *Phonemics: A Technique for Reducing Languages to Writing*, use symbols similar to those found in Kenyon and Thomas, although they both retain /ə/ for [ʌ] and [ə].[3] Fries uses /ər/ for both [ɝ] and [ɚ].

[2] (New York, Rinehart, 1957), pp. XIV–XV.

[3] (Ann Arbor, University of Michigan Press, 1945); (Ann Arbor, University of Michigan Press, 1947).

Pike uses /r/ for the same sounds. Phonemic treatments of the sounds of American English, using slight modifications of the International Phonetic Alphabet are probably the most common.

Suggestions that the Trager-Smith system show at least ten simple vowels and at least one or two other semivowels have been made by James Sledd, in the review of the *Outline* noted above, by Raven I. McDavid, Jr., in his chapter on "American English Dialects" in W. Nelson Francis, *The Structure of American English*,[4] and by Sumner Ives, in his presentation to the Texas Workshop on the phonemes of American English, in 1956. These three gentlemen are Southeasterners, and each is convinced that the nine simple vowels of the T-S system do not permit the contrasts they possess in their speech for such words as *fair, fire*, and *far* or *hide, hired, hod*, and *hard*. In a paper read by Ives at the Texas Workshop, a copy of which he was good enough to forward the author, he noted ten simple vowels /i, e, æ, a, ɨ, ʌ, ɑ, u, o, ɔ/ and five "secondary symbols" to be used after the primary or simple vowels: /w, y, ə, r, h/, where the /w/ and /y/ represent the close rounded and unrounded up-glides, the /ə/, the close in-glide, the /r/ for retroflexion, and the /h/ for lengthening and centralized transition. Both Sledd and McDavid agree that more than three semivowels are needed. W. Nelson Francis uses "fronting diphthongs" ending in /y/, "retracting diphthongs" ending in /w/, and "centering diphthongs" ending in /h/ or retroflexive /r/, thus adding four possible semivowels to form the complex nuclei. The superscript /ˇ/ symbol is used by Charles F. Hockett in his *A Course in Modern Linguistics*[5] for the T-S semivowel /h/. Hockett bases his phonological analysis on the Trager-Smith system and retains /h/ in prevocalic position. By not using the semivowel /h/ in postvocalic position, he avoids one of the criticisms launched at the *Outline*. One earlier text by Claude E. Kantner and Robert West, *Phonetics*,[6] used the regular IPA symbolization for the simple vowels as they appear in Kenyon and Thomas, but used the /w, j, r, ə/ for the diphthongal forms in *how, high, far, boa*.

Many arguments have been proposed against the Trager-Smith system. The strongest seem to be: (1) their use of the semivowel /h/ to represent both an off-glide as well as length; (2) the nine vowel—three semivowel—structure does not permit adequate representation of certain regional dialects of American speech; (3) a hesitancy to accept one over-all pattern of American English for a language which has as many differently structured major dialect types, unless the system permits constant expansion as additional contrasts turn up as a result of continuing in-

[4] (New York, Ronald, 1958).
[5] (New York, Macmillan, 1958).
[6] (New York, Harper, 1941).

vestigation; (4) their denial of long "pure" vowels such as those in *beat* and *boot*, showing them only as complex forms, when there is good phonetic evidence that shows them as both simple and complex forms; (5) the strong desire for a symmetrical structuring that, at times, seems to deny or overlook certain facts of usage, permitting certain conclusions that are difficult to substantiate. On this last point, some of our Canadian colleagues do not agree with the finding of four contrastive American English stresses and pitches, the separation of pitch and stress as discrete phenomena, and the use of /ɨ/ as a phonemic entity separate from /ə/. Still others of our Canadian colleagues find that such disagreements may be unwarranted.[7] Strong criticisms of the pitch-level system used in the *Outline* have been made by Dwight L. Bolinger in his "Intonation: Levels versus Configurations," and "A Theory of Pitch Accent in English."[8]

Perhaps the arguments in favor of the Trager-Smith system are even stronger. It is a careful and systematic structuring of the phonology of American English, based on a very wide range of experience with many American dialects. The result has been a phonemic analysis, not of a single dialect, as tried before, but an attempt at an "over-all analysis" of the phonemics of American English. It seems to be the best system for the analysis of the phonology of our language from the contrastive aspect of the phonemic principle. To many, the vowel and semivowel system of representation keeps to the fore the fact that vowels may be simple or complex. Ives answers one objection to the Trager-Smith system when he states that opposition to the vowel and semivowel analysis may result from a misunderstanding of the semivowel symbol and concept, that is, it may represent both an additional vowel segment, as well as something like a diacritic, such as length.[9]

There is little doubt that the influence of the Trager-Smith analysis has been considerable. Hardly any discussion of the phonology of American English can take place without the recognition of the Trager-Smith contribution to our thinking and the works of those upon whom Trager-Smith based their conclusions, tentative though they may be: particularly the earlier work of Bloomfield, Bernard Bloch, Morris Swadesh, Einar Haugen, W. Freeman Twadell, Rulon Wells, Stanley Newman, Kenneth Pike, Charles Hockett, and Benjamin Whorf. In his *Introduction to Linguistic Structures*, Archibald A. Hill defends his reason for adopting the Trager-Smith method of phonemic analysis by voicing an undoubtedly

[7] See *Journal of the Canadian Linguistic Association*, Vol. 4 (Fall, 1958), pp. 61–62; and Vol. 5 (Spring, 1959), pp. 8–16.

[8] *Word*, Vol. 7 (December, 1951), pp. 199–210; Vol. 14 (August–December, 1958), pp. 109–149.

[9] Letter to the author, October, 1958.

common feeling of many American linguists: "The phonemic analysis presented here is that of the Trager and Smith over-all pattern, and it has been chosen for the reason that it is the most complete, consistent, and simple analysis of English phonemes in existence. It is an analysis capable of being revised when revisions are shown to be needed, but it is not an analysis capable of being refuted except by another analysis more complete, more consistent, and more simple."[10]

It is too soon to know if the two vowel or vowel and semivowel method of representation for the complex nuclei will continue to be used in the literature, as they are at present. Both the IPA and the Trager-Smith symbolization are in common use. The IPA symbols are used by many for phonemic as well as phonetic symbols, and even those following the Trager-Smith phonemics retain the use of IPA symbols for phonetic discussions.

The following charts show ten different symbol systems for representing the phonology of American English. The first five follow the IPA symbolization rather closely. They all use two vowels to represent the complex nuclei. These sources are:

John S. Kenyon, *American Pronunciation*, 10th ed. (Ann Arbor, George Wahr Publishing Co., 1951);

Clifford H. Prator, Jr., *Manual of American English Pronunciation*, Revised Edition (New York, Rinehart, 1957);

Charles K. Thomas, *An Introduction to the Phonetics of American English*, 2nd ed. (New York, Ronald, 1958);

Allan F. Hubbell, *The Pronunciation of English in New York City* (New York, Kings Crown Press, 1950);

Kenneth Pike, *Phonemics: A Technique for Reducing Languages to Writing* (Ann Arbor, University of Michigan Press, 1947).

The second group follow the phonemic symbols used in the Trager-Smith *Outline*, with semivowels in the complex nuclei. In addition to the *Outline*, these sources are:

W. Nelson Francis, *The Structure of American English* (New York, Ronald, 1958);

Charles F. Hockett, *A Course in Modern Linguistics* (New York, Macmillan, 1958);

H. A. Gleason, Jr., *An Introduction to Descriptive Linguistics* (New York, Holt, 1955);

Sumner Ives. Work paper for Texas Conference on Linguistics, "Phonemics of American English." Unpublished. 1956.

[10] (New York, Harcourt, 1958), p. 61.

Key Word	Kenyon	Prator	Thomas	Hubbell	Pike
beet	i	i	i or ιi	iĭ	i
bit	ɪ	ɪ	ɪ	i	i
bait	e or eɪ	e	e or eɪ	eĭ	e
bet	ɛ	ɛ	ɛ	e	ɛ
bat	æ	æ	æ	æ	æ
part	ɑ or a	a	ɑ or a	aɝ̆	a
pot	ɒ	a	ɒ	ɑ	a
bought	ɔ	ɔ	ɔ	ɔɝ̆	ɔ
boat	o or ou	o	o or ou	oŭ	o
book	ʊ	ʊ	ʊ	u	ʊ
boot	u	u	u or uu	uŭ	u
bird	ɝ, ɝ̧	ər	ɝ, ɝ˞	3ɝ̆	ɹ̩
bett*er*,	ə, ɚ	ər	ə, ɚ	ə, r	ɹ̩
*a*bove	ə	ə	ə	ə	ə
but	ʌ	ə	ʌ	ʌ	ə

Complex Nuclei*

bite	aɪ	aɪ	aɪ	aĭ	aⁱ
bout	aʊ	aʊ	ɑʊ	aŭ	aᵘ
boy	ɔɪ	ɔɪ	ɔɪ	ɔĭ	oⁱ

Key Word	Trager-Smith	Francis	Hockett	Gleason	Ives
bit	i	i	i	i	i
bet	e	e	e	e	e
bat	æ	æ	æ	æ	æ
"jist"	ɨ	ɨ	ɨ	ɨ	ɨ
but	ə	ə	ə	ə	ʌ
blind (Southeast)	–	–	–	–	a
father, pot	a	a	a	a	ɑ
put	u	u	u	u	u
whole (NE)	o	o	o	o	o
"gonna" pot (NE)	ɔ	ɔ	ɔ	ɔ	ɔ

Complex Nuclei

simple vowels plus	w, y, h	w, y, h, r	w, j, ˇ	w, y, H	w, y, h, r, ə

* All except Prator use vowels plus schwa or vowels plus *r* for such words as *care*, *fear*, etc. Prator uses vowels plus schwa or vowels plus schwa plus *r*.

Index

References are to pages. Those followed by *n* refer to names appearing in footnotes. Authors' names appearing in the reference sections at the ends of chapters are not listed here. Symbols for the consonants and vowels appear under the appropriate headings, in the order in which they are discussed in the text.

317